Seeing Child Care

A Guide for Assessing the Effectiveness of Child Care Programs

Dedication

To my husband, Dr. Richard Frost, for your constant support and encouragement throughout my career. Also to my mother, Frances H. Bickett, whose own career in early childhood education and lifelong love of children have been a constant source of inspiration. ~ Marty Frost

And to all children, we hope that our book can make a positive difference in the lives of some of you.

Join us on the web at
EarlyChildEd.delmar.com

Seeing Child Care

A Guide for Assessing the
Effectiveness of Child Care Programs

Warren R. Bentzen   **Martha B. Frost**

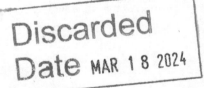
THOMSON

DELMAR LEARNING   Australia   Canada   Mexico   Singapore   Spain   United Kingdom   United States

THOMSON
DELMAR LEARNING

Seeing Child Care: A Guide for Assessing the Effectiveness of Child Care Programs
Warren R. Bentzen and Martha B. Frost

Business Unit Executive Director:
Susan L. Simpfenderfer

Executive Production Manager:
Wendy A. Troeger

Executive Marketing Manager:
Donna J. Lewis

Acquisitions Editor:
Erin O'Connor

Production Editor:
Joy Kocsis

Channel Manager:
Nigar Hale

Editorial Assistant:
Ivy Ip

Technology Project Manager:
Joseph Saba

Cover Design:
Joy Kocsis

Composition:
Carlisle Communications, Ltd

For permission to use material from this text or product, contact us by
Tel   (800) 730-2214
Fax   (800) 730-2215
www.thomsonrights.com

Library of Congress Cataloging-in-Publication Data

Bentzen, Warren R.
  Seeing child care : a guide for assessing the effectiveness of child care programs / Warren R. Bentzen, Martha B. Frost.
    p. cm.
Includes bibliographical references.
  ISBN 0-7668-4063-8
  1. Early childhood education. 2. Child development. I. Frost, Martha
B. II. Title.
  LB1139.23 .B46 2003
  372.21--dc21
                                    2002031237

NOTICE TO THE READER

Contents

Preface

Seeing Child Care is intended primarily for two audiences: professionals already working in an early childhood program, and college or university students who are preparing to become professional child care providers. That said, we strongly believe that sound practice must be based on sound knowledge of developmental principles and principles of child (developmentally) appropriate practice. If we wrote a manual or book consisting of nothing but practical recommendations—strictly a "how to" book—for providing caregivers and children with an effective, child appropriate program, such recommendations would lose their force if they were not implemented within an appropriate conceptual or theoretical framework. Practice must be informed by knowledge and ultimately by experience.

In his book *The Dancing Wu Li Masters: An Overview of the New Physics* (2001), author Gary Zukav describes a "Master" as follows:

> He begins from the center and not from the fringe. He imparts an understanding of the basic principles of the art before going on to the meticulous details, and he refuses to break down the tai chi movements into a one-two-three drill so as to make the student into a robot. The traditional way . . . is to teach by rote, and to give the impression that long periods of boredom are the most essential part of training. In that way a student may go on for years and years without ever getting the feel of what he is doing . . . A Master teaches essence. When the essence is perceived, he teaches what is necessary to expand the perception (p. 8).

We want you, the practitioner or student, to become a master in the field of early child care, if you haven't already achieved that level of competence. The "essence" of child care comprises the conceptual and theoretical content of Part I as well as the practical content of Part II. This knowledge is the "basic principles of the art," and the application of that knowledge is the "meticulous details." Because effective child care requires both knowledge and application, Parts I and II are inextricably linked.

Part II (Chapters 5 through 8) is the centerpiece of *Seeing Child Care;* in these last four chapters are the practical observation exercises. The information in the observation exercises emphasizes much of the material found in the various tables of the first four chapters, which will help you put the information to practical use. There are also a few learning activities in the first four chapters to help you apply some of the conceptual principles.

In this book, we alternate between gender pronouns to avoid the use of such cumbersome constructions as he/she, him/her, and his/hers. Also, when we use the term "child care" as an adjective, such as in the phrase "a child care facility," we wrote it as one word. When used as a noun, we wrote it as two words, "child" and "care," as in "proper child care is essential to our nation's welfare."

Regarding the references used in this book, we have drawn heavily on Carol Gestwicki's 1999 edition of *Developmentally Appropriate Practice: Curriculum and Development in Early Education.* (We have done this even though Bredekamp and Copple are probably generally acknowledged as the most recognized spokespersons for developmentally appropriate practice.) Such reliance on one source does not mean that we have no thoughts or ideas of our own. The *general* and *developmental environment, interaction effects,* as they pertain to early childhood programs, *child-appropriate practice,* our definition of *program effectiveness, first-category,* and *second category needs,* and the concept of a *general guideline,* among others, are original with us. So, readers need not think that they might as well read Gestwicki's book rather than ours, for unlike Gestwicki's book, *Seeing Child Care* uniquely blends the theoretical with the practical, and introduces concepts that are not found in Gestwicki's book or elsewhere. These two differences make *Seeing Child Care* eminently suitable for observing and evaluating the effectiveness of early child care programs.

One consequence of our heavy dependence on one source is that we will not give you an extensive bibliography. Given the purpose of *Seeing Child Care,* our primary concerns are more about the reliability, accuracy, and usefulness of the information we have provided than about its origins.

We speak of the "effectiveness" rather than the "quality" of early childhood programs. In the earlier versions of our manuscript, we arrived at what we thought was a definition of quality that was easy to understand and applicable to actual child care programs. On further consideration, we decided that quality has some connotations that might interfere with its usefulness as a descriptor of early childhood programs. We concluded that judging one program as more effective than another is not quite so critical as judging one program as being of higher quality than another.

In most instances, we use the term child appropriate practice in place of developmentally appropriate practice, and we discuss this substitution in Chapter 1. We want to emphasize here that the substitution is intended primarily to highlight the *child's central role* in everything that takes place in an early childhood program. The principles of development and developmentally appropriate practice are, of course, also central to any program. These principles are abstract, albeit useful concepts, but *one should never view the child as either an abstraction or a concept.* Therefore, as we explain in Chapter 1, child appropriate practice puts the focus where it rightly belongs—on the child.

The authors and Delmar Learning affirm that the Web site URLs referenced herein were accurate at the time of printing. However, due to the fluid nature of the Internet, we cannot guarantee their accuracy for the life of the edition.

Online Resources™

The Online Resources™ to accompany Seeing Child Care is your link to evaluating early childhood programs on the Internet. The Online Resources™ contain many features to help focus your understanding of quality child care:

- ✳ Web Links—these will direct you to helpful Web sites to allow you to conduct further research on the effectiveness of child care programs.

- ✳ Forms—you will find downloadable/printable versions of the forms located in this book.

- ✳ On-line Early Education Survey—this survey gives you the opportunity to respond to what features you like and what features you want to see improved on the Online Resources™.

The Online Resources™ icon appears at the end of each chapter to prompt you to go on-line and take advantage of the many features provided.

You can find the Online Resources™ at **www.earlychilded.delmar.com**

Acknowledgments

No one ever writes a book completely on his or her own, and we are no exception. There are many people we want to thank for assisting and guiding us through the completion of *Seeing Child Care*. We want to thank the editorial staff at Delmar Learning, especially Erin O'Connor, without whose initial and continuing support, *Seeing Child Care* would never have gotten off the ground. We also want to thank the reviewers who saw enough potential in the early manuscripts to recommend that Delmar Learning see this project through to the end. We are grateful to the following reviewers for their invaluable insights and recommendations, which helped make *Seeing Child Care* a much better book than it otherwise might have been.

Mary Banbury
Bellevue Community College
Bellevue, WA

Nancy Baptiste, Ed.D.
New Mexico State University
Las Cruces, NM

Gretchen Kolb
Rocking Unicorn Nursery School
West Chatham, MA

Judith Lindman
Rochester Community and Technical
    College
Rochester, MN

Jody Martin
Children's World Learning Centers
Golden, CO

Nina Mazloff
Becker College
Worcester, MA

Brenda Schin
Child Care Provider
Selkirk, NY

Evie Wexler
Governor's State University
University Park, IL

Fran Young, Ed.D.
Great Beginnings Child Development Center
Pennsauken, NJ

We owe special thanks and appreciation to our developmental editor, Amy Simcik Williams. Amy worked tirelessly to refine and hone our sometimes tedious, boring sentences, correct our grammatical mistakes, and help us overall to produce a book worth reading. We are especially grateful for the intelligent, sensitive, thoroughly competent, and decidedly hands-on way Amy discharged her responsibilities to this project.

Last, but not least, the first author wants to thank his friend, colleague, and co-author, Dr. Martha Frost, for agreeing to undertake this project. It is doubtful that either one of us could have fully predicted the amount of time and effort writing *Seeing Child Care* would eventually entail. Nevertheless, Dr. Frost remained undaunted, and not only wrote four critical chapters (5 through 8), but also offered her editorial skills when they were needed and kept our general level of motivation high. We also want to thank Dr. Richard Frost for taking some of his valuable time to edit our writing. His editorial and stylistic recommendations were very helpful.

About the Authors

Warren R. Bentzen earned his doctoral degree in child development and family relations from Pennsylvania State University in 1977. For three years before pursuing his doctorate, he was the director of a small rehabilitation center for brain-injured children in State College, Pennsylvania. Prior to that, he worked for four years as a counselor with the Pennsylvania State Bureau of Vocational Rehabilitation. In the fall of 1977, he joined the faculty of the Child Family Services program at Plattsburgh State University in Plattsburgh, New York. Dr. Bentzen taught courses in child development, the contemporary American family, parenting, and early childhood education, among others. He retired at the end of the spring 2000 semester.

Dr. Bentzen is also the author of the Delmar publication *Seeing Young Children: A Guide to Observing and Recording Behavior,* now in its fourth edition.

Kentucky native Martha B. Frost earned her doctoral degree in education from the University of Kentucky in 1977. She taught family and consumer sciences in Cincinnati, Ohio, and Rochester, New York, public schools before beginning her career in higher education at the University of Vermont in 1979. In 1980, Dr. Frost joined the faculty of the Child Family Services Program at Plattsburgh State University in Plattsburgh, New York. She is currently the CFS program coordinator. She has taught courses in early childhood education and child development, and currently specializes in child care administration.

Part I

Chapter 1

Seeing Child Care: The Essentials

See How To

* develop specific insights into effective child care

* differentiate between observation and interpretation in child care

* distinguish between the general environment and the developmental environment

* define the concept of interaction effects in a child care setting

* determine the role of development and developmental principles in highly effective child care

* distinguish among age appropriateness, individual appropriateness, and social/cultural appropriateness in child care

* discuss the role and importance of developmental needs

 ## Introduction

"The way to get the best out of something," writes Os Guiness, "is to find out what it is and treat it accordingly" (*In Two Minds*, 1976, p. 24). This advice is the guiding principle of our book. *If you want to get the best out of children, find out who they are and treat them accordingly. If you want to get the best out of an early childhood program, find out what it should look like and build it accordingly.*

Seeing Child Care is a practical resource. To some, "practical" connotes applicability to real-life situations, whereas "theoretical" often suggests formal, academic studies or research, and irrelevance to everyday affairs. Practical success requires an underpinning of theory or learned knowledge, the kind one learns in textbooks, for instance. Even the most practical activities—from brushing our teeth to driving a car, to balancing our checkbooks—require some sort of knowledge. Early child care is very practical, and to be effective, it must be based on special knowledge. You can know who little Juan is only if you know his present needs, abilities, interests, and personality characteristics, and how these will change over time. Likewise, you can know how an early childhood program should look only if you know what program practices optimally meet children's needs in the context of their unique personal, family, and cultural background and characteristics.

It takes time to learn about children's needs and to recognize an appropriate curriculum. Our goal is to provide you with the knowledge and practical skills needed to determine the effectiveness of early childhood programs. Our book is practical because it combines accepted principles of development and child (developmentally) appropriate practice with opportunities actually to observe and evaluate early childhood programs.

 ## Program Effectiveness

Effectiveness can be difficult to define and even more difficult to measure. Determining **program effectiveness** means either comparing programs with each other to reveal one program's effectiveness relative to others, or comparing programs with some standard of excellence. Both kinds of comparison involve evaluation.

Evaluation is not necessarily easy, because it is often subjective, and our feelings can significantly influence our judgments. For example, we could underevaluate programs we don't like and overevaluate those we do. How much or how little we know can also affect our evaluations; therefore, a solid foundation of knowledge will help a professional child care provider judge the effectiveness of any early childhood program.

A program's effectiveness is also seen in the particular behavioral and developmental outcomes the program produces. How does the program environment *interact* with each child's unique characteristics to achieve desirable outcomes? *Webster's New Universal Unabridged Dictionary* (1996) defines *effective* as "adequate to accomplish a purpose; producing the intended or expected result" (p. 622). An effective child care program is *one that understands children's changing abilities and developmental needs, and meets those needs by employing accepted standards of child (developmentally) appropriate practice (CAP/DAP) and accepted principles that describe and govern growth and developmental change.*

Evaluation, as we intend, does not mean assigning a numerical value to any program, as if to say "The Friendly Child care Center" is twice as good as "The Unfriendly Child care Center." Rather, we hope our tools will help you determine whether and where a program can improve.

To make practical use of our definition, you should

✳ know how to observe and interpret what goes on in an early childhood program

✳ understand the roles of the general and developmental environments

✳ understand the role of interaction effects

✳ know children's developmental needs and how they change over time

✳ understand the principles that guide and explain developmental change

✳ know what constitutes a child appropriate curriculum

 Observation and Interpretation

Observation

The physical and behavioral sciences depend on sensory information for understanding the phenomena they study. Physicists take measurements with various instruments; astronomers look at stars and planets through their telescopes; psychologists conduct interviews and administer various tests. Similarly, child care providers must also depend on observational information to learn about children's progress, spot trouble areas that need attention, and make appropriate changes in a program environment.

Observation is not merely looking *at* something, as when idly watching children play in a schoolyard. When you observe, you use your senses (look, listen, touch, taste, or smell) to discern the characteristics and practices that determine and reflect program effectiveness.

Interpretation

Interpretation gives purpose and meaning to your observations. Interpretation helps make sense out of something. Not to interpret children's behavior would make your observations pointless. For instance, if you could not reach a reasonable conclusion concerning a program's effect on Samantha's language development, how would you know whether or not to change certain aspects of the program, or if change were called for, what kind of changes to make.

Interpretation can be quite simple and immediate. We don't constantly have to make sense out of tables, chairs, family members, or friends. We already know what and who these objects and people are. There will be other situations, though, when it's difficult to recognize or understand a child's behavior or to know whether a particular experience is having a desired effect and, if not, how to change a child's expe-

Keen observation helps child care staff stay aware of both immediate and potential needs of each child and the direction of the program.

rience so that it does have a desired effect. For instance, can you be certain what kind of stimulation four-month-old Melinda is experiencing from a mobile hanging above her crib? She can't verbally tell you. By observing Melinda's responses to the mobile— looking at it or touching it with her hands or feet—you can reach a conclusion (interpretation) from her behavior toward the mobile. You can likewise interpret the effects of all children's interactions with their developmental environment.

When you observe an early child care program, try to objectively describe what occurs there. An objective description is one that records only what a child does or says, without drawing any conclusions or interpretations at that time. Such a description might look like the following: "Melinda walked over to the book and game area and pulled a puzzle down from the shelf. She sat down, poured the contents onto the table, and proceeded to put the puzzle together." Sometimes you will record your observations and later try to give meaning to your descriptions. At other times, you may have to make an on-the-spot decision about what you are witnessing. If, for example, you're looking for instances of good adult-child rapport, you would not record the behaviors of two children playing in the sandbox. Instead, you would observe and record whether Mrs. Garcia was establishing good rapport with Alice, and what Mrs. Garcia's interactions with Alice revealed about adult-child rapport. In many instances, observing and recording a behavior is considerably easier than interpreting the behavior's meaning or significance.

 SEE FOR YOURSELF

Observe your own early child care classroom and record the behaviors of the children and staff members as they interact. Can you observe clear instances of adult-child rapport? What signs or indications of rapport do you observe? Can you think of ways in which adult-child rapport could be improved in the situations you have observed?

General and Developmental Environments

Every child brings to any program a unique genetic inheritance, or **genotype,** over which child care providers have no direct control. Over a lifetime, genotypes express themselves within a number of different environments. These environments identify social, emotional, physical, language, and intellectual areas of growth and development that are the focus of early childhood curricula.

Heredity and environment never operate independently of each other; each plays a necessary role in the developmental process. Heredity sets the boundaries within which development takes place, and the environment exerts its influence within those genetic boundaries. If Carla has the genetically inherited potential to be an excellent artist, she will still need an appropriate environment to bring out that potential. Nevertheless, even in an artistically impoverished environment, Carla is likely to show greater potential or talent than Sophia, who has not inherited any special artistic ability. Heredity, then, provides every child with particular potential; environment helps this potential become possible.

Unlike heredity, child care providers have some control over children's environments. An effective program works toward maximizing the possibilities and minimizing the limitations of genotypes. This can be done only by providing environments that are appropriate to each child's genotype and individual characteristics. This is the essence of what we call **child appropriate practice,** or CAP.

Child Appropriate Practice

While the concept of **developmentally appropriate practice** (DAP) has justifiably gained a strong following among professional child care providers and early childhood educators in providing high-quality early childhood programs, we introduce the term *child appropriate practice,* or CAP, as an alternative to developmentally appropriate practice. This substitution in no way diminishes the role of DAP; its principles remain critical to our mission, and our alternative term leaves intact all of DAP's principles. Effective child care depends on dealing with children on their own terms, which requires an understanding of the developmental areas essential to their well-being.

A child's potential is heightened by an appropriate developmental environment.

In the term *child appropriate practice,* child consolidates into one word the three kinds of appropriateness central to the meaning of developmentally appropriate practice: (1) age appropriateness, (2) individual appropriateness, and (3) social/cultural appropriateness. In the context of early childhood programs, you can understand a *child* only in terms of what is age appropriate, individually appropriate, and socially/culturally appropriate. Developmentally appropriate practice is used, however, when referring to or quoting from sources that specifically use that term.

The single most important question child appropriate practice asks is, "What kind of environment will *promote the development and meet the needs* of each child in any given group of children?" Broadly speaking, there are two primary environments: the general environment and the developmental environment.

Two Kinds of Environments

The **general environment** is relatively fixed and constant. It's made up of the physical equipment and materials, together with their spatial arrangements and locations. It contains the cues or stimuli to which children and adults can respond. The general environment is the one that exists before anyone sets foot in the center or classroom and is an *objective* environment.

The **developmental environment** exists within the general environment and is an environment in action. Once established, the general environment does not depend on anyone for anything more (with such obvious exceptions as replacing broken or missing equipment and materials, adding new equipment, or rearranging equipment and materials). The developmental environment, however, is dynamic and constantly changing. For example, as part of the general environment, wooden blocks essentially remain constant, but as part of the developmental environment, blocks can assume as many meanings and uses as there are children who play with them. In an objective sense, wooden blocks are what they are; in a subjective sense, they are whatever children want them to be. The developmental environment is highly subjective.

These environments have various meanings and uses both for adults and for children. For experienced child care professionals, an environment is likely to have fairly well-established, well-regulated meanings. The child care staff certainly know what

An example of a general environment.

8

Think of ways to create a dynamic developmental environment.

wooden blocks are and how children can and perhaps will use them. Young children are less likely to enter the child care center with that same level of knowledge or understanding.

These two environments exist simultaneously insofar as a developmental environment necessarily exists within a general environment, but the developmental environment comes about through a process of transformation. The child care center's general environment becomes a developmental environment for adults as well as for children. The general environment thus challenges professional child care staff to move beyond preconceptions and construct a viable, dynamic developmental environment that results in desired interaction effects and meets the standards of child appropriate practice.

When you close the door at the end of the day, you leave a general environment that will be the same the next morning. The developmental environment will likely be quite different. Children will bring back what they experienced and learned on previous days, but their moods will likely differ from those of the day before. The child care staff will also bring what they have previously learned and experienced. All of these variables enter into the mix that is the developmental environment. It is this constantly shifting, dynamic character of the developmental environment that poses a challenge to child appropriate practice.

 ## Interaction Effects

The term interaction normally refers to two or more people getting together and talking, engaging in an activity, or in some way taking each other into account. Regarding child care, interaction has a deeper meaning than simple interpersonal exchanges. For example, not everyone learns best by reading. Some learn more easily by hearing or listening to books on tape than from the printed page. These differences are called **learning styles.** The way information is presented interacts with each individual's unique learning style and results either in faster, more efficient learning, or in slower, inefficient learning.

With regard to children, each child's responses to any given environment differ from another child's responses. Angela is fearful and shies away from new experiences, while Mark boldly seeks them. Chen Lee tends to focus on large-muscle activities like playing on the jungle gym or building with large wooden blocks, while John prefers fine-muscle movements like putting puzzles together or stringing beads. In other words, children cannot just be added to an environment and expected to show the same perceptions and responses. Rather, their individual characteristics—personality, temperament, level of development, experiences—interact with the characteristics of the environment and determine their own distinctive perceptions

Interaction effects include the relationship experienced between child and teacher.

Children's inward, individual responses to an activity shared in common can differ greatly.

A program's effectiveness can be determined by how many "right kinds" of interaction effects are accomplished.

and reactions. Children's characteristics influence *in unique ways* how they will respond to any particular environment.

Interaction effects, then, are the consequences—developmental changes, learning, emotions—that children experience from being in a particular child care setting at a particular time in their development. Effective child care attempts to maximize those interaction effects by providing children with experiences that are most compatible with their developmental needs, personalities, aptitudes, interests, and temperaments.

Although individual responses to features of the environment can outwardly look very similar, perceptions, understanding, and feelings can differ significantly. Paul and Miguel, both four years old, can show very similar behaviors when assembling a puzzle. Paul, however, dislikes playing with puzzles because he believes he is not very good at that activity. Miguel, on the other hand, thoroughly enjoys puzzles. He has very good eye-hand coordination, good spatial and shape perception; and consequently, believes he is very good with puzzles.

Understanding that each child's response to any environment is unique is essential to providing a child appropriate curriculum. Child appropriate practice tries to maximize the right kinds of interaction effects. A program's effectiveness is a function of how many of these right kinds of interaction effects are actually accomplished.

 SEE FOR YOURSELF

After observing individual children as well as groups of children in a child care setting, what, if any, interaction effects did you notice? Did you notice different interaction effects when you observed an individual child than when you observed a group of children? What interaction effects could occur in the case of a child playing by him or herself? Can you draw any conclusions about children's learning styles based on observable interaction effects?

≈≈ Through Their Eyes

Amy Scheels is the lead teacher in the preschool room at Suny Plattsburgh Early Care and Education Center. She observes several of the four year olds playing in the block area with plastic animals. Shameeka and Allen have sectioned off part of the space with large blocks and have built a zoo with a separate pen for each animal—the elephants with the elephants, the lions with the lions, the gorillas together, and so on. Noriko is the attending vet giving the animals their physical exams prior to allowing them into the zoo. Mr. Lion might need to take some vitamins—he seems run-down, she assesses. When Nicky tries to introduce his dog to the zoo, Shameeka explains that dogs are not zoo animals. Meanwhile, Emily and Arlie are discussing who will be the parents/caretakers of each animal. Amy recognizes the value of this dramatic play and how it fosters an appropriate learning environment to meet each child's individual needs.

 ## The Role of Developmental Needs

Developmental needs is the unifying theme of this book. Our primary premise is that *development is itself a need.* Development concerns two things: (1) children's *abilities* at particular times in their developmental histories, and how those abilities change, and (2) children's *needs* at particular times in their developmental histories, and how those needs change. Child care staff can foster children's proper growth and development by meeting the needs that development imposes during their various developmental stages. The key is to know what those needs are, both for children in general (age appropriateness) and for each child in particular (individual appropriateness).

Needs vs. Desires in the Developmental Environment

Needs are different from desires, yet the difference between the two can be difficult to distinguish. The difficulty lies partly in the fact that desires can mimic needs because they frequently stem from legitimate needs. For example, children need to eat. While adults know that wholesome foods will meet children's nutritional requirements, and junk foods offer empty calories, children often make their food choices based on taste. They can acquire strong desires for potato chips, soda, candy bars, and cookies, and fuss about eating fruits, vegetables, grains, protein, and dairy products. Junk food may satisfy an empty stomach or the need to eat, but it hardly satisfies the real need for nutritionally rich foods. Children also need to explore their environments, yet allowing them to poke metal paper clips into an electrical wall outlet—something they might greatly desire to do—would certainly not fulfill a legitimate developmental need and would be hazardous to their health.

Desires are important, though. There are desires that serve basic needs or that evolve from them. For instance, normal development dictates that children need to walk. But some children also ski, even though skiing is not a fundamental need universally imposed by developmental/maturational processes. For some, skiing becomes an essential part of life. It may become a passion and, for some select few, a profession. In some particular cases, therefore, skiing is part of the individual's identity, part of who he or she is. For these individuals, skiing is life fulfilling, and that makes skiing legitimate and worthy of pursuit.

In most instances, needs should be met before desires. This especially holds in the case of young children. At the very least, children's desires should be carefully assessed to ensure that granting them is within the framework of child appropriate practice.

In this book, *a need is any experience, opportunity, or task that is commensurate with a child's level of development and ability, which, if met, contributes beneficially to his growth and development, and, if not met, might interfere with, or negatively affect, his growth or development.* Also important, a child's true needs are the parents' and caregivers' obligations. This corollary establishes the proper attitude for early childhood program staff. Needs, by definition, are essential to children's well-being and sometimes their physical survival. This means that a child's needs are also her rights—a right to adequate nutrition, adequate health care, opportunities for optimal growth and development, and so on.

In this context, an early childhood program should (1) identify children's needs and abilities at various times in their lives, and (2) gauge the program's ability to meet those needs. It's important to remember that needs define and motivate program practices, program practices do not define needs.

 ## Two Categories of Needs

Think of needs as falling into two general categories. **First-category needs** are clearly delineated during children's development, such as physical/motor and cognitive/language development. They usually are highly specific, follow a fairly well-prescribed timetable and sequence, and are strongly influenced by maturational forces. These needs can be expressed as developmental skills or milestones, like rolling over, sitting up, crawling, creeping, walking, crying, cooing, babbling, talking, and so on.

A caregiver's ability to understand an infant's attachment behaviors and respond with sensitivity and consistency is the key to forming a secure attachment.

Second-category needs are those that are more broadly expressed and whose sequence and timing are not as clear-cut as the needs in the first category. These are needs such as adequate nutrition and health care, the need to explore, and the need for sensory stimulation. (These kinds of needs are discussed more in Chapter 2.)

Child care staff might require more ingenuity to meet second-category needs than to meet first-category needs. Providing children with opportunities to crawl, creep, and walk is more obvious than providing them with adequate health care or nutrition. As we discuss in Chapter 2, "adequate" has to be properly defined for each child, and evidence of adequacy is not always immediately discernible. For example, a child may not show the signs of poor nutrition for some time, which would delay actions to improve her diet.

Also, needs in the second category often require more intense participation or intervention on the part of early child care staff than do needs in the first group. Children need to form secure attachments or emotional bonds with significant adults, but this attachment does not simply happen. The formation of a secure attachment requires a caregiver to understand an infant's attachment behaviors and to respond to those behaviors with sensitivity and consistency. This is more complicated than putting an infant on a safe place on the floor and allowing him the freedom to move and explore his surroundings.

 ## The Role of Development and Developmental Principles

"Child development involves changes in physical, social, emotional, and intellectual functioning over time, from conception through adolescence" (Fabes and Martin, 2000, p. 5). This textbook definition provides only a glimpse into the meaning of development. To understand development, observe the workings of those biological, maturational processes that determine children's needs, abilities, and behaviors at particular stages. Their growth brings about reasonably predictable changes in their needs, abilities, and behaviors.

Knowledge of how children function and move through various stages is the basis of child appropriate practice. Well-established principles of child development determine and help us to know who a child is. See how these developmental principles become meaningful by using a behavioral definition.

Behavioral Definitions

Knowingly or unknowingly, we use **behavioral definitions** all the time. An object can be behaviorally defined in at least two ways: by what the object does, and by the ways the object is used. Ordinarily, we behaviorally define chair as something to sit in, but we can also define it as something to stand on to change a light bulb, prop open a door or fend off a lion in a circus act. Similarly, a child can be behaviorally defined by the skills and abilities he or she possesses (or lacks) and by how he or she is treated.

For example, 18-month-old Timothy rolls the round rubber object across the floor without knowing the object is called a ball. Timothy behaviorally defines "ball" by doing one of the things one can do with balls, namely roll it. Round objects like balls roll easily, but square objects like blocks do not. Round rubber objects bounce, but round *wooden* objects do not. A behavioral definition of ball depends upon certain characteristics of (rubber) balls—they roll easily and they bounce. Likewise, Timothy's caregiver can behaviorally define Timothy by his present level of development and maturation: he can roll a ball but cannot catch it or throw it with accuracy. The second kind of behavioral definition includes every use to which an object is put and every way in which a child is treated.

The most critical point is this: *Every early childhood program behaviorally defines children by the general and developmental environments it provides them.* Every interaction a professional caregiver has with a child is, at that moment, that caregiver's behavioral definition of that child. It may also be the program's behavioral definition of children, especially if the interactions are typical of that particular caregiver or of the program staff in general.

Some professional caregivers might be unfamiliar with the term *behavioral definition,* but it is almost certain they use behavioral definitions in their work with children. An experienced child care provider can distinguish one child from another based on his or her respective abilities, typical behavior patterns, strengths, and weaknesses. Three-year-old Jonathan shows precocious language skills, but three-year-old Sidney's language skills are behind the rest of the class. If Jonathan and Sidney's speech were described to child care staff, they would immediately know the identities of the two children.

Developmental norms follow the behavioral definition because they provide information on children's typical abilities at various ages. Children can be behaviorally defined by comparing their behavior to developmental norms. In this way, the life stages of newborns, infants, toddlers, and preschoolers are often distinguished. How often do we hear statements like, "He behaves that way because he is two"? A parent saying that about his or her two-year-old son is behaviorally defining not only his or her son, but to some extent, all two-year-olds.

It is also very important to know what children need relative to age appropriateness and individual appropriateness. Until Samuel is about three years old, he will need a chance to develop some independence, learn how to control his own behavior, and opportunities to learn self-care skills—all second-category needs.

Abilities and needs are often a matter of degree. Adolescents also need opportunities to develop independence, learn to control their own behavior, and provide for their own needs. Although Samuel's needs sound similar to those of an adolescent, they are qualitatively different and they are relatively immature. At Samuel's age, independence, control, and self-care form the foundation for mature independence, control, and self-care.

The importance of understanding development is apparent. As children mature, they require different environments. An environment suitable for Samuel at one year of age will not be completely suitable when he is three. The environment for one-year-old Samuel lacks the stimulation and learning opportunities that are appropriate to the older Samuel's more mature level of development and greater experience, abilities, and knowledge.

Because development follows certain patterns and timetables, these patterns and characteristics are considered developmental laws or principles. Bredekamp and Copple (1997), in the revised edition of *Developmentally Appropriate Practice in Early Childhood Programs,* discuss 12 developmental principles of developmentally appropriate practice. These principles are summarized and illustrated in Table 1–1.

The Three Kinds of Appropriateness

When you apply these developmental principles and principles of child appropriate practice, you lay the foundation for an effective early childhood program. An appropriate developmental environment is one that satisfies the conditions set by what is age appropriate, individually appropriate, and socially/culturally appropriate for each child. See what these three kinds of appropriateness include.

Age appropriateness refers to a child's level or stage of development. Age appropriateness is based on principles of development that apply to all children from all social and cultural backgrounds. Don't assume that chronological age *explains* all behavior and abilities. It wouldn't be entirely correct to say that Albert behaves as he does *because* he is two. Albert's age is a reasonable predictor of his needs, abilities, and overall level of development, but his age does not fully explain everything. One

TABLE 1–1 Twelve Developmental Principles

Developmental Principle # 1

All the areas or domains of children's development are interrelated.

Which Means:

Laura's social development influences and is influenced by her cognitive development, and so on for all of her developmental areas.

Developmental Principle # 2

Development is cumulative and occurs in a relatively orderly sequence.

Which Means:

Bobby's knowledge and abilities at four years, three months, one week, and two days of age are built on the knowledge and abilities he acquired up to four years, three months, one week, and one day of age (cumulative).

Among other things, before Bobby could speak any words, he cooed and babbled; he began with one word such as "mama," and progressed to two-word utterances such as "mama up." Most children's language development proceeds in much the same way. This orderly sequence also applies to other areas of development.

Developmental Principle # 3

The rate of development varies from child to child, and development proceeds unevenly within each child.

Which Means:

Emmanuel could grow faster physically than his same-age friend, Mark. Emmanuel's language development could be slower than his physical development, while Mark's language development could be faster than his physical development. These variations in rate of development apply to all functional areas.

Developmental Principle # 4

The effects of early experience on children's development are both cumulative and delayed. There are optimal periods for certain kinds of development and learning.

Which Means:

There is a second meaning of cumulative. If Carlos frequently has negative emotional experiences at home, they could adversely affect his emotional development. Frequent positive experiences could have beneficial effects on his emotional development. These effects don't necessarily occur immediately but can manifest themselves at a later stage in Carlos's development. For example, he could show no signs of emotional difficulty when in preschool, but could begin to have emotional problems in the first grade.

Carlos can learn some things more easily at certain development stages than at others—he will probably learn Spanish *and* English more easily at one year of age than at six years of age.

Developmental Principle # 5

Development is predictable and moves toward greater complexity, organization, and internalization.

Which Means:

Development doesn't occur in a haphazard way. If you know that Andrew is two years old, and if his development is typical, you can reasonably predict his future abilities and behaviors. Andrew's behavior will become more sophisticated and better organized, and he will become better able to deal mentally (cognitively) with his environment instead of having to deal with objects, people, and event in a direct, sensorimotor way.

continued

TABLE 1-1 Twelve Developmental Principles (Continued)

Developmental Principle # 6

Development and learning necessarily take place in, and are influenced by, a number of social and cultural contexts.

Which Means:

You cannot ignore Billy's family, social, and cultural backgrounds. These backgrounds serve as developmental environments, and they interact with his unique personal characteristics to make Billy who he is.

Developmental Principle # 7

Children are active, not passive, learners.

Which Means:

You should not think of Margaret as being like a sponge who simply waits for something to come along that she can respond to. Margaret will want to actively participate in her own learning, and she will voluntarily seek out stimulating activities and experiences.

Developmental Principle # 8

Biological maturation and the environment both interact to produce development and learning.

Which Means:

Jorge's development is a combination of his genetic potential and his experiences. If he inherits a special aptitude, he will require appropriate experiences (developmental environment) for that aptitude to show itself and to develop.

Developmental Principle # 9

Play contributes significantly to children's social, emotional, and cognitive development, and it also reflects their level of development.

Which Means:

It is through play that children construct their own developmental environments and thereby actively participate in their own development. Play can tell Frank how he compares to Lee with respect to physical speed, strength, and coordination. Play can help Tracy learn whether or not she has leadership qualities.

Although Howard and Stephen are both four, Howard tends to play with children who are one or two years younger than he, while Stephen plays with children his own age or older. His play is also more sophisticated or mature than Howard's. He engages in more symbolic play and more cooperative or socially interactive play than Stephen.

Developmental Principle # 10

Children need to practice their newly acquired skills and to experience challenges that appropriately exceed their present level of ability.

Which Means:

Even though Angela hopped on one foot for the first time, she still needs many more opportunities to hop on one foot. If Bethany identifies a triangle for the first time, she will still need many more opportunities to identify triangles of different sizes and types.

You should not bore Jerry by giving him things to do that are "old hat" to him or that are too far above his present ability. If he finally learns to put together a five-piece puzzle, don't make his next challenge a three-piece puzzle or a 100-piece puzzle. Rather, give him a puzzle that is slightly more difficult than he can presently handle.

TABLE 1–1 Twelve Developmental Principles (Continued)

Developmental Principle # 11
Children show different ways of knowing and learning and different ways of representing what they know.
Which Means:
Martha learns to read very easily, but Guilford learns best by hearing the information. Martha expresses what she knows by talking, while Guilford expresses his knowledge best through physical-motor actions.
Developmental Principle # 12
Children's development and learning are best accomplished when they are raised in a community that values them, keeps them safe, meets their physical needs, and makes them feel psychologically secure.
Which Means:
Children need to be and feel loved, valued, and respected, and to be and feel physically and psychologically safe. This principle needs no further explanation.

Adapted from Bredekamp and Copple, 1997.

certain thing a child's age does tell us is how long he has been alive, but it's not an infallible predictor of how much he has developed and matured, or what he has experienced. If age were a certain predictor, then two-year-old Albert would be virtually the same developmentally and maturationally as every other two-year-old. Age, therefore, indicates the amount of time a child has had for growth, development, and maturation to occur.

Individual appropriateness refers to those characteristics that are unique to each child. An individually appropriate developmental environment considers each child's needs, experiences, interests, temperament, personality, developmental level, and anything else that distinguishes her from everyone else. Individual appropriateness is never independent of age appropriateness. All children's unique characteristics are to some degree based on where they are developmentally.

Social/cultural appropriateness considers the child's social, cultural, and family background. Development always takes place within the context of family, culture, and social class. Bredekamp and Copple (1997) put it this way: "Rules of development are the same for all children, but social contexts shape children's development in different configurations" (p. 12). A child appropriate program takes into account these unique developmental "configurations." Table 1–2 briefly summarizes these three kinds of appropriateness.

According to the article "Guidelines for Developmentally Appropriate Practices. *Early Years Are Learning Years*" (NAEYC, 1997; on the Web site of the National Parent Information Network), developmentally appropriate practice does not follow a single formula that fits all situations. Principles of developmentally appropriate practice provide teachers with "strategies to make day-to-day decisions based on the individual children, their families, and social and cultural context" (p. 1). Gestwicki (1999) emphasizes that "programs designed *for* young children [should] be based on what is known *about* young children . . . It [DAP] is not based on what adults wish children were like, or hope they will be like, or even surmise they might be like" (p. 6, italics original). Developmentally appropriate practice, therefore, isn't a rigid curriculum or set of practices. Instead, the principles of developmentally appropriate practice are a perspective or philosophy that guide an effective early childhood program.

TABLE 1–2   The Conditions Necessary for Developmentally Appropriate Practice

Age Appropriateness	. . . what is known about child development and learning—knowledge of age-related human characteristics that permits general predictions within an age range about what activities, materials, interactions, or experiences will be safe, healthy, interesting, achievable, and also challenging to children;
Individual Appropriateness	. . . what is known about the strengths, interests, and needs of each individual child in the group to be able to adapt to and be responsive to inevitable individual variation;
Social/Cultural Appropriateness	. . . knowledge of the social and cultural contexts in which children live to ensure that learning experiences are meaningful, relevant, and respectful for participating children and their families.

(Verbatim from Bredekamp and Copple, 1997, p. 36)

The principles of developmentally appropriate practice guide an effective early childhood program.

Developmentally appropriate practice will not make all early childhood programs look and function alike. Instead, ". . . the intention is to focus philosophically on what we know about children and what we can learn about individual children as a basis for decision-making" (Gestwicki, 1999, p. 6). The simplest and most inclusive definition of developmentally (and child) appropriate practice we can offer is that DAP/CAP is any behaviors and activities that are in keeping with a child's level of development, unique personal characteristics, and family and cultural background, and that promote his or her optimal growth and physical, social, intellectual, language, and emotional development.

Specific principles of developmentally appropriate practice are incorporated into subsequent chapters. The principles of child/developmentally appropriate practice serve as guidelines for early childhood curricula and as such, they should be applied judiciously and intelligently. Refer to the 12 developmental principles as often as necessary to affirm their relationship with the principles of child appropriate practice. Child appropriate practice depends upon universal laws governing how children's needs and abilities change over time; these universal laws do not depend upon child appropriate practice.

Summary

The effectiveness of an early childhood program can be determined by observing how the program interacts with a child's unique characteristics. An effective program is one that understands children's changing abilities and developmental needs. Such a program meets those needs by employing accepted standards of child/developmentally appropriate practice (CAP/DAP) and accepted principles that describe and govern growth and developmental change.

To determine the effectiveness of the early childhood program, you should

1. know how to observe and interpret what happens in an early childhood program

2. understand the roles of the general and developmental environments

3. understand the role of interaction effects

4. know how children change over time

5. know what constitutes a child appropriate program (CAP)

Both heredity and environment play a significant role in a child's development. While child care professionals have no direct control over a child's genetic inheritance, they do have some control over his environment. Providing an appropriate environment is one essential feature of child appropriate practice.

Interaction effects are the consequences—developmental changes, learning, emotions—children experience from being in a particular child care setting at a particular time in their development. Child appropriate practice tries to ensure that the right kinds of interaction effects occur as much as possible.

Knowledge of children's needs and abilities and how they change over time is one basis of child appropriate practice. When properly applied, Bredekamp and Copple's (1997) 12 developmental principles lay the foundation for a high-quality early childhood program. Conditions necessary for child appropriate practice include age appropriateness, individual appropriateness, and social/cultural appropriateness. CAP/DAP depends upon the universal laws governing developmental change.

Questions to Consider

1. In the context of child care, what is meant by "finding out who a child is?"

2. Can you give examples of an interaction effect other than the ones given in the book?

3. What is the relationship between what we know about children's development and child appropriate practice?

4. Can you have a developmental environment without a general environment?

5. Can you have a general environment without a developmental environment?

6. What are the essential characteristics of child/developmentally appropriate practice as they have been discussed thus far?

7. Why are children's developmental needs so important in an effective early childhood program?

For additional information on assessing the effectiveness of child care programs, visit our Web site at **http://www.earlychilded.delmar.com**

Chapter 2

Observing and Evaluating the Infant Child Care Program

See How To

* differentiate between needs and desires in the developmental environment

* analyze the basic needs of infants (birth to one year of age)

* describe the characteristics of a safe infant environment

* summarize the nutrition needs of infants

* summarize the requirements of infants' sensory environment

* discuss child/developmentally appropriate social/emotional environment for infants

* discuss caregiving practices that indicate respect for infants

* recall characteristics of sensitive responsiveness

* discuss a child/developmentally appropriate cognitive/language environment for infants

* explain the principles of optimal cognitive and language development

Introduction

Seeing Child Care is not an exclusive authority on early childhood programs, because those in the child care profession, as well as students, must bring experience, knowledge, and skills acquired from a variety of sources. In Chapters 2 through 5 we present information that will help you distinguish between effective and ineffective early childhood programs.

Following Gestwicki's (1999) model, we divide the developmental environment into three domains: the *physical environment,* the *social/emotional environment,* and the *cognitive/language environment.* Remember that we define the physical environment as part of the general environment. Although important, the physical environment only provides the resources and opportunities for constructing the more important developmental environment. Wooden blocks and sand tables, then, are never merely objects; they are among the many tools in the general environment that help build a developmental environment. The best possible general environment is useless if it's not transformed into an effective developmental environment.

Using Developmental Needs in Child Appropriate Practice: A General Guideline

Recall from Chapter 1 that development is primarily about children's abilities and needs at particular times in their developmental histories. Also, a major premise of child appropriate practice is that you can promote children's proper growth and development only if you satisfy the needs that development imposes during the various developmental stages.

Development is the prime mover. It is nature's way of telling children, and us, what they need and when they need it. Maturation determines children's developmental needs, the developmental tasks they will accomplish, and the sequence in which those needs and tasks occur. These needs and their sequences are called *developmental patterns.* They are the elements of what can be considered a *general guideline,* which is stated as follows: *Use maturationally and culturally prescribed developmental patterns as definitions of need and as the basis for child appropriate practice.*

This guideline should be practiced intelligently and patiently. Because of individual differences, developmental patterns will not always clearly identify every child's

TABLE 2–1 Infants' Motor Development—An Abbreviated Sample

Motor Skill	Average Age Achieved
Holds head steady and erect when held upright.	Six weeks
Lifts self by the arms when in the prone (face down) position.	Two months
Rolls from side to back	Two months
Grasps cube	Three months, three weeks
Rolls from back to side	Four and one-half months
Sits alone	Seven months
Crawls	Seven months
Pulls to stand	Eight months
Plays pat-a-cake	Nine months, three weeks
Stands alone	Eleven months

Adapted and excerpted from Berk (2000, p. 145)

needs. When you know, for example, how most infants progress in their motor development, each projected and actual step in the process is an occasion for opportunity and encouragement. To illustrate, early motor development follows a fairly well-defined course, making it reasonably easy to discern the developmental needs an infant will exhibit. Table 2–1 identifies 10 motor skills or milestones normally achieved in the first 11 months of life and the average age at which each is reached.

Not all developmental patterns are so clearly delineated, but the general guideline still applies. Consider each of the motor skills to be a developmental need. (Pat-a-cake might seem a strange need, but in this case, it's the ability that the activity represents that is important, not the activity itself.) As four-month-old Ronny's child care provider, you would give him as many opportunities as possible to acquire and perfect skills and abilities that you know are likely to unfold during his next seven months or so. You also know that Ronny will not acquire and perfect his motor skills without or apart from a social/emotional and cognitive/language developmental environment. So, while providing Ronny with an appropriate environment for meeting his physical/motor needs, you would also attend to his other developmental needs. This might mean talking to him, explaining things to him, showing him various objects, and allowing him physical proximity to other children.

As Ronny grows and develops, and for whatever length of time he is in your program, he will need opportunities to learn and practice all the skills and behaviors that for him are age appropriate and individually appropriate. You would take advantage of his built-in "drive" to accomplish the developmental tasks nature has set before him. This principle applies to all areas of his development.

 ## Specific Developmental Needs of Infants: What Do They Need?

Unlike the developmental needs shown in Table 2–1, other developmental needs are broader in scope; in Chapter 1 these were referred to as second-category needs. These needs often make up general groups of events, opportunities, and experiences

Infants need opportunities to learn and practice skills and behaviors that are appropriate for their age and individuality.

that children must have for proper development. Using the criteria of age appropriateness, individual appropriateness, and social/cultural appropriateness, you can convert these general needs into specific, practical applications. Consider the following example.

Although adequate health care is a true need, "adequate" can be ambiguous, open-ended, and different for each child. By itself, it doesn't say anything about what adequate health care would be for 18-month-old Robin, who has diabetes. You could give Robin the care she needs only if you understood her medical condition and followed through on its prescribed treatment—injections, oral medication, diet, etc. These treatment regimens are individually appropriate for Robin, but not for nondiabetic Alisandro.

There are also situations that are less obvious than a pronounced disease, situations of which even the parents might initially be unaware. Horace, at 16 months of age, has undiagnosed food allergies causing reactions that puzzle the parents and the child care staff. Food allergies concern both health care and nutrition. For Horace, adequate health care and nutrition would require a physician diagnosing his allergies and giving him an appropriate treatment and diet. The need is expressed in general terms, but Horace's need would have to be met in ways that are specific to his situation.

The needs we discuss apply to children of all ages. As illustrated by the examples of Robin and Horace, the unique characteristics of the individual child guide how such needs are to be met. This means there are many paths to the same end, and no two children should necessarily be put onto the same path. For instance, our society gen-

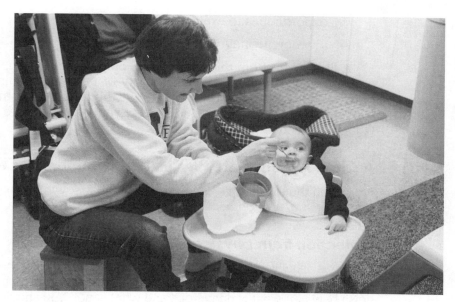

Adequate nutrition and healthcare is unique to each infant.

erally accepts each child's need to become independent, but shy Miguel may require a slower journey toward independence than Luis, his bold and more assertive brother. Ideally, Miguel and Luis would reach independence in the way that best suits their respective developmental pace, temperaments, and personalities.

A lot has been written about children's needs that is relevant to child appropriate practice. The Web site of "The Consultative Group on Early Childhood Care and Development" is one source of such information. A 1992 publication by the Christian Children's Fund (christianchildrensfund.org) authored by N. Donohue-Colletta, states the following:

> In terms of physical, intellectual, emotional and social well-being, the period from conception to age 6 is the key to subsequent growth, development and ultimate productivity. Pre-natally through the sixth year there are several distinct stages. They include: . . . postpartum (birth to 1 month), early infancy (the first six months), late infancy (6–12 months), toddler (1 to 3 years), and the pre-school child (3–6 years of age). Children have different needs, depending on where they are within these stages.

The article continues, "In order to create a programme [sic] for young children, it is critical to have more specific information on their needs" (p. 1). The article refers to "A delineation of developmental differences" (Donohue-Colletta, 1992, p. 1). Notice how the following needs are stated more broadly than the needs described in Table 2–1.

According to Donohue-Colletta, infants (birth to age one) need

* protection from physical danger
* adequate nutrition
* adequate health care
* adults with whom to form attachments
* adults who can understand and respond to their signals
* things to look at, touch, hear, smell, and taste

* opportunities to explore the world

* appropriate language stimulation

A final quote from this same article emphasizes the importance of a good developmental environment: "A wide variety of inputs is required to support children's growth and development. An important thing to note is that all the inputs require someone to interact with the child. Very young children are not capable of obtaining what they need on their own" (p. 1).

 ## A Child Appropriate Physical Environment for Infants

From Donahue-Colletta's list, we identify the following as belonging to a child appropriate *physical environment* for infants.

Protection from physical danger

Danger is usually relative to a child's developmental level or maturity—what is dangerous for a one-year-old might pose no threat to a two-year-old. Sometimes it is hard to distinguish between what is dangerous and what is not. You should consider not just age appropriateness but also individual appropriateness when dealing with issues of physical safety. For example, Michael and Johnny, both fourteen months old, can walk, but Michael is more skilled and surefooted than Johnny, who tends to fall if he walks more than a few feet, especially if he is carrying something. Child care staff should be more cautious about letting Johnny walk where he could hit his head against hard objects if he fell.

Because others have to bring the environment *to* a nonmobile infant, keeping a nonmobile infant safe is in many respects easier than keeping an older, mobile infant safe. Physical safety therefore becomes a matter of monitoring such things as the objects the child can put into his mouth, to prevent choking; his interactions with older children who could inadvertently play too roughly with him; her position on the diapering table to prevent her from rolling off; or every moment you are bathing her, to prevent drowning.

An infant needs the protection of a physically safe environment.

A safe physical environment may seem easy to distinguish from a safe emotional environment, but a safe emotional environment depends to some degree on safe physical surroundings. For example, it's hard to imagine 16-month-old Rebecca feeling emotionally safe in an environment filled with loud, strange noises, or furniture that is unstable and likely to collapse under her weight. Such an environment would hardly foster feelings of psychological well-being. Feelings of insecurity come not only from the physical environment but also from the social environment. Young children, for example, can find older children's larger size or rough-and-tumble play threatening and overwhelming.

 SEE FOR YOURSELF

Observe the interaction of infants and their caregiver in a child appropriate infant room. What distinguishes a healthy environment from one lacking in this area? An emotionally safe environment from one that is threatening to the child? A physically safe environment from one where the child is in danger?

A safe physical environment should also provide infants with opportunities to explore the world and to look, hear, taste, touch, and smell. Gestwicki's (1999) characteristics of a safe infant environment are summarized in Table 2–2.

Table 2–2   Characteristics of a Safe Infant Environment

- ❑ Mirrors and windows that will not break, and windows that open only from the top or protection from windows that open at the bottom.
- ❑ No electrical cords to trip or chew on; electrical outlets that are covered.
- ❑ Protection from anything that could burn or scald (for example, light bulbs, heaters, radiators, hot water faucets).
- ❑ Plants that are not poisonous.
- ❑ Unreachable hazardous chemicals such as medicines, cleaning substances.
- ❑ No broken or damaged toys, toys with easily removable small parts, or toys painted with lead or other toxic materials.
- ❑ Furniture that is stable and cannot be pulled over or fall; furniture should meet consumer protection standards to prevent infants from getting their heads stuck.
- ❑ Any sharp edges that could injure if fallen on or bumped into are covered or padded.
- ❑ Staff that is knowledgeable about emergency procedures, such as CPR and first aid; location of emergency numbers and equipment; and evacuation procedures, such as fire drill.
- ❑ Constant supervision of infants who are never left unattended; high-chairs, strollers, and changing tables are fitted with proper restraints.
- ❑ Infants are supervised as they eat and drink; they are never left with a propped up bottle and are given properly sized finger foods.
- ❑ Infants are not overprotected; they are provided with safe ways to practice a challenging skill (for example, cushioning with a pillow a child's possible fall from a step he is interested in, rather than prohibiting him from climbing at all).

Adapted from Gestwicki (1999, pp. 75–76).

≋ Through Their Eyes

Cathy Bentley is the lead teacher in the infant room at Suny Plattsburgh Early Care and Education Center. Today she has seven-month-old Molly busily crawling along the carpeted floor near the wall that has an infant-safe mirror mounted behind a wooden grab bar. Molly delights at catching her own reflection in the mirror. "Who is that friendly girl in the mirror?" Cathy teases. Molly gurgles her approval and scoots toward the small, soft climber made of vinyl-covered high-density foam. The soft mats underneath the climber provide a safe area for the infants to test their climbing and stretching skills. The low teacher-child ratio in the room also contributes to the safe physical environment in the infant room.

Adequate Nutrition

This need involves both the physical and the social/emotional environments, because without basic nutrition even an optimum social/emotional or cognitive/language environment will not keep a child alive and well. The caregiver and the food he or she provides are physical, but the act of feeding is such an important social and emotional event that adequate nutrition becomes more than just giving a baby something to eat. Table 2–3 (adapted from an article titled "Appropriate diet for age" found at http://www.WebMD.com) outlines the elements of adequate nutrition for infants from birth to one year of age.

SEE FOR YOURSELF

Observe lunchtime in a room for infants ranging in age from six weeks to 11 months. Critique the contents of their lunches and evaluate the appropriateness for the infants' various ages. Afterwards, when the children are napping, discuss with the caregiver what you have observed.

Adequate Health Care

Like nutrition, health care also involves both the physical and the social/emotional environments, as biological health also depends on things provided by the physical environment, like immunizations, medications, and physicians and caregivers to administer them. Table 2–4 outlines the characteristics of a healthy infant environment.

Things to Look At, Touch, Hear, Smell, and Taste

We learn about the world through our five physical senses. Much of what we think and feel is based on what we have seen, touched, heard, smelled, or tasted. Piaget

TABLE 2–3   Adequate Nutrition for Infants from Birth to One Year of Age

Birth to Four Months

❑ During the first four to six months of life, breast milk or formula will meet infant's nutritional needs.

❑ Breast milk is recommended for the first six months, but a fortified formula is satisfactory.

❑ A breast-fed newborn may nurse 8 to 12 times per day (every two to four hours) or on demand.

❑ By four months, frequency of breast feeding is likely to reduce to four to six times per day, but quantity per feeding will increase.

❑ Formula fed infant may need to eat six to eight times per day, beginning with two to five ounces of formula per feeding (16 to 35 ounces per day).

❑ With age, frequency of formula feeding decreases and quantity increases to about six to eight ounces per feeding.

Four to Six Months

❑ Infant should consume 28 to 45 ounces of formula; transition to solid foods imminent.

Developmental Indicators of Readiness for Solid Food

❑ When birth weight has doubled.

❑ When infant has good control of head and neck.

❑ When infant can sit up with some support.

❑ When infant can show she is full by turning her head away or not opening her mouth.

❑ When infant shows interest in food when others are eating.

Recommendations for Feeding Solid Food

❑ Start with iron-fortified baby rice cereal; mix with breast milk or formula to a thin consistency. With greater mouth control, mix to a thicker consistency.

❑ Give cereal two times per day, starting with one or two tablespoons of dry cereal prior to mixing with milk. Increase gradually to three or four tablespoons of cereal.

❑ CAUTION: Do not give cereal in a bottle unless recommended by a pediatrician.

❑ Introduce other iron-fortified instant cereals when infant is routinely eating rice cereal. Introduce only one new cereal per week and watch for any intolerance.

Six to Eight Months

❑ Offer breast milk or formula three to five times per day. Milk consumption will decrease as solid food becomes a source of nutrition.

❑ Following a variety of baby cereals, introduce fruit juices, strained fruits, and vegetables. "Use infant-packed juices or unsweetened vitamin C rich juices such as apple, grape, and orange." CAUTION: To avoid tooth decay, do not give juices in a bottle at bedtime. Also, do not give orange juice until infant is at least nine months of age if the family has a history of allergy to orange juice.

❑ Introduce one strained fruit or vegetable at a time; wait two to three days in between to check for allergic reactions.

❑ Begin with plain vegetables and plain fruits; for example, green peas, potatoes, carrots, sweet potatoes, squash, beans, beets, bananas, applesauce, apricots, pears, peaches, and melons.

❑ Offer fruits and vegetables in servings of two to three tablespoons; offer about four servings per day.

continued

TABLE 2–3 Adequate Nutrition for Infants from Birth to One Year of Age (Continued)

Eight to Twelve Months
❑ Offer breast milk or formula three to four times per day.
❑ Introduce strained or finely chopped meats. If the infant is breast-fed, start meats at eight months of age in order to get iron into his or her diet.
❑ Offer only one new meat per week in three to four tablespoon servings.
❑ Increase servings of fruits and vegetables to three to four tablespoons, four times per day.
❑ Offer eggs three to four times per week, but only the yolk to avoid possible sensitivity to egg whites.
❑ Do not give children under the age of one any dairy products, although cheese, cottage cheese, and yogurt may be given in small amounts.
One Year
❑ After one year of age, vitamin D or four percent whole milk may replace formula or breast milk. Do not give children younger than two years of age low-fat milk (two percent or skim).
❑ The one-year-old child should be getting much of his or her nutrition from "meats, fruits and vegetables, breads and grains, and the dairy group."
❑ Provide a variety of foods to ensure adequate intake of vitamins and minerals.

Adapted from a WebMD.com article titled "Appropriate diet for age."

TABLE 2–4 Characteristics of a Healthy Infant Environment

❑ Staff religiously adhere to standards of "adult hand-washing after coughing, sneezing, wiping a child's nose, changing diapers, and before handling food or bottles; after washing, adults use paper towels to touch faucets or waste containers " (p. 76).
❑ There is strict adherence to licensing standards for cleanliness of the diaper changing area; staff provide a clean and covered surface for each diaper change.
❑ Food and bottles are refrigerated until they are used.
❑ Infants' hands are washed frequently, with individual washcloths.
❑ Toys and surfaces are washed every day, or more frequently when children are sharing and mouthing toys.
❑ Parents and staff remove street shoes before they walk on floors where infants lie.
❑ Individual cribs are kept clean.
❑ Accurate records of up-to-date infant immunizations are kept.
❑ Infants who show signs of illness are excluded in keeping with the "standards and symptoms defined by the program" (p. 50).
❑ Only prescribed medicines are administered to infants with permission and instructions from the parents.

Adapted from Gestwicki (1999, p. 76).

deduced that children are held hostage by their senses for about the first 18 months of life. They respond to what they perceive primarily through physical-motor actions, so he called the first stage of cognitive development the *sensorimotor stage.* Reports and studies of children raised in bland and unstimulating environments (such as certain orphanages) attest to the detrimental effects such environments have on growth and development.

Gestwicki (1999) believes infants' environments should duplicate as much as possible the rich and varied kinds of sensory stimulation ordinarily found in their homes. There are good reasons for doing this. New experiences are best understood when they occur in the context of familiar ones, because later learning is built on earlier learning. Familiar surroundings also give infants a sense of security and confidence to explore new aspects of their environment. Mixing the familiar with the unfamiliar can also lead to beneficial interaction effects. How is this so?

In Piaget's theory of cognitive development, learning takes place through two complementary processes, *assimilation* and *accommodation.* When one-year-old Melanie experiences something familiar to her, she assimilates it into what she already knows, and she learns little if anything new. However, when Melanie experiences something that is a little out of the ordinary for her, she tries to make sense out of it, and in so doing, she

Familiar surroundings provide the security and confidence an infant needs to explore new aspects of the environment.

TABLE 2–5   Infants' Sensory Environment

❑ Provide infants with materials they can explore independently, "using the areas and furniture twenty-four inches above the floor" (p. 74).

❑ Prepare an environment that uses all the infant's senses.

❑ Use commercial toys as well as homemade ones that appeal to infants' senses. Continually check all toys for safety.

❑ Remove things that infants cannot directly understand to avoid sensory overload.

❑ Do not use cribs as an environment for sensory stimulation. Authors' note: A stimulating sensory environment is not conducive to sleeping, which is usually a crib's primary purpose. An infant is likely to fall asleep more quickly if his crib becomes only a place where he sleeps and not also a place where he can play.

Adapted from Gestwicki (1999, p. 74).

learns something new—she accommodates. This new learning, or accommodation, is an interaction effect. In an effective early childhood program, optimal growth and development depend on the interaction between children's levels of development and maturation; their skills, abilities, temperaments, and cultural backgrounds; and a child appropriate developmental environment. Table 2–5 summarizes some of the requirements of an appropriate sensory environment.

It would be impossible to duplicate every aspect of an infant's home sensory environment, and this is where staff-parent communication becomes important. Parents certainly can give child care staff useful suggestions regarding the kinds of sensory stimulation their infants find interesting. It's also possible that several infants will share some interesting stimuli in common.

Opportunities to Explore the World

Animals often depend on exploration for their survival and may explore ways to escape their immediate surroundings should they feel endangered. Have you ever seen a cat put into a strange room and watched how it walks around the space, sniffing and looking into every nook and cranny? Unless in unusual circumstances, adults do not ordinarily look for ways to escape their immediate surroundings, but they may show a natural curiosity or even fear when they are in unfamiliar places. Because children have had less experience with the world, they show even more curiosity or fear in a strange environment than do adults.

Exploration allows infants to find interesting ways to use their senses. Research and experience tell us that infants' healthy, anxiety-free, spontaneous exploration depends on the formation of secure emotional attachments to another person or persons, because security of this kind gives infants a safe physical and psychological base from which to explore. This connection between the physical and the emotional domains highlights the interdependence of all the developmental areas.

Since our sensory modalities are the pathway for all our learning, opportunities to explore the world are critical. To paraphrase Abraham Kaplan (1964), we are not pure intelligence operating outside of our physical senses. We have bodies with eyes, ears, noses, taste buds, and the capacity to recognize objects through touch. Children of all ages absolutely need to interact with their environments using all aspects of their physical beings.

An environment that promotes mobility gives infants the freedom to learn how to crawl, creep, cruise, and eventually walk and run.

TABLE 2–6 An Environment for Fostering Infants' Mobility

❏ Infants are confined to cribs only when necessary for their safety or when they do not need extra space to roll over. Otherwise, they are placed in a safe space on the floor where they can play and move about freely.

❏ Nonmobile infants are protected from mobile ones. Creative solutions include the use of movable barriers such as cushions, boxes, or gates.

❏ Adults regularly lie down on the floor to get the infant's perspective on her environment. Potential hazards and the "need for verbal restrictions" are eliminated before they become an issue. This makes the environment "an inviting place, rather than one where babies continually have to be removed or restricted" (p. 72).

❏ Adults keep in mind that the size a space needs to be is relative to the size of the infant. Adults help infants feel secure by sectioning larger spaces into smaller spaces that are appropriate to their needs and abilities.

Adapted from Gestwicki (1999, p. 72).

Exploration, however, ultimately requires the ability to move from one place to another. The general environment should also support a developmental environment that gives infants the freedom to learn how to crawl, creep, walk while holding onto furniture (cruise), and eventually walk and run. Gonzalez-Mena and Eyer (2001) advise putting infants "in the position in which they are freest and least helpless during their waking hours" (p. 109). Infants need a wide range of safe opportunities to learn new movements, and to practice movements and physical skills they have already acquired.

Table 2–6 outlines some characteristics of an environment that encourages mobility.

A Child Appropriate Social/Emotional Environment for Infants

Donohue-Coletta identifies two needs that are relevant to an appropriate social/emotional environment for infants: adults with whom to form attachments, and adults who can understand and respond to infants' signals. The second need, though, is an integral part of attachment. Trust, respect, and attachment have been noted as central features of infants' social/emotional environment, so please take note of how these are discussed.

The Formation of Attachments

Muzi (2000) defines attachment as "the emotional bond between infants and their caregivers" (p. 551). Most psychologists believe that early secure attachments are vital to healthy development, as these attachments form the foundation for healthy interpersonal relationships later on. Also recall that an infant's exploratory behavior relies on her feeling that she has a secure physical and psychological base from which to venture out into the surrounding environment.

From both an evolutionary and contemporary perspective, attachment also has survival benefits. When Michelle is strongly attached to her mother, and her mother feels a strong bond with Michelle, her mother is far more likely to meet Michelle's needs appropriately and consistently than if the attachment and the bond are weak, insecure, or nonexistent. Attachment is not only a need but can serve as a diagnostic tool for evaluating the effectiveness of the child/caregiver relationship and, by logical extension, the effectiveness of an early childhood program. Let's see why.

Conceptually and behaviorally, attachment is not simple or straightforward. It involves several dynamics, such as interactional synchrony and attachment behaviors. Interactional synchrony refers to a caregiver coordinating his or her behaviors with those of the infant, thereby allowing the infant to "lead the dance," so to speak (see Table 2–9 for a further discussion of interactional synchrony). Related to interactional synchrony are the various behaviors an infant uses to signal her needs and get the attention of the caregiver—behaviors such as crying, smiling, and watching the caregiver as he or she moves about the room.

The quality of attachment also varies. Mary Ainsworth, prominent among attachment researchers, identified three basic attachment patterns: *securely attached, avoidantly attached,* and *ambivalently attached* (Muzi, 2000, page 206). Mary Main, who was a student of Ainsworth's, identified a fourth pattern of attachment, which she called *disorganized-disoriented attachment.*

These patterns can be useful in at least two ways: (1) they indicate the possible characteristics of the parent-child relationship that led to a particular pattern, and (2) they can be used to identify the kinds of adult-child interactions that are most and least likely to contribute to an effective, child appropriate social/emotional developmental environment. Please refer to Tables 2–7 and 2–8.

Attachment and trust go hand-in-hand. As you can see from the behavioral descriptions of the four attachment patterns in Table 2–7, trust is an essential ingredient of the adult-child relationship and must be nurtured environmentally as well. One of Gonzalez-Mena and Eyer's (2001) 10 principles of caregiving is "build security by teaching trust" (p. 21). They write, "For infants to learn to trust they need dependable adults. They need to know that they will get their needs met in a reasonable amount of time. Learning to predict what will happen is an important part of building trust" (p. 21). Recall that the mothers of avoidantly and ambivalently attached infants were not predictable (consistent), dependable, or timely in meeting their infants' needs. Table 2–9 summarizes the characteristics of an environment that nurtures trust.

Gonzales-Mena and Eyer (2001) and Gestwicki (1999) include respect as a critical element of trust. Gestwicki writes, "Caregivers must respect infants needs as real and

TABLE 2–7 Attachment Patterns—Their Characteristics and Causes

Securely Attached

Child's Typical Behavior

- ❑ Uses mother/caregiver as a secure base for exploration. He comes back to caregiver if he needs reassurance.
- ❑ Becomes upset when caregiver leaves the room, and play decreases. Greets caregiver with pleasure when she returns; is easily comforted and stays close to caregiver for a period of time, then resumes play. Definitely prefers the company of the caregiver to that of a stranger.
- ❑ Child is "usually cooperative and free of anger" (Papalia, p. 246).

Contributing Caregiver Behavior

- ❑ Caregiver is very responsive to child's signals and needs. She feeds child when he is hungry and comforts him when he is distressed.
- ❑ Care is reliable and consistent. Mothers of securely attached infants "responded promptly, consistently, and appropriately to infant signals and held their babies tenderly and carefully" (Berk, 2000, p. 426).

Avoidantly Attached

Child's Typical Behavior

- ❑ Child ignores or is unresponsive to the caregiver while playing with toys.
- ❑ Child may or may not appear distressed when caregiver leaves the room (Papalia, et al., 1999, report that babies who are avoidantly attached rarely cry when the mother/caregiver leaves); in either case, the child does not seek contact when the caregiver returns.
- ❑ Child turns away or averts his eyes when caregiver tries to pick him up. If picked up, child often fails to cling to the caregiver (Berk, 2000, p. 424).
- ❑ Child tends to be angry, does not to reach out when in need (Papalia, p. 246).
- ❑ Child does not like to be held, but dislikes being put down even more (Papalia, p. 246).

Cautionary Note to Early Childhood Program Staff

- ❑ Muzi (2000) notes that "What is often interpreted as independence and autonomy is in actuality a lack of trust in others and an inability to share in a close relationship" (p. 206). The avoidantly attached child can thus protect herself emotionally by staying uninvolved with the caregiver.

Contributing Caregiver Behavior

- ❑ Caregiver is insensitive to and rejects the child's needs.

Ambivalently Attached

Child's Typical Behavior

- ❑ Child rarely explores his environment.
- ❑ Child shows distress when caregiver leaves the room, but is ambivalent or uncertain when caregiver returns.
- ❑ Upon caregiver's return, child reaches out and clings to her, then quickly and angrily pushes caregiver away, "sometimes kicking and swiping at them" (Muzi, p. 207).
- ❑ Child shows two essentially contradictory behaviors: Because of her uncertainty, the child wants her mother around continually; at the same time, the child angrily rejects her mother because of her unreliability and inconsistency.

continued

TABLE 2–7 Attachment Patterns—Their Characteristics and Causes (Continued)

Contributing Caregiver Behavior
❑ Caregiver is insensitive to and rejects the child's needs.

Disorganized-Disoriented Attachment
Child's Typical Behavior
❑ Main found that in a laboratory situation (the Strange Situation experiment), disorganized-disoriented infants "appeared dazed or disoriented and sometimes depressed" (Muzi, p. 207).
❑ These children cannot seem to find ways to get close to their mothers. "Sometimes they approach her backward and even stand still and stare into space when she is coming close" (Muzi, p. 207).
❑ Papalia, Olds, and Feldman report that disorganized-disoriented infants ". . . often show inconsistent, contradictory behaviors. They greet the mother brightly when she returns but then turn away or approach without looking at her. They seem confused and afraid. This may be the least secure pattern" (p. 246).
Contributing Caregiver Behavior
❑ According to Muzi, disorganized-disoriented children often have been abused.
❑ Papalia, Olds, and Feldman, on the other hand, note that it is often the parents who have ". . . suffered unresolved trauma, such as loss or abuse" (p. 247).

Adapted from Muzi (2000, pp. 206–207) and Papalia, Olds, and Feldman (1999, pp. 246–247).

TABLE 2–8 An Environment for Attachment

❑ Facility contains comfortable chairs and floor spaces that allow adults to focus on their interactions with the infants.

❑ There is a designated place for parents to interact privately with their infants.
  ❑ Meeting this condition avoids distractions that work against parents and their infants focusing exclusively on each other, an important part of the attachment process.

❑ Location of work areas is such that staff can supervise the room and still care for an individual infant and have access to all necessary materials.
  ❑ This is what Gonzales-Mena (2001) calls "soft eyes," the ability to pay appropriate attention to a particular child while still being aware of what is happening in the rest of the room.

❑ Caregiving areas where feeding and diapering take place contain nothing that would distract infants from focusing on the adult.
  ❑ This condition not only helps attachment but also helps the infant pay attention to what the caregiver is doing. In turn, it provides the caregiver the opportunity to explain what she is doing: "Now I'm taking off your dirty diaper, and I'm going to give you a nice, clean one. You will feel so much better."

Adapted from Gestwicki (1999, p. 71).

TABLE 2–9   The Characteristics of a Trustworthy Environment for Infants

- ❑ Infants' needs are consistently responded to, and by the same adults.

- ❑ Daily schedules for feeding, sleeping, and playing are individually appropriate to each infant's unique personality, temperament, and biological rhythms.

- ❑ One primary caregiver is assigned to the same group of infants in order to facilitate the caregiver's close relationship with the infant and his or her family. A special, primary relationship with their caregivers helps infants and caregivers establish mutual respect and trust. It also allows caregivers to establish a special relationship with infants' families.

- ❑ The program adheres to a small adult-child ratio—DAP recommends one adult caring for three infants (see, for example, Bredekamp and Copple, p. 80).

- ❑ In order to ensure that responsiveness is consistent and that infants' needs are met, there is regular communication between all staff members and parents.

- ❑ Staff see a trustworthy environment as a safe, familiar place for infants. The patterns and locations of things in the environment are predictable and consistent. Special places are provided for equipment and materials that even infants can become familiar with and reliably return to, to retrieve and store their playthings.

- ❑ In order to protect infants from constant verbal restrictions, which might threaten their emotional security, restrictions and prohibitions such as gates or the removal of forbidden or dangerous objects, are built into the physical environment.

- ❑ Berk reports that *interactional synchrony,* which is a "special form of communication," supports babies' feelings of trust. Interactional synchrony is described as "a sensitively tuned 'emotional dance,' in which caregiver-infant interaction appears to be mutually rewarding. The caregiver responds to infants' signals in a well-timed, appropriate fashion. In addition, both partners match emotional states, especially the positive ones" (p. 426).

Adapted from Gestwicki (1999, pp. 68–69; also see Berk, 2000, p. 426).

important. Babies are treated with an appropriate degree of seriousness" (p. 138). "Respect for infants and toddlers as worthy people" is among Gonzales-Mena and Eyer's 10 principles of caregiving (Gonzales-Mena and Eyer, 2001, pp. 11–22). Respect includes explaining even to the youngest infant what you are about to do and what the child can expect. They note, for example, that "the natural tendency is to pick up a child without saying anything. Babies are often carried around like objects—even when they are old enough to walk and talk" (p. 16). A possible reason for this kind of behavior toward young infants is that "Respect is not a word usually used with very young children. . . Usually worries about respect go the other way, as adults demand (or wish for) children to respect them" (Gonzales-Mena and Eyer, 2001, p. 16).

Respect for infants has important implications for caregiving. See what these are in Table 2–10.

 SEE FOR YOURSELF

Observe staff/child relationships in an infant room. How many caregiving practices that indicate respect for infants (summarized in Table 2–10) can you observe? Can you suggest any improvements that could be made in the staff/child relationships you have observed?

TABLE 2–10   Caregiving Practices That Indicate Respect for Infants

❏ Infants are allowed to establish their own schedules for sleeping, feeding, and playing. Adults do not assume that they know best and that infants should conform to adults' timetables. Caregiver also respects the needs and decisions of individual families.

❏ Caregiver always assumes that infants' needs are real, and he or she responds promptly to infants' cries. Caregiver makes it clear to the infant that his message has been received.

❏ Infants are allowed to take the lead when communicating their needs and desires; caregiver tries to interpret their communication. Caregiver also assumes that nonverbal infants will have their own means of communicating. (Gonzales-Mena and Eyer [2001, p. 14] include this advice in their third principle of caregiving: "Learn Each Child's Unique Ways of Communicating and Teach Them Yours.")

❏ Before intervening, caregiver allows infants time to do things for themselves—find solutions to a problem, find interesting things to do, or quiet themselves when distressed.

❏ Caregiver assumes and allows infants' active participation in routine caregiving activities. Caregiver gives infants cues and observes their readiness to participate.

❏ Infants' preferences for, and aversions to, particular people are respected, especially when they are able to exhibit stranger anxiety.

❏ Caregiver takes infants' emotions seriously; he or she helps infants find ways of coping with, and acknowledging, their feelings.

❏ Caregiver respects cultural differences regarding what is appropriate care for infants. Such differences are explored with the families, and compromises are reached to accommodate the families' views and the standard practices of the child care facility.

Adapted from Gestwicki (1999, pp. 138–139).

From the foregoing, responsiveness and sensitivity play a prominent role in infants' emotional environment, and every aspect of child appropriate practice demands them. At issue here are concerns about infants' temperaments, moods and feelings, and communication styles. In any given instance, the specific characteristics of responsiveness and sensitivity are determined by each child's unique characteristics. Some children's temperaments might make them very tolerant of caregiving behavior that other children might perceive as unresponsive. For some children, being picked up and cuddled is an important element of sensitive responsiveness, whereas other children resist such caregiving behaviors.

Gestwicki's reference to sensitivity of responsiveness gives a specific meaning to responsiveness. A caregiver can be insensitively responsive to a child's needs. For example, Phyllis is a caregiver in charge of three infants ranging in age from three to eight months. It has been a particularly trying day for Phyllis, and she is feeling fatigued and irritable. Five-month-old Lucinda has not had an especially good day, either, and she shows her displeasure by crying and demanding attention. Phyllis attends to Lucinda every time she cries, but it is without warmth, and she makes little or no effort to discover why Lucinda is so fussy. No one could accuse Phyllis of being unresponsive, but she certainly is not sensitively so.

Sensitive responsiveness exhibits the characteristics shown in Table 2–11.

A Child Appropriate Cognitive/Language Environment for Infants

Donohue-Colletta (1992) says simply that infants need "appropriate language stimulation." This is true, but infants need far more if their language skills are to develop

Child care staff should strive to respond sensitively to the needs of each child.

TABLE 2–11   The Characteristics of Sensitive Responsiveness

❑ Caregiver lets infants determine for themselves what kinds and degrees of physical stimulation they can tolerate and enjoy. Caregiver is sensitive to what the infant actually likes and dislikes and does not impose his or her own preconceptions of what the child should like or dislike.

❑ Caregiver uses what others have learned about infants' styles and experiences. Caregiver communicates with parents and others to enhance his or her own understanding of infants' individual personalities.

❑ Caregiver recognizes that sensitive responsiveness necessarily involves "reciprocal interaction. Caregivers have to practice turn-taking behavior, taking time in play and caregiving interaction to pause and allow the baby to participate and respond" (p. 140). Such "pauses" permit the caregiver to observe how the infant is reacting and to modify her behavior accordingly.

Adapted from Gestwicki (1999, p. 140).

properly. Moreover, "appropriate" has to be meaningfully defined if it's to have any practical application in an effective early childhood program.

Children's cognitive development, as described by Piaget's sensorimotor stage, consists of first-category needs and developmental patterns. The sensorimotor stage's six substages have reasonably defined characteristics, a predictable sequence, and predictable ages at which they usually occur. As a result, infants' newly emerging skills, behaviors, and activity preferences define their developmental needs during the sensorimotor period. See how the first four substages of Piaget's sensorimotor stage are outlined in Table 2–12.

Our general guideline is applicable to these four substages. Sensitive responsiveness means being alert to an infant's changing abilities and behaviors. A sensitively responsive caregiver would provide an infant with appropriate objects and opportunities for interacting with the external environment.

TABLE 2–12: The Four Substages of Piaget's Sensorimotor Period

Substage	Age	Principal Characteristics
I: Reflexive substage	0–1 mos.	Infant mostly uses her reflexes, over which she gradually gains control. She cannot yet demonstrate sensory coordination—she cannot, for example, recognize the same object by using information coming from two or more of the five physical senses at the same time.
II: Primary Circular Reactions	1–4 mos.	Infant capitalizes on chance occurrences of actions. He engages in repetitive behaviors (thus the term "circular") that primarily involve his own body—e.g., sucking the fingers, watching his hands and feet—rather than the external environment.
III: Secondary Circular Reactions	4–8 mos.	Interactions with the external environment assume importance. Infant repeats behaviors that involve objects in the environment. Infant shows the beginning of *intentional* behavior, which she repeats because she enjoys the consequences of her actions. Infant shows the beginning of object permanence by starting to grasp for objects, although he will not continue to search for an object that is hidden.
IV: Coordination of Secondary Schema. (Schema are concepts or patterns of behavior)	8–12 mos.	Infant now combines existing behaviors in order to achieve some goal. He uses specific behaviors as a means to achieve a goal (ends). Infant will now continue to search for hidden objects, but his search is not organized or methodical, but random and haphazard.

Reprinted with permission from Delmar Learning. Partially excerpted from Bentzen, W. R. *Seeing Young Children: A Guide to Observing and Recording Behavior,* 4th edition (2000, p. 246)

The Elements of Cognitive Development

Principles to Guide Child Appropriate Practice

Virtually every activity or action contributes in some way to cognitive and language development. It would be easy to believe that development in these areas will simply happen on its own. Such a laissez-faire policy should not be part of an effective early childhood program. Intellectual and language growth are the products of a reasonably clear, well-thought-out strategy or series of strategies that motivate and define children's developmental environment.

This is not to say that every adult-child interaction is preplanned. Rather, the developmental environment and the interactions that occur there are guided by principles and conditions known to maximize children's intellectual and language growth. Table 2–13 summarizes 10 principles, which we call "conditions."

TABLE 2–13 The Conditions (Principles) for Optimal Cognitive and Language Development

Condition 1: Relationships Are of Paramount Importance

Recall again that early child care is about behavior—the behavior of the developmental environment and the adults and children in the environment. Gestwicki emphasizes relationships, which are particular kinds of behavior, as the vehicle for forming secure child-adult attachments. Attachments are the basis for exploration, learning, self-affirmation, and generally healthy social-emotional development later on in life.

Relationships with other people are more important than relationships with things, and this first condition affirms that fact. But relationships are also important for their role in interaction effects. A child's relationship with just any caregiver may not necessarily lead to the *best* interaction effects. If Phyllis, our hypothetical caregiver mentioned previously, consistently responded without warmth or sensitivity, it would not bode particularly well for five-month-old Lucinda. Moreover, children sometimes get along better with some adults than with others, just as some adults get along better with some children than with others—there is a sort of "chemistry" operating.

We recognize that most child care programs do not have the luxury of custom fitting their adult-child pairings. We would only recommend that there be the best possible fit between each child and his or her primary caregiver.

Condition 2: Learning Depends on Interaction

Nearly everything depends on interaction. Interaction in this context takes its more usual meaning as some sort of exchange between people or between people and objects. Child appropriate practice assumes that children are active participants in their own development, and active participation requires interaction. As with relationships, interaction should not be allowed simply to occur. Sensitive responsiveness should characterize at least some of an infant's interactions during the day.

The idea of children being active participants in their own development is very important. Active participation means involvement with the environment, and involvement means interaction with resulting interaction effects. Two things are needed here, a sensitive caregiver, and autonomy for the infant. When an infant may choose her own age appropriate and individually appropriate activities, she will interact with things that interest her, and she will make choices that are legitimate expressions of autonomy. A sensitive caregiver is alert to the infant's signals and knows when to interact directly with the infant and when to let her explore on her own.

Condition 3: "Learning is Sensorimotor "

Physical play and exploration pretty much define Piaget's sensorimotor stage, which means that physical play and exploration also pretty much define the infant's motor and cognitive behavior for the first 12 to 18 months of life. Sensorimotor learning is highly active learning (see Condition 2 regarding active participation).

During this stage, infants construct reality through direct involvement with people and objects. They are learning to think, but most of their dealings with the environment are action-oriented, not thought-oriented. Consequently, even though you need to talk *to* infants, don't try to teach them by talking *at* them. Just as important, don't interrupt their play or other self-initiated activity on the assumption that they're not learning anything and their behavior is unproductive.

continued

TABLE 2–13 The Conditions (Principles) for Optimal Cognitive and Language Development (Continued)

Condition 4: "Learning is Playful"

In an effective early childhood program, even important caregiving activities—such as feeding, diapering, or removing a child from a dangerous situation—can be cloaked in a playful attitude. Much depends on how the adult approaches these activities or situations. In a child appropriate environment, infants' learning should not be the dull, tedious thing it sometimes can be for older children and adults. Play has long been recognized as an essential activity for children. Caregivers must recognize that although play and sensorimotor activity in general are serious business from a developmental point of view, they are very pleasurable from the infant's point of view. Gestwicki makes the point that adults can also derive a great deal of pleasure and satisfaction from watching children play. This should be particularly true when adults realize that this play is contributing significantly to infants' development.

Condition 5: Learning Requires Repetition

Somewhere in his writings, Piaget argued that children need massive general experience. Even we adults seldom learn complicated things in only one try. Gonzales-Mena (1996) notes that "Children cannot push themselves on until they have done very thoroughly what it is they need to do" (p. 70). In Piaget's terms, infants need time and repeated experiences for growth and development to occur.

Repetition also seems to be a natural part of sensorimotor activity and play, but it is repetition voluntarily chosen by the infant herself. This is a caution against trying to teach infants things in an adult way. "Adult-directed repetition quickly exhausts and frustrates infants. This is shown by the fretful baby, who rubs her eyes, and keeps looking away from the 'lesson' " (p. 215).

Condition 6: Learning is Sequential

This means that the infant has to learn certain things before he can learn other things, or he has to go through earlier stages before going through later stages. Piaget argued that the child has to accomplish the tasks of the sensorimotor stage before she can move on to the preoperational stage, and the tasks of the preoperational stage before moving on to the concrete operational stage, and so on. Also, the child cannot temporarily or permanently skip a stage.

Adults should not try to accelerate a child's progress through the various stages of learning. Instead, adults are aware that cognitive stages have a reasonably predictable pattern, and they can be sensitive and responsive to the developmental needs and tasks that are dominant at a given time in the child's life.

Condition 7: "Learning Is Unique to the Learner"

Infants have individualized learning styles (see Chapter 1), and they learn and develop cognitively at their own pace. Again, interaction effects and age and individual appropriateness become important. One-year-old Brian's developmental level and experiences set him apart from other children, and optimal learning experiences for him will likely differ from anyone else's.

Infants derive their own unique kind of pleasure from their learning experiences. For example, eight-month-old Jonathan might find auditory stimulation more pleasurable than does Stephen, who prefers visual stimulation. When they are older, Jonathan will prefer listening to music and Stephen will prefer watching a movie. Jonathan's preferred auditory learning style partly defines his uniqueness relative to Stephen, and vice versa.

TABLE 2–13 The Conditions (Principles) for Optimal Cognitive and Language Development (Continued)

Condition 8: Infants Are the Leaders

In the traditional school classroom, the teacher generally takes the lead. Students sit in neat rows and listen to the teacher dispense information she thinks the students need to know. Students in this situation seem to be more passive than active. As Piaget pointed out, young children—infants—are active, not passive, learners. They seek stimulation and deliberately confront their environment as if to extract from it every possible pleasure, piece of information, and meaning.

Sensitivity of responsiveness, which we discussed in relation to attachment, also applies to infants' cognitive development and is especially relevant to infants' leadership role in this domain. The infant takes the lead by providing the cues to which adults respond. This message is repeated again and again in the literature and is essential to an effective early childhood program.

Gonzales-Mena and Eyer (2001) address this issue in their first principle of caregiving: "Involve Infants and Toddlers in Things That Concern Them" (p. 11). The key phrase here is "things that *concern them*." This is what taking the lead is all about. The infant decides what she wants to do and how she wants to do it (within limits established by concerns for safety and developmental appropriateness). Gestwicki states it this way: "Caregivers follow the lead of infants, rather than intruding on their exploration and play interests. They recognize that their role is that of supporter, offering attention and encouragement as babies proceed with their self-imposed tasks" (p. 216).

Condition 9: "Caregivers Provide the World"

This condition is one of the essential features or characteristics of an effective developmental environment. If adults only provided infants with a general environment, and no more, they would be leaving the developmental environment to chance. A general environment is a necessary and inevitable part of an infant's world. However, it is only the framework that potentially contains the infant's truly important world—the world of sights, sounds, smells, tastes, objects, people, and interactions.

With nonmobile infants, providing takes on a more direct meaning than with mobile infants who can take themselves to the environment rather than needing an adult to bring the environment to them. In either case, infants need a world of opportunities, relative freedom, consistencies, and sensitive, responsive adults who understand infants' needs and how to help them meet them.

Condition 10: No Learning Without Communication

"Communication" does not only mean talking and listening. Communication takes many forms. Physical objects and their locations in space communicate with infants. "Look at me," says a bright, shiny mobile hanging above five-month-old Jamie's crib. The mobile invites Jamie to reach up and touch it and make it move.

Adults and infants communicate with each other nonverbally in such ways as smiling, frowning, pointing, and giving and taking toys and other objects. It is impossible not to communicate. An adult's sensitive responsiveness tells Sylvia that she is loved, cherished, and deemed a worthy person. Another adult's insensitivity and unresponsiveness give Sylvia a totally different message. Infants learn the names for things and what they do when caregivers verbalize about the activities that involve them. "Oh," says Marsha, "Alfred likes that big, red ball. Look, Alfred, see how it rolls across the floor." Children do not invent the language they speak, so adults must not only provide them with the names of things, but they must let children hear a lot of speech so they can acquire the language skills needed to express feelings and complex ideas.

Adapted from Gestwicki (1999, pp. 214–217).

Summary

Child care professionals can foster children's proper growth and development when they satisfy the needs imposed by the developmental stages. Maturationally prescribed developmental patterns are used as definitions of need and as the basis for child appropriate practice.

Specific developmental needs of infants include:

* a child appropriate and safe physical environment

* adequate nutrition

* a healthy infant environment that provides opportunities to explore and fosters infants' mobility

* an appropriate social/emotional environment that respects infants and includes sensitive responsiveness on the part of caregivers

* an appropriate cognitive/language developmental environment

Questions to Consider

1. What would you say is the most critical difference between a need and a desire?

2. What is the General Guideline; that is, what role does it play in an early childhood program? What is its most important component?

3. Under what circumstances might desires become important?

4. Why are responsiveness and sensitivity so important in an effective early childhood program?

5. How does nearly everything children do contribute to their cognitive and language development? Do you think this is an accurate assumption?

6. Why is safety partly a function of the infant's age or developmental level?

For additional information on assessing the effectiveness of child care programs, visit our Web site at **http://www.earlychilded.delmar.com**

Chapter 3
Observing and Evaluating the Toddler Child Care Program

See How To

* differentiate between first- and second-category needs in the toddler child care program

* describe the relationship between first- and second-category needs in the toddler child care program

* examine specific needs of toddlers

* evaluate the components of a child appropriate physical environment for toddlers

* evaluate the components of a child appropriate social/emotional environment for toddlers

* evaluate the components of a child appropriate cognitive/language environment for toddlers

Introduction

Toddlerhood consists of the period from one to three years of age. The transition from infancy to toddlerhood is almost a quantum leap and, though it doesn't happen overnight, some changes are rapid enough to be noticeable over the course of several weeks. This pace of change can challenge early childhood program staff. For example, once 18-month-old Jeremy discovers how many interesting objects he can locate and grab, there will be no holding back his need and desire to explore. Jeremy's attention span will be relatively brief, and he is likely to move rather quickly from one object to another, giving each object only fleeting attention.

This characteristically short attention span is a developmental phase dictated by Jeremy's normal maturational processes. Don't try to slow Jeremy down or force him to attend to just a few things for longer periods. That would not be Jeremy at this stage of his development.

First-Category vs. Second-Category Needs in the Toddler Child Care Program

First-category and second-category needs are interdependent and interactive. Second-category needs directly or indirectly serve first-category needs. First-category needs or developmental tasks, when met, also enable the accomplishment of second-category needs. For instance, toddlers' ability to walk helps them meet their second-category need to explore the environment.

Some of the relationships between the two categories are obvious. Clearly, adequate health care and adequate nutrition serve all other needs at any age. The toddler's need to be accepted for who he or she is (see Table 3–1) can be subtler than health care or nutrition. Nevertheless, acceptance serves such first-category needs as the freedom to move about and explore, or to develop cognitive and language skills. Acceptance of the toddler implies adults' willingness to allow her to do the things she needs to do when she needs to do them. The ability to speak and to walk paves the way for many social interactions that are difficult or impossible for the prelinguistic, nonmobile child. Speaking and understanding language lead to understanding and expressing increasingly complex ideas essential for proper intellectual development and formal education.

Newly-acquired skills like speaking and walking stimulate toddlers to explore their environment and engage in more activities.

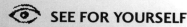 **SEE FOR YOURSELF**

What other relationships between second-category and first-category needs can you think of? What are the implications of these relationships for caregivers and early childhood program staff?

Physical/motor skills serve an especially broad array of second-category needs. Look again at the need to walk and run. Walking and running are capstone skills required for such second-category needs as autonomy, separateness (from the caregiver), sensorimotor exploration, and acquisition of self-help skills. Mobility opens the child up to more interaction effects than are possible for the nonmobile child. Mobility doesn't grant any child (or adult) unlimited access to the environment, but the child who can walk will experience far more of the richness and variety of his environment than the child who must have the environment brought to him.

The Changing Character of First-Category and Second-Category Needs

Although the needs in both these categories are important during all stages of development, the particular content of the categories changes from one stage to another. While infants exhibit first-category developmental needs to roll over, sit up, crawl, creep, and pull to a standing position, toddlers' first-category physical/motor needs

TABLE 3–1   What Toddlers Do and What They Need

A Toddler Typically Can and Does	A Toddler Needs
❑ Mimic (imitate) adult actions • Caregivers might model appropriate behaviors that are in the toddler's repertory or within her ability to acquire—such as throwing a ball, using a spoon, petting a dog, etc. ❑ Speak and understand words and ideas • Caregivers might engage the toddler in conversation, listen attentively and sensitively to his efforts to communicate, comment on what he is doing, apply labels to common objects in the environment ❑ Experiment with objects and enjoy listening to stories • Caregivers might provide the toddler with child appropriate objects in situations that are conducive to experimentation; read age appropriate and individually appropriate stories to the child ❑ Walk with a steady gait, climb stairs, and run • Caregivers might provide the toddler with safe opportunities to practice these motor skills under a reasonable variety of conditions; these activities could also be structured to result in meaningful consequences or objectives—walk to get a toy from a shelf, climb a short flight of stairs to retrieve an object, run in a game of "I'm gonna getcha!" ❑ Assert his independence, although he prefers familiar people • A toddler's strivings for independence must take place within the boundaries of age and individual appropriateness; a familiar caregiver should always be nearby to provide the toddler with feelings of security and self-confidence ❑ Recognize possession or ownership of objects • Caregivers should not demand that a toddler share his toys with others, since sharing is still beyond his conceptual grasp; however, the toddler's understanding of possession can be added to by such statements as "Yes, that's Bobby's ball," or "Let's ask Paula if we can play with her blocks."	❑ All the things an infant needs (protection from physical danger, adequate nutrition and health care, etc.) ❑ Opportunities to acquire motor, language, and cognitive skills ❑ To develop independence ❑ To learn self-control ❑ Opportunities for exploration and play ❑ Opportunities to play with other children ❑ Acceptance for who he or she is ❑ ". . . adults who can enjoy the exuberance and striving of the toddler to move to a sense of self" ❑ Help with achieving separation or detachment from the persons to whom she is attached ❑ Help to achieve a sense of individuality, "while maintaining safety and rights" of the toddler as a member of a group ❑ Protection from his or her "immaturity and impulsiveness," while at the same time assurance that she will be allowed to explore and learn "while still in Piaget's sensorimotor stage" ❑ Safety, but without unnecessary restrictions that frustrate him ❑ Flexibility that accounts for and meets her changing needs ❑ Flexibility of space and equipment that will allow the accomplishment of several purposes—"play as well as routine caregiving, practicing skills of new walkers, and relentless climbers" ❑ Variety to "provide for different toddlers doing different things and individual exploring, as well as for expanding the world beyond the confines of the four walls of the toddler room" ❑ An environment that can be easily restored to order so as to provide him with the "security of familiar objects being in familiar places"

continued

TABLE 3–1 What Toddlers Do and What They Need (Continued)

A Toddler Typically Can and Does	A Toddler Needs

❑ Establish friendships
  • Caregivers might provide opportunities for social interactions during various curriculum activities such as play and snack time
 	
❑ Solve problems
  • Many of the things a toddler encounters during the day might pose problems for her to solve: for the one-year-old—how to open a container that has something inside that rattles, how to make a mechanical object work after seeing someone else do it, or how to maneuver around furniture or other objects; for the two-year-old—discovering simple cause and effect or opening a door with an unfamiliar knob
 	
❑ Take pride in accomplishments
 	
❑ Help with tasks
 	
❑ Begin pretend play
  • Caregiver can give the toddler various objects that might encourage pretend or fantasy play—small blocks of wood that can become cars or boats
 	
❑ Move constantly
 	
❑ Manipulate objects to the full extent of his ability
 	
❑ Try to do everything by herself, even tasks that are beyond her ability
	❑ A challenging environment that prevents boredom and promotes further growth and development
	
	❑ An organized environment to help her acquire self-help skills and avoid frustrating delays

Adapted from the Web site http://www.worldbank.org/children/what/stages.htm and from Gestwicki (1999, pp. 83–84).

are different. Having already mastered the physical/motor needs of infancy, toddlers devote their attention to walking, running, and other more advanced motor activities.

Infants' second-category needs include protection from danger, adequate nutrition and health care, opportunities for exploration, and sensory stimulation. Toddlers also have these needs, but they differ from those of infants. Toddlers typically are no longer breast- or bottle-fed, and their nutritional needs in general are met with different foods than infants. Some of the things that are dangerous to an infant are not dangerous to a toddler. Toddlers explore differently than infants, largely because of their increased mobility.

There is another important aspect to meeting toddler's physical/motor needs. At 18 months of age, Corinne's cognitive, social, perceptual, speech, and language abilities are more advanced than they were in infancy. As a toddler, she enjoys a number of interaction effects previously unavailable to her. She becomes increasingly capable of representing her environment mentally rather than depending upon the direct,

Walking and running help toddlers to develop other skills.

immediate involvement of her physical senses (especially as she gets closer to the end of Piaget's sensorimotor stage). Corinne has more of her world "in her head," and she is increasingly capable of talking about her world and the things and people in it, even when that world is not directly present. Consequently, Corinne can walk into the kitchen with the intention of grabbing some pots and pans from under the kitchen sink, or alternatively, she might simply point to the cabinet and say to an adult, "pot, pot."

 SEE FOR YOURSELF

Observe children in a toddler classroom. Cite examples of the children's first- and second-category needs. Record any children's activities or behaviors that might demonstrate the interdependence and interactivity of first- and second-category needs.

 ## More About Needs

As noted in Chapter 1, development is itself a need. Recall that you can estimate a child's developmental level by observing his abilities. A given ability might constitute a developmental need if its expression is individually and culturally appropriate.

To clarify, not all the things a child can do are beneficial. Three-year-old Joshua opens a kitchen drawer and plays with a sharp knife. Fourteen-month-old Barbara toddles to the top of a flight of stairs and wants to go down them before she is capable of doing so safely. Two-year-old Arnold holds a fragile glass above his head with one hand and drops it, shattering it to pieces.

Each of these potentially dangerous scenarios illustrates a developmentally based ability: Joshua can open a drawer, Barbara can walk (toddle) from one place to another, and Arnold can hold a glass in one hand. However, the specific actions are not necessarily important, but the skill the action requires is. For example, a child who lives in a culture where there are no drawers will not demonstrate drawer-opening skills. She will acquire the ability necessary to open drawers but use that ability to perform comparable activities relevant to her culture.

Consider two important things here. First, don't associate only a few particular activities or actions with the underlying ability needed to perform them. Joshua's ability to open a drawer and Arnold's ability to hold a glass with one hand are simply behaviors that reflect underlying sets of abilities. There is nothing critically significant *per se* about opening drawers or holding a glass with one hand. However, Barbara's walking is a critical ability in its own right.

Second, the context and consequences of a child's behavior should be age appropriate, individually appropriate, and culturally appropriate. Opening drawers is good, playing with knives might not be; holding an object with one hand is good, dropping a glass and getting cut on its fragments is not; walking is good, falling down stairs is not.

We accept the skills and abilities cited in the literature as indicating growth and developmental change. Allen and Marotz (1999) report that the one-year-old "enjoys looking at picture books," a sign of perceptual-cognitive development (p. 75). An Aboriginal child living in the Australian outback may not have picture books to capture his interest, but that same child will be able to name everyday objects, also a sign of perceptual-cognitive development. This example illustrates the need to exercise good judgment when deciding what developmental patterns and needs are being expressed by particular behaviors. It also illustrates the importance of cultural appropriateness. The Aboriginal child in Australia is no less mature or capable than his American counterpart simply because picture books are not a part of his culture.

What Toddlers Do and What They Need

Before discussing the three specific developmental environments—physical/motor, social/emotional, and cognitive/language—let's briefly examine what toddlers typically are able to do. Their abilities also potentially identify their developmental needs. Table 3–1 summarizes this information and suggests some implications for caregiver behavior.

What Toddlers Need: Motive and Means

Any given behavior requires a *motive* (or purpose), and the *means* (or resources, ability) needed to perform the behavior. We are especially interested in the motives provided by development and maturation. Because development is a need, it provides motives for behaving in particular ways. Hunger motivates us to eat, fear motivates us to run away from or avoid a situation. In addition to being a need in its own right, development sets into motion a number of specific needs that contribute to the overall course of development. Children need to grow and mature as total beings, but they also need to grow and develop as a combination of "smaller" beings that make up the various functional domains (growing physically in size, walking, speaking, playing, interacting socially, developing and expressing emotions, etc.)

Development also provides the means to behave in particular ways. The need to walk motivates a child's efforts to walk, and maturation eventually leads to the ability to walk. Development and maturation provide both motives and means that govern or direct children's changing behaviors and abilities.

Although we discuss toddlers' needs as though they appear for the first time during toddlerhood, they actually develop out of infants' needs. Autonomy, for instance, is strongly associated with toddlers, but infants also need opportunities to achieve autonomy. Infants' autonomy is different from toddlers', but it is autonomy nonetheless.

A Child Appropriate Physical Environment for Toddlers

Gestwicki (1999) writes, ". . . adults need to consider the toddler developmental tasks they want to support. These include autonomy, separateness, movement ability, self-help skills, and sensorimotor exploration" (p. 84). She assigns these needs to the physical environment, but several of them also fall into the social/emotional and cognitive/language environment. This overlap again points out the interconnectedness of all the developmental domains. But why assign these tasks to the physical environment? Let's explore this question by providing a context within which to think about toddlers' developmental tasks or needs.

 ## The Need for Autonomy

The general environment must become an adequate developmental environment in order to achieve a child appropriate program. All of the developmental tasks discussed in this book need a general (physical) environment. The toddler's autonomy depends partly on having a physical environment that allows him to do things on his own without adult help; for example, shelves that are accessible. (See Table 3–2). An appropriate developmental environment, in turn, provides the toddler with encouragement and opportunities to do things on his own. These two environments necessarily work together.

Child care staff can unknowingly violate this relationship between the two environments. Staff can have a "proper" developmental environment attitude to foster autonomy, but provide a general environment that works against it. Toddlers achieve autonomy when the general and developmental environment permit an appropriate degree of independence and give them the feeling they are doing things for themselves. Children can do things for themselves if places for toys, equipment, and personal possessions (storage bins, cubbies, coathooks), and items they need for practicing self-help skills (mirrors, washcloths) are accessible to them without adult intervention. These conditions are not difficult to meet, but meeting them requires alertness and sensitivity.

Why Autonomy is an Important Need

All the toddler's needs or developmental tasks are important, but when their expressions are age appropriate, individually appropriate, and culturally appropriate, autonomy can become the cornerstone for accomplishing other developmental tasks. It would be hard to envision a toddler accomplishing such tasks as movement, self-help skills, and sensorimotor exploration, if she were not granted a reasonable degree of independence. Two-year-old Melinda wants to feed herself, but learning

TABLE 3–2   An Environment for Toddler Autonomy

❏ Appropriately sized furniture and an environment that encourages toddlers to do things for themselves

❏ Materials arranged in ways familiar and accessible to toddlers so they can get them on their own

❏ Provisions for toddlers to carry out responsibilities, such as picking up their blocks, putting games back on shelves, and other ways to restore order

❏ Opportunities to make age and individually appropriate choices

❏ Places where the toddler can be alone

❏ Environments that are physically and emotionally safe so as not to unduly restrict exploration

Adapted from Gestwicki (1999, p. 85).

Child care staff should foster an environment that provides toddlers with the encouragement and opportunity to do things on their own.

Learning how to eat can be a messy but important process of independence for a toddler.

to do this efficiently requires opportunities to feed herself, even though she may make a mess. Sixteen-month-old Paul's increasing ability to move about on his own creates opportunities to get into things that might be harmful or forbidden. Granting Paul reasonable autonomy might require childproofing his immediate space, rather than constantly restricting his explorations with such statements as, "No, no, don't touch that." Gestwicki (1999) advises against such "overt [verbal] restrictions," recommending instead that limits on where toddlers can go and what they can do be "built into the environment" (p. 84).

Autonomy usually implies the freedom to make choices from among a number of options. Gonzales-Mena and Eyer's (2001) first principle of caregiving is "involve infants and toddlers in things that concern them" (p. 10). This principle involves choice, and legitimate choice requires a reasonable number and variety of options. Twenty-two-month-old Arthur's autonomy is better served if he is free to choose from among six widely different objects rather than between only two objects. Moreover, given a choice of six objects, he is more likely to find something that really interests him. In keeping with Gonzales-Mena and Eyer's first principle, toddlers' interests and needs *are* the things that concern them. See what constitutes an appropriate environment for toddler autonomy in Table 3–2.

The Need for Separateness

Separateness and autonomy are closely related. Autonomy requires a certain kind of separateness or separation from outside influences or control. Autonomy and separateness do differ in some important respects. Autonomy refers to the toddler's ability and freedom to *do things for himself,* while separateness refers to the toddler's need and desire *to be by himself.* Being by himself means not only being alone physically, but perhaps more importantly, acquiring an identity or self-concept that eventually allows the toddler to perceive himself as psychologically, emotionally, and intellectually distinct from others.

Gestwicki's view of separateness includes toddlers choosing their own activities, materials, and spaces that "suit [their] particular moods or activity levels" (p. 85). The other side of the coin includes experiences as part of a group, which should always be offset by the toddler's freedom to be separate when he or she chooses. Separateness also includes the moving-away or independence phase of the earlier attachment process. The toddler must learn to leave the familiar surroundings of her home and family and adjust to the initially unfamiliar people and physical surroundings of the child care center. See Table 3–3 for the characteristics of an environment for separateness.

≈≈≈ Though Their Eyes

Kristina Jackson is the lead teacher in the wobbler room at Plattsburgh State University's Child Care Center. She has noticed that 18-month-old Tyler enjoys playing on the soft climbing toy. While Tyler engages in solo play in "her house," 15-month-old Sherry offers her a blanket. "I see Sherry bringing a blanket over for Tyler," Kristina comments to the group. This encourages Sean to volunteer to give Tyler his Teddy bear. Since he is not yet able to climb up to Tyler's house, Kristina asks if he would like her to help. When Sean nods she hands the bear up to a smiling Tyler. The toys and equipment in the wobbler room are arranged in ways that are familiar and accessible to the children so they can help themselves and make their own choices. Besides the loft, there are several other places where the children can have private space visible to the caregiver, further complementing the children's need for autonomy and separateness.

TABLE 3–3 An Environment to Foster Separateness

❑ Spaces for play and exploration that are clearly separated and allow each toddler his or her own area away from the other children

❑ A number of different materials that allow each toddler to make his or her own choice

❑ Brief opportunities for group interaction, such as singing, listening to songs and stories, or eating

❑ A number of similar toys to permit parallel play while still separate from other children

❑ "Pictures of family, home, and self to encourage toddlers to feel comfortable with separation and feelings of self" (p. 86)

Adapted from Gestwicki (1999, pp. 85–86).

 ## The Need for Movement

The importance of movement is apparent by its frequent appearance in discussions of children's developmental needs. As discussed in Chapter 2, most of the infant's earliest mobility skills prepare him for walking and running. Toddlers' movements are virtually nonstop, and they can appear to move just for the sake of moving. Movement also gets toddlers to various parts of the room where they can encounter interesting objects and sample interesting activities. This is understandable, since their expanded ability to move combines with their need and desire to learn about so many new objects and places. They do not linger very long in any one place and often prefer to stand or squat rather than sit while exploring and manipulating objects. To accommodate this pattern, the general environment should be free of objects that interfere with movement and should contain as many interesting objects as possible.

Toddlers' freedom of movement necessarily creates concerns for their safety. Legitimate or child appropriate freedom of movement goes hand in hand with child appropriate autonomy. Freedom of movement and autonomy frequently arouses anxieties regarding safety, which can lead to the tendency to overprotect. Overprotection, in turn, can send toddlers the message that they are incompetent. In Erik Erikson's theory of psychosocial development, failure to grant autonomy, or limiting autonomy by overprotecting, leads to feelings of shame and doubt. Thus, little Sean comes to believe he is incapable of doing things on his own, that adults do not trust his ability. He consequently doubts himself and develops a sense of shame because of his perceived incompetence. Table 3–4 summarizes the characteristics of an appropriate environment for movement.

TABLE 3–4 An Environment for Movement

❑ Classroom furnishings and their spatial arrangements provide clear paths for toddlers' movements and accommodate their very active exploration style.

❑ Gross motor activities are encouraged by providing proper space and equipment in the classroom.

❑ Toddlers are provided places and accompanying cues that suggest a quiet place where they can be alone.

❑ Toddlers are provided safe outdoor areas and equipment that are commensurate with their skills.

❑ Adults help toddlers acquire physical skills that allow self-management and lessen adults' tendency to overprotect.

Adapted from Gestwicki (1999, pp. 87–88).

The Need for Self-Help Skills

Self-help skills are inherent parts of autonomy. Autonomy has two aspects: the *ability* to behave autonomously, and the *opportunity* and *freedom* to behave autonomously. If either aspect is missing, autonomy does not exist. Thus, if two-year-old Alex has the ability to make certain kinds of appropriate choices, but his caregiver, Margaret, typically makes choices for him, she effectively stifles his autonomy. Conversely, if Margaret allows Alex to make choices he is not yet capable of making, the choices he makes will not be legitimate expressions of autonomy. Freedom without structure or direction is not freedom, but chaos.

A child also cannot be truly autonomous if she cannot accomplish certain routine activities such as eating, dressing, toileting, and self-hygiene. The toddler's messiness and relative inefficiency can cause concern, but it takes time to gain competence in these skills, and sensitive responsiveness makes caregivers aware and tolerant of a toddler's progress toward mastering these skills.

David Elkind cautions against what he calls *developmental exploitation.* Developmental exploitation can occur either by expecting a child to do more than she is capable of doing, or by expecting a child to do less than she is capable of doing. Parents or child care staff, in order to save time, might zip up two-year-old Brenda's coat or pull on her boots rather than let her accomplish these tasks on her own. An appropriate developmental environment allows ample time and opportunity for Brenda to learn and perform these activities. See Table 3–5 for the conditions that foster the learning of self-help skills.

The Need for Sensorimotor Exploration

Adequate and appropriate sensorimotor exploration requires adequate mobility and autonomy. One might think that providing a proper environment for movement would automatically meet the need for sensorimotor exploration. Adequate space to move about allows the "motor" part of sensorimotor, but the "sensory" part requires objects that the toddler can grab, drop, feel, mouth, stand up, knock down, put into containers, and drag around the room.

Also keep in mind that the toddler's perceptual, cognitive, and motor abilities are becoming increasingly more sophisticated. He can unbutton large buttons, unzip large zippers, open doors by turning doorknobs, climb up on chairs, turn around and sit down, and stack four to six objects on top of one another. His eye-hand movements are more coordinated. He can sort objects according to such simple classification schemes as putting all red things in one pile and all blue things in another. He is discovering simple cause-and-effect relationships. These increasing skills mean the toddler will need a sufficient number and variety of objects to keep his interest and challenge his new abilities.

TABLE 3–5   An Environment for Learning Self-Help Skills

- ❏ Toddlers are given durable, child-sized eating utensils and an eating area that is easy to clean.
- ❏ Toddlers are provided stools or other physical structures that help them reach toilets, sinks, and mirrors.
- ❏ Toddlers are given as much time as they need or want to participate in self-help activities.
- ❏ Adults approach toddlers' learning of self-help skills with a positive, accepting attitude.

Adapted from Gestwicki (1999, p. 89).

Toddlers increase their perceptual, cognitive, and motor skills by playing with a variety of objects that challenge their abilities.

Toddlers are in a transitional phase, and though their behavior is largely sensorimotor, they are gaining the ability to represent the world through concepts or symbols. Their interactions with the world become increasingly mental, and so available objects should satisfy their need to explore and manipulate physically and intellectually. Intellectual exploration and manipulation for the toddler include an expanding ability to imitate the actions of others and to engage in symbolic play. Imitation and symbolic play require suitable props or cues, which could include realistic-looking furniture and household utensils (beds, stoves, chairs, pots and pans), items of clothing, anatomically correct and racially representative dolls, and small cars and trucks. (Gestwicki, 1999, p. 90).

Gestwicki's term "open ended" best describes the kinds of objects to which toddlers should have access. An open-ended object is one that has many uses beyond the obvious ones. For adults, the most obvious use for a cardboard box might be as a container for things, but for a toddler, a box is something to stack on top of another box, kick or push across the room, lie on top of, climb into, or crawl under. Table 3–6 summarizes the most important characteristics of an appropriate sensorimotor environment.

TABLE 3–6:   An Environment for Sensorimotor Exploration

❑ Toddlers are provided a variety of open-ended objects and materials that foster sensorimotor exploration; these objects and materials are changed when necessary.

❑ Imitative and symbolic play are encouraged by providing realistic toys and props.

❑ Toddlers are in an environment they can understand, with special areas for active, hands-on learning.

❑ Toddlers are offered meaningful experiences with people together with opportunities to observe their physical surroundings.

Adapted from Gestwicki (1999, p. 91).

SEE FOR YOURSELF

After observing in a toddler setting, record any observable behaviors that may illustrate their developmental tasks, including autonomy, separateness, movement ability, self-help skills, and the like. How do the adult caregivers appropriately respond to the children's needs? What do other examples illustrate?

 ## A Child Appropriate Social/Emotional Environment for Toddlers

Social and emotional development is important at any age. The toddler's struggle for independence, a self-concept, and a sense of identity, result in what Arnold Gesell called "the terrible two's." Caregivers should remember that the child who is striving for independence and identity lacks self-control, has limited communication skills, and has mastered only elementary interpersonal skills. She probably is uncertain whether she really wants to be separated from her primary caregiver or other persons to whom she has become emotionally attached.

The label "terrible two's" refers to the resistance that toddlers often exhibit when an adult tries to tell them what to do or when and where to do it—they seem to be contrary for its own sake. Developing a sense of self is a critical task for toddlers, and accomplishing that task depends upon meeting such needs as autonomy, separateness, and acquiring self-help skills. For the toddler, however, autonomy, separateness, and self-help come at a time of relative immaturity, dependency, and uncertainty. Gestwicki appropriately notes that ". . . developing a positive sense of self is a critical task of toddlerhood, dependent on a social/emotional environment of appropriate guidance and interaction" (page 146).

A toddler's coming of age.

Revisiting Interaction Effects

This is a good time to reintroduce the concept of interaction effects and their role in understanding and dealing with the toddler's characteristic behavior. Think of the toddler's striving for independence and a sense of self as a "drive" that he simply cannot ignore. This drive interacts with fluctuating feelings of security and insecurity, confidence and lack of confidence, and other variables that make satisfying this drive somewhat risky and uncertain. Consider the following example.

Thirteen-year-old Sandra has a strong desire to sing solos on a concert stage; she has a real drive to perform. At the same time, her confidence rises and falls, sometimes because of her mood, sometimes because of the inconsistent quality of her tone. As a result, she occasionally doubts her basic vocal talent. For Sandra, singing is never merely a matter of opening her mouth and producing sound. Her strong desire to sing inevitably interacts with her feelings of uncertainty on any given occasion. The quality of her performance depends on her level of confidence—the greater her confidence, the better her performance; the lower her confidence, the worse her performance. Most simply put, Sandra's singing, with all that that involves, interacts with her confidence level to produce a performance of a particular quality. This quality is an interaction effect.

Sandra's situation roughly parallels the situation faced by most toddlers. The toddler's confidence also rises and falls. His independence shifts to dependence, and his efforts at maturity give way to immaturity. He never expresses his striving for independence and separateness in a simple, straightforward way. His unique physical, emotional, and intellectual characteristics always interact with the developmental tasks he must accomplish at any given time or developmental stage.

Child Appropriate Social/Emotional Concerns of Toddlerhood

Recall from Chapter 1 that an effective early childhood program understands children's developmental needs, then meets those needs by employing accepted standards of child appropriate practice and by following principles that describe and govern developmental change. Developmental needs essentially have two origins. First, they come from the individual. They are self-defined in the sense that each child's unique characteristics determine, in part, who he is and how he will express and meet his needs during the developmental process.

Self-defined needs are the concern of *individual appropriateness*. In our culture, for example, we believe that children need autonomy, but how Dorothea specifically achieves autonomy is a matter of what is individually appropriate for her. What she has to do to achieve autonomy, how long it takes her, and how she eventually expresses autonomy will be unique to her. What needs are met and tasks are accomplished, and how this is done, are also influenced by what the culture considers appropriate. For instance, not every culture shares our view of how children should express emotions, or how much autonomy or separateness is proper for children.

The universal principles and patterns of growth and development are the second origin of developmental needs. Recall that all children require adequate nutrition and health care—second-category needs that exist from birth and persist throughout life. All children need to form an emotional bond with a significant other person or persons (attachment), but the attachment process follows a developmental/maturational schedule. Children typically begin to form attachments at around six to eight months of age. Until then, they usually will not show signs of stranger anxiety or separation anxiety, two behavioral indications that attachment has begun.

Gestwicki (1999) refers to "social/emotional issues of toddlerhood" (p. 147). These issues are "autonomy, negativism and resistance, separation, egocentric behavior with peers, social learning, and emotional responsiveness" (pp. 147–148). These issues are a combination of *developmental tasks* (autonomy, separation, social learning, and emotional responsiveness) and *behavioral characteristics* (negativism and resistance, and egocentric behavior with peers). Together, they define the toddler and are the framework for a child appropriate early childhood program. The behavioral characteristics might make more sense if you see their connection with toddlers' abilities to behave autonomously, separate from others, learn socially appropriate behavior, and express emotions. Let's briefly examine these social/emotional issues.

 Autonomy

It's enough to say here that toddlers' striving for autonomy is largely an attempt to put their abilities to the test, to demonstrate their competence to do things on their own. Eventually, toddlers move from autonomy in performing physical actions to emotional and intellectual autonomy. This latter form of autonomy signals the ability to express emotions and have thoughts and make decisions that are distinctly their own. To help toddlers achieve autonomy, adults should approve and support their early strivings toward independence. Autonomy and a positive self-concept go hand in hand, so a child appropriate social/emotional environment should help toddlers gain a positive sense of self. Table 3–7 summarizes some suggestions on fostering toddlers' autonomy.

TABLE 3–7   Promoting Autonomy

❑ Adults allow toddlers to complete their self-chosen, age appropriate and individually appropriate tasks. Just the right amount of help is offered if a task is beyond the toddler's present level of ability—a response that is in keeping with Vygotsky's **zone of proximal development.**

❑ Adults respond to toddlers' accomplishments with appreciation, admiration, and specific meaningful comments.

❑ Adults allow toddlers to make choices that are within their capabilities and control—such as choices among food items, toys to play with, or activities to participate in.

❑ Adults "encourage independent play requiring exploration and mastery" (p. 149).

• Recall our premise that autonomy is truly achieved only when the child's behavior is reasonably freely chosen and under his or her control.

❑ Adults help toddlers achieve a sense of identity (or self-concept) by calling them by their names, identifying and playing games involving awareness of their body parts, and using mirrors and photographs to enhance toddlers' self-perceptions.

• We recommend helping each child recognize the names of the other children, which should help the child recognize him or herself as distinct from others.

❑ Adults avoid being overprotective by allowing toddlers as much freedom "as they can safely use," which requires you to consider what is age appropriate and individually appropriate for each child.

❑ Adults arrange equipment and materials to be accessible to the children with little or no adult help.

❑ Adults look for signs of a toddler's readiness for toilet training and then gently and patiently accustom him to the toilet and assist him in using it.

❑ Adults accept and respond sensitively to toddlers' strivings for autonomy. They recognize that toddlers' abilities and needs are changing, and they anticipate these changes and respond accordingly—"anticipatory socialization." Adults also greet these changes with genuine enthusiasm, an indication of sensitive responsiveness.

Adapted from Gestwicki (1999, pp. 149–150).

A Child Appropriate Cognitive/Language Environment for Toddlers

Toddlers' cognitive development essentially occurs during the fifth (12 to 18 months) and sixth (18 to 24 months) substages of Piaget's sensorimotor stage. These substages are summarized in Table 3–8. There are dramatic differences between the toddler's and the infant's intellectual abilities. Between 12 and 18 months of age, the toddler begins purposely to make things happen—new things she has not experienced before. At first, she achieves these novel experiences predominantly by trial and error, with no idea of what the consequences of her behavior will be. She has no mental representations of the outcomes of her actions.

The toddler also begins to see his own distinctiveness more clearly. He can deliberately vary his actions to produce different effects, a sign of greater flexibility in his thinking. He also recognizes the results of his behavior, which he begins to understand are separate and distinct from himself.

Between 18 and 24 months, the toddler starts to show that she is actually thinking. She acquires what Piaget called the symbolic function, the ability to represent the world through symbols. The ability to **defer imitation** signals the presence of the symbolic function, as well as a much-improved memory. Katrina can now remember her own or other people's actions and reproduce (imitate) them later. She can also solve simple problems mentally without first trying a number of solutions and finally stumbling onto the correct one. Thinking at this stage, however, still has a way to go before it resembles that of older children and adults.

Pretend or symbolic play is now also possible. An important feature of pretend play is that the toddler can see an association between two objects and use one object to represent the other. Thus, a stick becomes a sword or an airplane; wooden blocks laid end to end in a sandbox become a road for toy trucks. The toddler's language also reflects representational thought, and just as a stick can stand for an airplane, "ba" can stand for a ball. This is an important accomplishment, because it

TABLE 3–8 Piaget's Fifth and Sixth Sensorimotor Substages of Cognitive Development

V. Tertiary Circular Reactions	12–18 months	Child repeats actions because they are novel or unfamiliar. She devises and experiments with new means to achieve various ends.
		Child can search for and successfully find hidden objects in one location, but is confused if the object is moved to a different place.
VI. Beginning of Thought	18–24 months	Child is ready to enter the preoperational stage of cognitive development. He moves from sensorimotor intelligence to representational intelligence, which means he can deal with symbolic or mental representations of objects. He uses thought to develop and achieve new goals.
		Child has a true concept of the object and will search for it even if it is moved from one location to another and she does not witness the transfer.

Excerpted from Bentzen, W. R. (2001).

Toddlers associate one or more objects for other objects in pretend play.

indicates that the toddler's representations, though still largely expressed through concrete physical actions, are becoming increasingly more abstract (mental).

Toward the end of infancy and near the beginning of toddlerhood, an expressive vocabulary starts to appear. The toddler's first words predominantly name things that are tied in some way to his actions and experiences. For about six months, speech typically consists of single words or **holophrases.** The toddler conveys different meanings through inflection, context, and adults' interpretive skills. Between 18 and 24 months, toddlers' language skills increase dramatically, and vocabulary expands at a phenomenal rate. According to Cowley (1997), vocabulary increases at the rate of one word every two hours. Toddlers' curiosity appears boundless, and they seem intent on applying a label to virtually everything in their environment.

As their second birthdays approach, toddlers begin to speak in two or three word combinations called **telegraphic speech**—telegraphic because they leave out words that are not essential to meaning. Language development during the second year needs adults who act as "language partners," and it builds on the language stimulation and brain development that occurred during infancy (Gestwicki, 1999, p. 230).

Some Abilities Required for Cognitive Development

Developmental/maturational processes lay the foundation for cognitive development. This is the premise of Piaget's stage theory of cognitive development. Even though Piaget believed that development results from the interaction between maturation and experience (nature and nurture), he placed greater emphasis on the role of maturation than of experience. Of course, both are required for development to occur at all (discussed in Chapter 1).

As you now know, each succeeding stage of development has requirements and opportunities (interaction effects) that were not present or relevant during the previous stages. This suggests that there are critical or sensitive periods during which certain needs must be met and certain tasks accomplished. If they are not, some "harm" could come to the child's future development. Gestwicki (1999) discusses the abilities Burton White (1995, 1988) identifies as crucial for toddlers' continuing intellectual development. These abilities are listed in Table 3–9, together with our comments.

TABLE 3–9 Burton White's Prerequisites for Intellectual Competence

❑ **"Good language development."**

- This ability, as stated, appears to link intelligence directly with language function. Piaget argued, however, that cognitive ability precedes language ability; for example, a child will not use such words as *before, after,* or *under* until he understands the temporal and spatial relationships to which these words refer. Vygotsky, on the other hand, believed that intelligence and language develop more in parallel with each other, rather than one coming before the other. However, intelligence and language are related developmentally. A significant aspect of cognitive functioning is the ability to deal with symbolic representations of the world, and language is, after all, a codified set of symbols.

❑ **"The ability to notice small details or discrepancies."**

- This ability would appear critical to learning to read, such as in seeing the difference between *b* and *d,* or *p* and *q.*

❑ **"The ability to anticipate consequences."**

- This ability has a number of implications. It certainly plays a role in impulse control and in the ability to understand cause and effect relationships. It also plays a role in the ability to formulate hypotheses—"educated guesses" about possible relationships between variables: "If I do A, B is likely to occur."

❑ **"The ability to deal with abstractions."**

- Language is a set of abstractions. The word *dog* bears no resemblance to four-legged, tail-wagging Fido. A child has to learn that the word *dog* is an abstraction or concept that stands for a real, live animal. Abstractions are an integral part of cognitive functioning.

❑ **"The ability to put oneself in the place of another person."**

- This ability is necessary for good social relationships. It is a key element of such human sentiments as empathy and sympathy. It also indicates a child's ability to anticipate consequences or to understand cause-effect relationships.

❑ **"The ability to make interesting associations."**

- This ability is also related to cognitive functioning—the ability to see connections between objects and events, or to classify objects along particular dimensions or attributes. Interesting associations motivate the toddler to continue her physical and intellectual exploration of the environment.

❑ **"The ability to plan and carry out complicated activities."**

- Again, there is a strong relationship with cognitive ability. This ability encompasses the ability to deal with abstractions, notice small differences and discrepancies, and anticipate consequences. It also helps make life interesting.

❑ **"The ability to use resources effectively."**

- This ability seems particularly relevant to "learning to learn." Resources refer to the child's intellectual abilities, knowledge, experiences, and the equipment and materials that are available to him. Knowing how to learn requires knowing how to use all the resources that contribute to the learning process.

❑ **"The ability to maintain concentration on a task while simultaneously keeping track of what is going on around one in a fairly busy situation."**

- This ability reflects the child's increasing maturity as an active explorer, seeking information through manipulating and observing her world. As a problem-solver, she can now mentally manipulate ideas and focus her attention for longer periods of time.

Adapted from Gestwicki (1999, pp. 230–231). Bold-faced text in quotation marks are quoted verbatim.

Teaching Toddlers

To some degree or another, all children learn on their own. Adults must at various times leave infants, toddlers, and preschoolers to their own devices, with the expectation that learning will occur. What adults should do, however, is provide all children with general and developmental environments that are conducive to learning. Recall that the developmental environment is virtually everything that is in and takes place in the general environment. Consequently, toddlers' learning depends on the developmental environment provided to them.

Curriculum is another term for developmental environment. Any early child care curriculum is synonymous with everything that takes place in the program. "Everything," however, raises the issue of intended and unintended interaction effects. The developmental environment can produce unplanned, unexpected, and undesirable interaction effects. Not everything that occurs in even the best early childhood programs is always good or beneficial to children.

Gestwicki (1999) discusses six "principles of teaching toddlers" that contribute to child (developmentally) appropriate practice. We have summarized these principles in Table 3–10.

TABLE 3–10 Six Principles of Teaching Toddlers

First Principle: "Environment is Everything"
Gestwicki thinks that her first principle might be a "slight overstatement." She regains her confidence, however, by noting that ". . . it is important to realize just how important are the decisions teachers make regarding the materials arranged in the classroom" (p. 232). She stresses the physical arrangement of play spaces that make adults available to toddlers while still giving them the freedom to do things on their own.
The present authors are not so cautious about saying that the environment is everything. Gestwicki is concerned with what we call the general environment—the environment that contains physical equipment and materials and their particular arrangements in space. That environment, however, is only the foundation for the all-important developmental environment. The developmental environment is everything. Keep in mind that the developmental environment consists not just of physical objects, but also of people, sounds, smells, tastes, emotions and moods, and anything else that can contribute to the interaction effects children experience.
Second Principle: "Curriculum is Materials"
"The choice of materials that are interesting, novel, and challenging," Gestwicki writes, "is a key to extending the toddlers' sensorimotor investigations" (p. 232). Gestwicki here emphasizes materials that neither bore the toddler because they are too simple, nor frustrate her because they are too difficult. Open-ended equipment and materials are recommended.
Again, our view of curriculum differs somewhat from Gestwicki's. As stated, her second principle is largely relevant to the general environment (thus the term *materials*), whereas we see curriculum as synonymous with the developmental environment *and* the general environment. Admittedly, it is easier to construct and control the physical aspects of a general environment than it is to construct and control the social and emotional aspects of a developmental environment. Nevertheless, we still urge the importance of our definition of curriculum, while at the same time we agree with the basic intent of Gestwicki's second principle.

continued

TABLE 3–10   Six Principles of Teaching Toddlers (Continued)

Third Principle: "Toddlers Initiate"

On this principle we have no disagreement. Gestwicki makes the important point that it is sometimes difficult for teachers not to "tell things" and simply allow toddlers to engage in their own self-chosen activities. We again invoke Gonzales-Mena and Eyer's first principle of infant-toddler caregiving—involve infants and toddlers in things that concern them. A generally reasonable assumption is that age appropriateness and individual appropriateness will define what toddlers find interesting. Of course, they can initiate a harmful activity or one of no particular value to their growth and development. Consequently, you must impose some constraints on toddlers' initiatives when it is appropriate to do so.

Fourth Principle: "Adults Observe"

This principle should be self-evident. Our premise is that observation is at the center of a child appropriate early childhood program. Without observation, nearly everything else is pointless. It is only through observation that you can determine a child's level of development, knowledge, experiences, temperament, needs, and desires.

Gestwicki acknowledges the role of observation in learning "the toddler's level of ability and interest, before making first decisions about materials. . . ." (p. 232). She seems to stress the relationship between observation and curriculum materials, especially observing the role of materials in fostering a toddler's learning. We stress the role of observation in every aspect of an early childhood program. The need to observe toddlers' interpersonal relations with their peers and adults is just as critical as observing how they interact with physical objects. Additionally, adults need to observe and make sense of the multilateral interactions of child-child, child-object, and child-object-child that inevitably occur among toddlers.

Multilateral interactions make intuitive sense if you imagine the scenario of two-year-old Kirby interacting with three-year-old Foster, and a second scenario of Kirby holding a toy that Foster would like to have. Merely adding a toy potentially produces a significantly different interaction effect.

Fifth Principle: "Adults Scaffold"

"Scaffolding" refers to giving a child only as much assistance as she needs to accomplish a task. J. McVicker Hunt's (1966) "problem of the match" is a scaffolding problem: giving a child a task or problem that is far enough above her present level of ability to force her to "stretch" mentally, but not so far above as to discourage her from even trying. Gestwicki discusses five components of effective scaffolding.

❑ *"Joint problem solving"* This is really the crux of effective scaffolding, but the adult must be careful not to overemphasize "joint" by providing more of a solution than is necessary from the toddler's point of view. This is not an issue if several toddlers are collaborating on reaching a goal or solving a problem. There is a difference between showing a child a solution, which he can subsequently repeat, and providing him with just enough of what he needs to find the solution on his own. This latter process characterizes effective scaffolding.

❑ *"Intersubjectivity"* This refers to a convergence of different understandings into essentially one understanding or agreement. This is an element of joint problem solving, inasmuch as two or more individuals are likely to have different perspectives on any given problem and how to solve it. A solution emerges when the participants (toddlers) reach some kind of consensus. Incidentally, consensus need not be verbal, but can take the form of agreed-upon actions or behaviors, which are most likely with toddlers whose language skills cannot support discussions or verbal solutions to problems.

continued

TABLE 3–10   Six Principles of Teaching Toddlers (Continued)

❑ *"Warm and responsive emotional tones"* This is important to every aspect of an early childhood program. It is akin to sensitive responsiveness. In the case of scaffolding, warm and responsive emotional tones imply a genuine and enthusiastic involvement with toddlers' efforts to solve problems and reach objectives.

❑ *"Keeping the child in the ZPD"* The ZPD is the zone of proximal development. Scaffolding is an activity that depends on, or works within, the child's ZPD. The ZPD describes or reflects the child's level of ability or accomplishment. For Gestwicki, this principle structures "the environment and tasks so that demands are at appropriately challenging levels. . . ." and requires adults to constantly adjust "the amount of adult intervention in the child's 'momentary competence' " (p. 233).

Our view is that scaffolding and the ZPD must operate within the boundaries established by age and individual appropriateness. The "stretch" we referred to earlier must be possible for the child, but not yet accomplished. The purpose of this stretch (the result of scaffolding) is to expand the boundaries of what is individually appropriate for the child. Put another way, keeping the child in the ZPD is keeping the child engaged in the alternating processes of assimilation and accommodation (Piaget), or in the alternating circumstances of "I can't quite do it/I need a little bit of help/now I can do it."

❑ *"Promoting self-regulation"* Self-regulation plays a number of roles, some of them outside the arena of cognitive/language development. Self-regulation is essentially synonymous with impulse control, a social/emotional as well as a cognitive issue. But self-regulation refers also to the toddler's ability to choose equipment, materials, and activities with a minimum of adult intervention. Effective scaffolding, we think, must contain the element of self-regulation.

Sixth Principle: "Adults Play as Partners"

True play is self-chosen and spontaneous. When adults play as partners, it should not be as senior partners who dictate to the junior partner (toddler). Allowing the toddler to regulate his play can give you information about his level of development, interests, temperament, knowledge, and other characteristics that help paint a picture of who the child is.

Adapted from Gestwicki (1999, pp. 232–233). Bold-faced text in quotation marks is quoted verbatim.

 ## Fostering Language Development

For the toddler, language becomes an increasingly important function. Not only is she learning the names for things, she is also learning to express her needs, desires, and feelings. This ultimately results in the ability to express complex ideas. There are differing views regarding how children acquire language. Learning theorists place a lot of importance on imitation, while theories at the other end of the continuum see complex linguistic structures as being self-generated. The self-generation view argues that adults could not possibly utter all the verbal expressions that children eventually learn to speak. This is not to say that imitation plays no part in language acquisition (for instance, learning the names of things and people involves imitation), only that its role is more limited than learning theorists believe.

Gestwicki (1999) discusses 10 "principles of teaching language to toddlers" (p. 239). We need to qualify the term "teaching." No parent or professional child care provider has ever sat down with a toddler and said, "Today I am going to teach you language." Young children are natural linguists and, given sufficient exposure, they will learn the language they hear spoken. It's true that they must hear the language they are to learn; they will not invent English, German, French, or any other language. It's also true that adults do engage in some direct teaching—helping the child pronounce certain difficult words, naming objects and people, and so on. Typically, however, adults do not try to teach syntax and grammar: "No, Bobby, you want to put the adjective as close to the noun as possible," is not something you are likely to overhear an adult say to a toddler.

We make this point in order to make adults' role in the language acquisition process clear. Rather than adults teaching toddlers language, we prefer to think of adults as providing a developmental environment that supports and encourages language acquisition. Teaching language need not be a highly structured task. Table 3-11 addresses the conditions necessary for fostering toddlers' language development.

TABLE 3–11 Conditions for Fostering Toddlers' Language Development

First Principle: "Language Teachers Respond"

Responsiveness is the critical component of virtually every aspect of effective child care. Gestwicki, however, notes its special importance in toddlers' efforts to learn language. If 13-month-old Brandon's initially unsuccessful efforts to pronounce his older brother Anthony's name are met with sensitive responsiveness, Brandon will experience several benefits. His efforts will be positively reinforced, and he will learn that language is important and valued; his sense of initiative will be strengthened; and reinforcement of successive approximations to the correct pronunciation will eventually result in Brandon's ability to say Anthony correctly.

Second Principle: "Language Teachers Model"

Given our earlier discussion regarding teaching language, we support Gestwicki's perspective on modeling. As she so rightly points out, ". . . toddlers depend on adult speech for their example of vocabulary, as well as for extracting their own understanding of grammar usage. . . ." (p. 239).

Providing examples of vocabulary comes closer to the usual meaning of teaching than does providing examples of speech from which children can extract "their own understanding of grammar usage." By repeating words and phrases, adults help toddlers with pronunciation. By emphasizing key words, adults help toddlers learn the names of objects and people. By making clear to whom they are speaking and by waiting for a response, adults help toddlers learn what Gestwicki calls "the logistics of conversation" (p. 239). Except for such instances of special emphasis, modeling entails fairly ordinary speech under fairly ordinary circumstances. We believe, in other words, that most language modeling occurs when adults simply speak, although their speech must be commensurate with the toddler's ability to understand. It must be age appropriate and individually appropriate.

Children must hear the language they are to learn, and so, adults must meet the child's need to hear language. Young children do not learn a first language the way adults generally learn a second language—by poring over textbooks, memorizing vocabulary and rules of grammar and syntax. We deemphasize this aspect of language teaching.

Third Principle: "Language Teachers Simplify"

Simplification does not mean talking baby talk to the toddler. It means avoiding overuse of complex sentences but not avoiding them entirely. Judicious use of complex sentences helps the toddler acquire an understanding of grammatical structures. Appropriate speech simplification occurs within the child's zone of proximal development. Adults' speech should be just far enough above the child's present level of ability to provide him with a model for further learning.

continued

TABLE 3–11 Conditions for Fostering Toddlers' Language Development (Continued)

Fourth Principle: "Language Teachers Expand"

Expansion is related to the zone of proximal development and is a very effective way of providing children with a language model. Adults expand when they add vocabulary and ideas to a toddler's original utterances; such expansions are important for language and cognitive development. By expanding on the toddler's original utterances, you provide the child with a model or pattern for her own speech. You also scaffold by relating the child's ideas and experiences to additional ideas and experiences that are not quite familiar to her, thus requiring her to "stretch" cognitively and linguistically.

Fifth Principle: "Language Teachers Link Words with Actions and Experience"

We believe this principle has a great deal to do with explicitness and the power of actions to command a toddler's attention. Verbs—action words—are what give life to writing and speaking. Action words tend to be concrete and specific, especially if adults model or describe the actions the words represent. "Here, Jimmy, let's roll the ball back and forth," says Francine, who then rolls the ball to Jimmy using clear, distinct arm motions. "Now," Francine says, "roll the ball back to me." Gestwicki cautions that although gestures, pointing, and other nonverbal cues can aid toddlers' language learning, adults should never replace words with gestures. If anything, gestures should accompany words. She notes further that adults' choice of words should be explicit; for example, by making specific reference to object nouns rather than their pronoun referents ("Take the ball," rather than "Take this").

Sixth Principle: "Language Teachers Correct Indirectly"

Proper grammar and word usage are achieved over time. They are fairly consistently preceded by such mistakes as overgeneralization of the rules governing the formation of past tense, and plurals that are formed by adding *ed* and *s,* respectively: "he goed" for "he went," or "my foots" for "my feet." Correcting indirectly reflects, we think, the different character of teaching language as opposed to teaching arithmetic or history. When correcting indirectly, the adult simply recasts the toddler's original utterance into the correct form—"Yes, those are your two feet." He does not say such things as, "No, Billy, the plural of foot is an irregular construction, and the singular 'foot' becomes 'feet.' " You can see how ridiculous such a statement would be, given the toddler's relatively immature cognitive and language ability. Moreover, the well-known pediatrician, Dr. Terry Brazelton (1974), attributes language delay to undue emphasis on correct speech, when correctness is attempted through repeated direct instruction (p. 240). This principle again illustrates the easy, nonstressful communication style that should be used in "teaching" language.

Seventh Principle: "Language Teachers Encourage Speech"

Encouraging speech in this context is a natural, almost spontaneous behavior. Although most of us do not talk constantly, a significant part of many adults' day involves speaking. For the professional child care provider, speech patterns and the occasions for speaking have to be adjusted to be commensurate with what is age appropriate and individually appropriate for each child. Adults also encourage speech by patiently allowing toddlers to verbalize their needs and desires rather than prematurely anticipating them and precluding their need to talk.

Encouraging speech is really not much different than encouraging any other child appropriate behavior. All encouragement ultimately depends on providing children with an adequate and appropriate general and developmental environment.

continued

TABLE 3–11   Conditions for Fostering Toddlers' Language Development (Continued)

Eighth Principle: "Language Teachers Talk Face to Face"
In some respects, talking face to face with toddlers is the equivalent of adults looking each other in the eye when having a conversation. One could argue that talking face to face is a sign of respect, interest, and sensitive responsiveness. Toddlers can benefit greatly from this intimate experience with adults. Getting physically down to the toddler's level helps him feel that he is worthy of your personal attention. He can more easily watch your mouth as you pronounce words with which he might have difficulty. Face-to-face conversation gives a toddler the sense that you are talking *to* him in a personal, meaningful way, rather than *at* him in an impersonal, distracted way.
As with infants and older children, toddlers need quality time with their primary caregiver. Feeding an infant is a caregiving activity that meets a developmental need. Infants benefit most when caregivers interact with them in a direct, personal way during the feeding process. Learning language is also a developmental need, and if you meet that need with the same sensitivity as you would an infant's nutritional needs, you will immediately recognize the importance of face-to-face interactions and communications with toddlers.
Ninth Principle: "Language Teachers Sing, Recite, and Play Games"
Singing, reciting, and playing games are, at the very least, interesting ways of using language. Moreover, as Gestwicki points out, "traditional nursery songs, rhymes, and games have lasted" because they are appropriate "for [the] language experiences of toddlers. The rhythm, rhyme repetition, and linking of action and meaning help toddlers acquire understanding and vocabulary" (p. 241).
Tenth Principle: "Language Teachers Read Books"
The ability to speak does not automatically entail the ability to read; hearing words and seeing them on the printed page are two quite different things. Among other benefits, reading to toddlers helps them see the connection between the spoken and the printed word. Sustained interest in actual stories will not occur until the toddler is well into the second year, but picture books play a vital role in forming associations between words and pictures, thus increasing the toddler's vocabulary. Reading to toddlers, especially on a one-on-one basis, provides another opportunity for adults to spend high-quality time with a child, and such time is another avenue for enhancing a toddler's feelings of self-worth as well as providing him or her with a source of pleasure.

Adapted from Gestwicki (1999, pp. 239–241). Bold-faced text in quotation marks is quoted verbatim.

  SEE FOR YOURSELF

After observing individual toddlers as well as a group of toddlers in a child care setting, record specific actions of the children and suggest appropriate caregiver responses to each action. For example, if the toddler is trying to speak about a favorite toy, the caregiver might engage the child in conversation about that toy, listening attentively and sensitively to the child's efforts to communicate, comment on what the toddler is doing, etc.

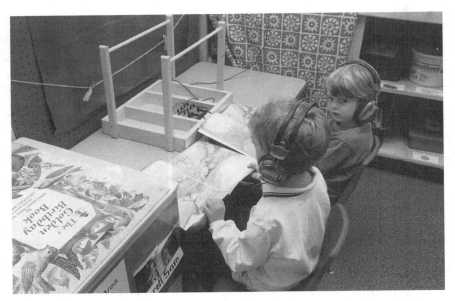

A developmental environment supports and encourages ways in which children learn language.

Summary

Toddlerhood is the period from one to three years of age. The first-category and second-category needs of toddlers are interdependent and interactive. Second-category needs contribute to first-category needs, and vice versa. For example, the toddler's need to be accepted serves such first-category needs as the freedom to explore or to develop language skills. Acceptance of the toddler implies adults' willingness to allow the freedom needed by the toddler. The second-category need for sensitive responsiveness plays a similar role as the need for unconditional acceptance.

Some of the toddler's behaviors include imitating adult actions; speaking and understanding words and ideas; experimenting with objects; walking with a steady gait, climbing stairs, and running; asserting independence; establishing friendships; solving problems; taking pride in accomplishments; helping with tasks; beginning pretend play; manipulating objects to the full extent of her ability; and trying to do everything by himself. Some of the toddler's needs include receiving adequate nutrition and health care; acquiring motor, language, and cognitive skills; learning self-control; developing autonomy; having opportunities for exploration and play with other children; being accepted for whom he or she is; achieving separation from those to whom she is attached; achieving a sense of individuality; safety, flexibility, and variety; and an organized and challenging environment.

Also important is an environment that promotes toddler autonomy, fosters separateness, allows the development of self-help skills, provides for sensorimotor exploration, encourages the development of intellectual competence, and fosters language development.

Six principles of teaching toddlers include:

1. environment is everything

2. curriculum is materials

3. toddlers imitate

4. adults observe

5. adults scaffold

6. adults play as partners

There are 10 principles for fostering toddlers' language development. Within the context of these 10 principles, language teachers do the following:

1. respond

2. model

3. simplify

4. expand

5. link words with actions and experience

6. correct indirectly

7. encourage speech

8. talk face-to-face

9. sing, recite, and play games

10. read books

Questions to Consider

1. What does it mean to say that first-category and second-category needs are interdependent and interactive?

2. In terms of toddlers' needs, what are the roles of motive and means?

3. What is the relationship between a toddler's general environment and autonomy? Between the developmental environment and autonomy; that is, what factors are involved in this relationship?

4. In your opinion, is there any one second-category need that is more important than all the others?

5. What qualification(s) did the authors put on the idea of teaching toddlers language? Why?

6. What is the self-generation view of language acquisition? How does it differ from, say, the learning theory view?

7. What is the relationship between a toddler's specific actions and the skills or abilities necessary to perform those actions?

For additional information on assessing the effectiveness of child care programs, visit our Web site at **http://www.earlychilded.delmar.com**

Chapter 4

Observing and Evaluating the Preschool Child Care Program

See How To

- describe the characteristics of appropriate care for three-, four-, and five-year-olds, and of preschoolers themselves

- examine children's abilities and needs from two to six years of age

- analyze the components of a child appropriate physical environment for preschoolers

- examine the components of a child appropriate social/emotional environment for preschoolers

- examine child appropriate social/emotional interactions

- evaluate the components of a child appropriate cognitive/language environment for preschoolers

 Introduction

The child in the early childhood or preschool stage is an altogether different person from the toddler. Even among themselves, preschoolers show a wider range of individual differences than do toddlers. The years from three through five lend themselves to a greater variety of experiences. The early childhood stage is longer than the toddler stage, which provides opportunities for more experiences. The preschooler also has more knowledge, skills, and abilities than the toddler, and the interaction effects available to the preschooler are significantly greater than those available to the toddler.

The cumulative character of development and learning also plays a role. A child's knowledge and ability are the foundations for acquiring more knowledge and ability. The child who has a concept of numbers can learn to count; the child who can walk can learn to ski, and so on.

Infancy is a period of particularly rapid change. Toddlers also experience rather rapid changes, but the pace of change begins to slow by the end of toddlerhood. Though changes during the preschool years are not as rapid as during the two earlier stages, in some respects they seem more dramatic. Especially noticeable are the preschoolers' communication and cognitive skills. The three-year-old has begun Piaget's preoperational stage of cognitive development, and his speech is considerably more like that of an adult.

Everything three-year-olds know and can do, and everything they will come to know and do during the next two years, constitutes the basis for a child appropriate early childhood program. An effective developmental environment will keep abreast of each child's personal characteristics, performances, and developmental patterns as these unfold. First-category needs retain their importance as the young child continues to refine his existing motor skills and learn new ones, improve his physical coordination, and gain strength and agility.

Such second-category needs as adequate nutrition and health care are still very important, but some of their specific characteristics change as the child grows older. The three- to five-year-old child's need for autonomy, separateness, exploration, and movement changes with developmental maturity. With each passing year, there is the potential for increasingly greater changes in the number and variety of interaction effects that can occur, because the child possesses abilities, experiences, and knowledge he did not previously have. In effect, interactions between the preschool child and his developmental environment have a greater number of potential "paths" to follow than they did during infancy and toddlerhood.

What Preschoolers Do

The development that occurs during the three or so years of the preschool stage reveals significant differences from one year to the next. The term "preschooler," therefore, does not refer to a period of uniform, consistent behaviors and abilities. Rather it refers to a series of significant developmental advancements that, at about age six, transition into the stage of the school-aged child.

A major requirement for an effective preschool program is to understand and accept each child's level of development and maturity at any given moment and proceed from there. The principles that govern developmental change, as well as what is typically age-appropriate for the children in your program, continue to be important. Developmental principles and the age-appropriate components of child appropriate practice are the standards by which you assess where three-year-old Gregory is likely to be if his developmental progress approaches developmental norms. If he is functioning below the norms in any areas, you will know what he still has to do to reach the developmental level typical for his age.

Descriptions of preschoolers' abilities can be quite lengthy, primarily because preschoolers are becoming increasingly more knowledgeable and capable. Look at one description of typical preschoolers.

> Typically, three-, four-, and five-year-olds are full of energy, eagerness, and curiosity. They seem to be constantly on the move as they totally engross themselves in whatever captures their interest at the moment. During these years, preschoolers are perfecting their motor skills. Creativity and imagination come into everything, from dramatic play to artwork to storytelling. Vocabulary and intellectual skills expand rapidly, allowing the child to express ideas, solve problems, and plan ahead. . . . (Allen and Marotz, 2003, p. 88).

Gestwicki (1999) confirms the breadth of preschoolers' abilities by answering the question, "What do preschoolers do?" with the question, "What *don't* they do?" It's not necessary to plan the developmental environment to account for every subtlety and nuance of preschoolers' actions and abilities. Although you should be familiar with some typical abilities and behaviors, preschoolers themselves will make evident the full scope of their characteristics and capacities. Our assumption is that child appropriate general and developmental environments will accommodate virtually the full range of preschoolers' abilities and developmental needs.

Sprain (1990), and Bredekamp (1987) describe some of the characteristics of appropriate care for three- to five-year-olds, as well as some characteristics of preschoolers' themselves. This information is summarized in Table 4–1.

Table 4–2 offers another perspective on preschoolers' abilities and needs. The source of this information is the "Early Child Development" Web site.

 SEE FOR YOURSELF

Which of the needs in Table 4–2 could qualify as first-category needs, and which as second-category needs? Would knowing this have any bearing on how you would meet those needs? Explain.

Additionally, after observing in a preschool child care setting, record children's behaviors that may illustrate typical characteristics, abilities, and needs of three and one-half to five-year-old preschoolers, using the information in Table 4–2 as a guide.

TABLE 4–1 Appropriate Care for Preschoolers

Appropriate Care for Three-Year-Olds Would Include
❑ A developmental environment that provides activities that emphasize language, gross motor physical activity, and movement.
❑ Such activities include "puzzles and blocks, wheel toys and climbers, [areas for] dramatic play acting and story telling" (Sprain, 1990). Bredekamp includes "opportunities to talk and listen to simple stories."
Appropriate Care for Four-Year-Olds Would Include
❑ A developmental environment that accommodates four-year-olds' enjoyment of "a greater variety of experiences and more small motor activities like scissors, art, manipulatives, and cooking" (Bredekamp).
❑ A developmental environment that accommodates four-year-olds' improved memory and concentration and ability to recognize the shape, color, and size of objects.
❑ A developmental environment that provides opportunities for four-year-olds to develop problem-solving skill and basic math concepts (Bredekamp; Sprain).
Appropriate Care for Five-Year-Olds Would Include
❑ A developmental environment that accommodates most five-year-olds' ability to understand more complex relations (for instance, such concepts of number as one-to-one correspondence), increased memory capacity, and improved fine motor skills.
❑ A developmental environment that recognizes most five-year-olds' increasing interest "in the functional aspects of written language, such as recognizing meaningful words and trying to write their own names" (Bredekamp).

Adapted from Sprain, J. (1990) and Bredekamp (1987).

This preschooler has developed an interest in books.

TABLE 4–2 Children's Abilities and Needs from 2 to 8 Years

Approximate Age	Children's Typical Characteristics and Abilities	Children Need...
Two to Three and One-Half Years	❑ Take pleasure in learning new skills ❑ Acquire language quickly ❑ Constantly on the go ❑ Gains increasing control of hands and fingers ❑ Are easily frustrated ❑ Behave more independently but are still dependent in certain situations ❑ "Act out familiar scenes"	In addition to the needs of previous stages, they need opportunities to: ❑ Make developmentally appropriate choices ❑ Engage in dramatic or fantasy play ❑ Read books of increasing complexity ❑ "Sing favorite songs" ❑ Assemble simple puzzles
Three and One-Half to Five Years	❑ Attention span is longer ❑ Are sometimes silly and boisterous; may use language that shocks adults ❑ Talk a lot and constantly question ❑ Desire adult things, will keep art and other projects ❑ Cautiously test their courage and physical/motor skills ❑ Disclose their feelings through dramatic play ❑ Enjoy playing with friends; hate to lose games or other kinds of contests ❑ Will sometimes share and take turns	In addition to the needs of the previous stages or age periods, they need opportunities to: ❑ Develop and refine fine motor skills ❑ Further expand language skills through "talking, reading, and singing" ❑ "Learn cooperation by helping and sharing" ❑ "Experiment with prewriting and prereading skills"
Five to Eight Years	❑ Are increasingly curious about the world and the people in it ❑ Numbers, letters, reading, and writing are of increasing interest to them ❑ Become more concerned about final products or goals ❑ Exhibit physical skills with greater confidence ❑ "Use words to express feelings and cope" with various situations ❑ Enjoy adult activities ❑ Play becomes more outgoing and cooperative	In addition to the needs of the previous stages or age periods, they need opportunities to: ❑ Develop a concept of numbers; develop reading skills ❑ Solve problems ❑ "Practice teamwork" ❑ Acquire and refine a sense of competency ❑ Question and observe ❑ "Acquire basic life skills" ❑ "Attend basic education"

Adapted from the "Early Child Development" Web site.

Gestwicki (1999) discusses preschoolers' needs in terms of forming a *sense of initiative* versus a *sense of guilt* (Erik Erikson), and Piaget's stage of preoperational thought. A preschooler who has a sense of initiative is confident in her autonomy, makes choices easily, and feels competent, energetic, enthusiastic, and eager to explore the world (Gestwicki, 1999). If the child does not adequately resolve this issue in favor of initiative, according to Erikson, he will feel guilty for trying to be competent and independent.

≋≋ Through Their Eyes

Amy Scheels, lead teacher in the preschool room at Suny Plattsburgh Early Care and Education Center, overhears Noriko challenging Nicky at the water table. "Look! This plastic bottle floats!" she exclaims. "Why?" Nicky has to think about Noriko's question for a few moments before conjecturing, "Because it's empty?" Amy asks both children, "What do you think would happen if we filled the bottle with water?" Both children are eager to try the experiment. Quickly, they discover that the water-filled bottle sinks. "Why did the bottle sink?" Amy follows up. Both children pause, repeat the experiment with predictable results. Amy's open-ended questions encourage the children to use their problem-solving skills. And while she encourages their play she does not give them the answer, challenging them to think through the puzzle and draw their own conclusions.

The preoperational child thinks intuitively, not logically. Her thinking is concrete, egocentric (largely in terms of her own perspective), and lacks focus. A child appropriate developmental environment provides learning experiences that fit those characteristics. Play is the single most important way for preschoolers to learn. Preschoolers must accomplish particular developmental tasks to develop properly. They must be socialized to behave according to accepted norms, form a sense of identity appropriate to their social context, develop a conscience and self-control, and understand where and how they fit into the world. These tasks depend on continuing language competency. The developmental environment should provide opportunities for these kinds of learning.

A Child Appropriate Physical Environment for Preschoolers

Developmental needs and tasks that follow a fairly clear maturational pattern offer different challenges to early child care staff than those that are more ambiguous or open-ended. Open-ended tasks and needs can still follow a maturational timetable, but the timetable's precise boundaries can be a bit unclear. For example, it's hard to mistake a child's efforts to pull herself to a standing position, to walk, or to say her first word, and it's not too hard to provide an environment that supports and encourages these activities. In the same fashion, it's relatively easy to provide infants with a physically safe environment, since their limited mobility reduces their chances of getting into mischief through their own actions. However, as children's mobility and other physical skills increase, and they are able to get into dangerous situations on their own, physical safety becomes a more crucial issue. As a result, creating a safe environment for older children becomes more difficult, because preschoolers' safety becomes more ambiguous or open-ended than infants' safety. This lack of clear boundaries requires adults to exercise ingenuity and alertness.

There are three physical environments for preschoolers that the present authors view as open-ended: an "environment for initiative," an "environment for learning through play," and an "environment for self-control" (Gestwicki, 1999, pp. 101–107). In Erikson's theory of personality development, the task of developing a sense of initiative rather than a sense of guilt follows a developmental/maturational schedule. Nonetheless, an environment for initiative is still somewhat open-ended, because the developmental environment must support interaction effects that are age appropriate and individually appropriate, and that result in children actually developing initiative. This process is open-ended because developing initiative allows more variations in the developmental environment than does supporting a child's efforts to walk. There is also more room for error in the former than in the latter.

Virtually all children play, but the characteristics of their play change as they mature. Consequently, the general and developmental environments intended to support children's learning through play must be tailor-made to fit their developmental level and the individually appropriate characteristics of their play behavior. This requirement effectively defines open-endedness.

A safety conscious caregiver.

SEE FOR YOURSELF

Observe in a preschool classroom and describe several characteristics of the developmentally appropriate preschool environment that you can observe there. Record any of the children's activities or behaviors that might demonstrate that they are receiving appropriate care.

An Environment for Developing Initiative

Initiative shares autonomy's two important characteristics (see Chapter 3). The child should be capable of the behaviors she initiates, and adults should approve of and encourage the child's initiative. Secondly, the behaviors should be age appropriate, individually appropriate, and socially/culturally appropriate. Social and cultural approval of children's initiative also contributes to their socialization to accepted behavioral norms—finding a sense of identity appropriate to their social context, developing a conscience and self-control, and understanding where and how they fit into the world.

Initiative is discussed in the context of a physical environment. Initiative is influenced by social, emotional, cognitive, and language factors, but these other factors can play a supportive role only if the physical environment is conducive to children making their own choices. Four-year-old Bethany does not gain very much if she is permitted to show initiative in a physical environment that thwarts her efforts. A poorly structured environment would include games and toys stored on unreachable shelves, activity areas that are unclearly marked and confusing, and any other arrangements that force Bethany to ask for help when it would otherwise be unnecessary. Table 4–3 summarizes the characteristics of a child appropriate environment for initiative.

 SEE FOR YOURSELF

Observe caregivers' and children's interactions with one another in a preschool child care setting. Using Table 4–3 as a guide, evaluate whether the room provides a child-appropriate environment for initiative. Cite specific examples to justify your evaluation.

An Environment for Play

The assumption that children need to play is virtually unchallenged. It's said that play is children's work, which is true. Let's briefly explore some of the characteristics of play and work (nonplay) to see where they are alike and where they differ.

Most of us probably hold some stereotypes about play and work that influence our perspectives on these two activities. Some view all play as fun, and all work as drudgery or unpleasant. Some work at jobs or professions they consider so pleasant or rewarding that working is akin to playing. Play is often characterized as spontaneous or self-chosen activity performed for its own sake, without any necessary goal or objective in mind. Work, on the other hand, is often characterized as something we must do, at least to survive economically. In many instances our work defines who we are, which for some goes well beyond monetary gains.

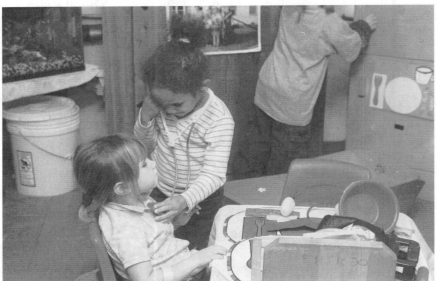

A physical environment promotes initiative if it is conducive to children making their own choices about play and learning.

There are probably those who look at play as frivolous activity, as a diversion from the unpleasant demands of work. Some might believe that children play too much and need to engage in more serious, productive activities. Yet, young children's play is anything but frivolous or diversionary. Play is a developmental need and a means by which children accomplish various important developmental tasks. Play is children's natural activity. We should be careful, though, not to paint play with so broad a brush as to define play as everything children do, even though they might approach nonplay activities in a playful manner. There are occasions when even young children must learn there is a serious side to behaviors they consider play.

In this book, play is natural, spontaneous, and essentially self-chosen behaviors that are child appropriate and can reasonably be expected to result in desirable interaction effects. These criteria rule out behaviors or activities that are dangerous to the individual

TABLE 4–3   A Child Appropriate Environment for Initiative

An Environment for Initiative:

❑ Allows and encourages children to freely choose their own play activities by providing activity areas that are clearly defined and labeled.
  - Clearly defined and labeled activity areas help prevent confusion. Confusion should be avoided because it places undue limits on children's initiative. There are times, of course, when even children have to demonstrate initiative in uncertain or ambiguous circumstances. Nevertheless, their play in an early childhood program should not predominantly be one of those times.

❑ Puts materials and equipment where children can get them for themselves.
  - Initiative and autonomy go hand-in-hand. Initiative probably is not possible without autonomy. In the case of this second characteristic, suitably placed equipment and materials gives the child overall freedom (autonomy) to choose and the initiative to make particular choices from among a number of options.

❑ Lets children "display their work in the classroom."
  - Initiative has to be reinforced or rewarded; otherwise it will be discouraged and possibly stifled altogether. When children produce things through their own initiative, adults give value to their productions and their efforts by proudly displaying their work for all to see.

❑ Provides open-ended materials that foster creativity and accommodate all levels of ability.
  - The advantages of open-ended materials are that they simultaneously serve a number of different levels of ability and interest, and they allow varying degrees of initiative. Creativity is really a form of initiative, and to some extent, initiative is a form of creativity. Open-ended materials contribute to both aspects.

❑ "Establishes systems that help children make conscious choices for play."
  - "Systems" appears to mean more or less formal or structured ways for children to plan their activities—by signing up for particular activities, or by putting their names on lists to indicate an interest in a particular activity. Probably no choice is more conscious than one a child has planned ahead of time. The preschooler gains cognitive and social benefits by such planning—foreseeing future events and their possible consequences, and delaying gratification or waiting one's turn, for example.

❑ Provides opportunities for independent behavior and responsible classroom participation.
  - You can see how closely related all these characteristics of an environment for initiative are; all of them have something to do with independence and responsible participation.
  - The first characteristic emphasizes clear definition and labeling of activity areas, which supports independence and participation.
  - The second emphasizes easy accessibility to the equipment and materials, which also supports independence.
  - The third emphasizes displaying children's work or productions, which certainly would seem to foster responsible participation.
  - The fourth emphasizes open-ended materials, again fostering independence by allowing the child to make choices.
  - The fifth characteristic emphasizes systems for allowing the child to make conscious choices for play, and again, independence is the foundation of conscious choice.

Adapted from Gestwicki (1999, p. 102).

Play is a developmental need and is important for children.

Play supportive environments encourage initiative and autonomy and offer adequate periods of time and various places for children to play.

child or to others, and activities that are foisted on the child for the convenience of an adult. Thus, playing with objects or under conditions that could lead to injury should not be acceptable to early child care staff. Additionally, saying to a child, "Here, go play with this puzzle and stop bothering me!" is not a child appropriate invitation to play. This doesn't mean adults should not suggest play ideas to children, or that activities suggested under duress are inappropriate in their own right. Playing with a puzzle is a perfectly acceptable activity, but it's not a spontaneous, self-chosen activity when the child does it at your command. Rather than telling Kathy to play with a puzzle, a better approach might be: "Don't you know what to do, Kathy? Look, here are some puzzles, some picture books, and even some materials to do fingerprinting. Do you think one of these would be fun to do?" You will have made some suggestions that allow Kathy to exercise her autonomy and initiative.

It is not important that you make subtle distinctions between play and nonplay. It is important that you distinguish between behaviors and activities that are likely to benefit children and those that are not. It's also important that, when necessary, you see play from children's points of view and not just your own. Young children are unlikely to compare play with nonplay. They simply do the things they enjoy doing. Recognizing this helps you to see play from the children's perspective. This requires patience and acceptance of children's choices of play activities. Bear in mind that if their play leads to learning, and if they enjoy it, it is not frivolous or unproductive behavior.

Table 4–4 summarizes the characteristics of a play supportive environment. Notice the strong role autonomy and initiative play in this environment.

 SEE FOR YOURSELF

Using Table 4–4 as a guide, judge whether the caregivers in a preschool child care setting demonstrate appropriate characteristics of adults in a play-supportive environment. Give examples to clarify.

An Environment for Self-Control

"Stability, order, and predictability" are the environmental characteristics Gestwicki proposes as beneficial for children who are learning self-control. To some extent, controlling oneself depends on feeling that one has some control over the external environment. As children mature, they establish consistent behavioral patterns in response to familiar situations. With increasing age, experience, and developmental maturity, more and more situations become familiar, or at least decipherable, so that the child can adjust his responses to meet demands made by a situation's unfamiliar aspects.

Self-control essentially involves knowing what to do, when to do it, wanting to do it, and conforming to what one's society and culture consider appropriate behavior under particular circumstances. When we drive our cars, for instance, traffic laws and rules make our behavior and other drivers' behaviors orderly and predictable. Each driver exhibits self-control in the context of laws, rules, and the self-controlled behaviors of other drivers. If someone seriously violates an established, expected driving pattern, our own self-control becomes more difficult or sometimes impossible, and an accident occurs. If, even under the best of conditions, a driver does not want to stop at a red light or stop sign, he will not drive in a self-controlled manner.

Adults typically want children to behave in socially acceptable ways, which is the primary meaning of self-control for many adults. If four-year-old Jake acts out in the classroom, some would describe his behavior as "out of control." We are not diminishing the importance of children behaving appropriately, but we want to emphasize the importance of the underlying foundation of self-control.

This foundation is a child's knowledge and understanding of what to do, when to do it, and the ability and motivation to do what she needs to do. You cannot put a complete novice behind the wheel of a car and expect him to drive with self-control. Likewise, you cannot expect three-year-old Brit to exercise self-control in an activity area that contains confusing, ambiguous behavioral cues. Even adults tend to function poorly in disorderly environments. Most of us, for instance, need to know what behaviors are

TABLE 4–4   Characteristics of a Play-Supportive Environment

Adults in a Play-supportive Environment:

❑ Send a clear message that play is the primary means by which learning occurs
- A clear message involves a carefully structured general environment containing equipment and materials that lend themselves to play. Since the physical (general) environment sets the stage for the developmental environment, the children have to use these places to play, and materials to play with, in ways that are meaningful to them. Moreover, autonomy and initiative are at least two second-category needs that should be met by children's play.

❑ Protect play and minimize distractions through carefully designed interest or activity centers
- This particular criterion helps children focus their attention, but we think it also helps children learn that sometimes environments are designated for specific purposes—that situations are defined in particular ways and therefore suggest or encourage particular behaviors.

❑ Invite active participation and play through proper arrangement of equipment and materials
- Proper arrangement does not only mean where equipment and materials are located in the classroom, although that is important with respect to accessibility, visibility, and establishing meaningful relationships between different activity centers. Particular arrangements can also suggest related activities within a given activity center. Gestwicki, for instance, notes that, "The scales and a box of rocks on a science table suggest an activity; a notepad and pencil arranged beside the telephone in the house corner suggest a beginning plot line" (p. 104). This is a form of scaffolding that encourages children to use their initiative and imagination without direct suggestions from adults.

❑ Set up activity areas whose size promotes small-group interactive play, but also allows for secluded or solitary play
- This criterion recognizes that play spaces can be larger than is appropriate for the activity and the developmental level of the children in those spaces. Space that is too large invites children to physically distance themselves from one another, so that relatively intimate, interactive play becomes difficult. We believe large spaces also tend to scatter children's attention away from the activities at hand. Large, unoccupied spaces also encourage running and intrusion by children who are not directly involved in the ongoing activity.
- Allowing for secluded or solitary play enables children to exercise their initiative and autonomy by freely choosing not to participate in a group activity.

❑ Provide adequate periods of time for play
- This criterion recognizes the importance of play in children's development. If play is children's work, then they must be given enough time to finish the "jobs" they have undertaken. Ample time also allows the children to terminate play when it suits them, rather than being forced to stop because of externally imposed (and possibly artificial) time constraints.

❑ Facilitate play
- This criterion illustrates the interrelationship between the general and the developmental environment. Although this criterion apparently is meant to stand on its own, everything discussed in this table is intended to facilitate play. For the present authors, however, facilitating play incorporates all of the other characteristics of a play-supportive environment while also emphasizing the critical function of an appropriate developmental environment. None of these things is likely to happen on its own.

❑ Treat outdoor and indoor play areas and materials as equals
- This is only to say that play is no less important outdoors than indoors. Play is important wherever it occurs.

Adapted from Gestwicki (1999, pp. 104–106).

TABLE 4–5 An Environment for Self-Control

An Environment for Self-control
❑ Is a general and developmental environment that foresee and prevent problems caused by negative emotions—tiredness, anxiety, boredom, crowded classrooms, frustration
❑ Is a general and developmental environment that provide clear signals and expectations for appropriate behavior
❑ "Uses posters and other visual clues to remind children of appropriate classroom behavior."
❑ Provides children with places for private retreat or withdrawal
❑ Respects individual rights and differences and uses equipment and materials that convey such respect
❑ Provides children with the means to express strong emotions—toys and other objects made for vigorous use, for example
❑ "Model[s] opportunities for children to meet for problem solving"   • This last feature provides a way for children to discuss problems and disagreements and try to reach agreeable solutions. This is similar to a "family council" that meets to solve problems within the family group.

Adapted from Gestwicki (1999, p. 107).

appropriate or inappropriate in particular circumstances. We want the rules to be clear. Children need behavioral cues that are age, individually, and socially/culturally appropriate. What is clear to program staff might be very unclear to one or more of the preschoolers in the classroom.

There is also the emotional component of self-control. The tired or upset driver is more likely to run a red light or stop sign, or to speed through congested traffic. The tired or angry four-year-old is more likely to act out, behave aggressively, or resist instructions. This is why children need a personal space to go to when they feel out of sorts. Table 4–5 summarizes the characteristics of an environment that fosters self-control.

 SEE FOR YOURSELF

After observing in a preschool room, record any characteristics of the setting that provide evidence of an appropriate environment for self-control. Use the information in Table 4–5 as a guide.

 ## A Child Appropriate Social/Emotional Environment for Preschoolers

Preschoolers' social and emotional functioning are considerably more sophisticated than toddlers' or infants'. Preschoolers are increasingly capable of taking other people's points of view, asserting their own points of view, forming friendships and alliances, moving away from attachment figures, and behaving independently. They are increasingly capable of understanding and anticipating the effects their behavior will have on others. They are developing personalities that yield interaction effects that are often dependent on the personalities of others with whom they are relating. For

Preschoolers' developing personalities make them more aware of the effects their behaviors have on others.

preschoolers, these interaction effects are more complex and varied than has previously been possible. The world's complexity does not increase with children's increasing age and maturity, but older children become more aware of it. They must learn how to deal with complexity and how and where they fit in physically, socially, intellectually, and emotionally.

Preschoolers' social horizons are much wider than toddlers' or infants' because their contacts with peers are more extensive and varied. Their more advanced cognitive abilities and larger behavioral repertoires give them more options for social relationships. Relationships among preschoolers begin to show subtleties that were not present in the earlier stages of their development. For example, three- to five-year-olds can discern characteristics in others that they either like or dislike, which promotes or prohibits the formation of certain friendships. More sophisticated language skills accompany and influence social relationships and emotional expressions.

Preschoolers experience a developmental environment that either promotes or interferes with these developmental advancements. There are seven "social/emotional issues of the preschool years" (Gestwicki, 1999, p. 165). These issues are the preschooler's developmental needs or tasks, and meeting them lays the foundation for healthy social and emotional development. In Table 4–6, see what a child-appropriate social/emotional developmental environment would look like in the context of the previously mentioned issues.

 SEE FOR YOURSELF

Observe some groups of three-, four-, and five-year-olds playing or interacting socially. Do these children exhibit any of the characteristics of play or social interaction described by Parten in Table 4–6? If you observe younger and older children playing together, do the older children modify their play in any way to conform to the younger children's typical play behavior? Do the younger children modify their behavior in any way?

TABLE 4–6 Preschoolers' Social/Emotional Issues/Tasks

"Identification"

Identification is a psychological process by which a child wants to be like another person, such as a parent, teacher, or close friend. Although identification involves imitation, it is more profound than merely copying someone's overt behaviors or mannerisms. Identification can involve adopting someone's attitudes, opinions, values, looks, behaviors, and feelings.

Identification generally requires observation, sufficient intellectual capacity, and possibly what Gestwicki refers to as "affectionate affiliation," (p. 165), although this last aspect is not strictly necessary. Children can identify with rock singers, movie stars, or even fictitious characters. One essential criterion is that the model possesses some characteristics that the child wants to possess and emulate.

Identification is a significant task because it is associated with establishing gender, cultural, or racial identity. Identification also helps children internalize adult standards for behavior, because they want to be like the adults with whom they are identifying.

"Gender Identity"

There is a distinction between biologically determined sexual identity and culturally determined sex-role behavior. By age four, boys and girls become increasingly aware of their differences, particularly the different expectations held out for gender-based behavior. There are those who favor raising children to be androgynous, or neutral, with respect to sex-role behavior. Thus, boys would play with dolls and girls would play with trucks. Others argue that boys are genetically wired to behave like boys and girls to behave like girls.

Parents and teachers are aware of the differences between males and females and socialize them accordingly. Most would agree that children need to establish a complete and appropriate conception of what is acceptable behavior relative to their biological sex. As a professional child care provider, you should also recognize and be sensitive to how different cultures define appropriate sex-role behavior. This is where frequent communication with children's families becomes so important.

"Cultural and Racial Identity"

Children identify not only with particular individuals, but also with their families and the ethnic or cultural groups to which they belong. Cultural and ethnic diversity are a permanent characteristic of our society and should be given proper respect and consideration. Individual families and cultures might argue that a child has an obligation to identify with his or her family, culture, or ethnic group. In the final analysis, each individual eventually has to decide for him or herself whether or not to establish such an identification. Without a doubt, however, an early child care developmental environment is obligated to support, encourage, and assist all children to acquire and understand their respective cultural and racial identities.

"Initiative"

We have already discussed initiative in the context of a child appropriate physical environment for preschoolers. The essence of that discussion is that the physical aspects of a developmental environment need to be conducive to children exercising their initiative—equipment and materials easily accessible to the children, encouragement and opportunities to make choices from among a number of options, and the like.

We call these physical initiatives. Healthy social and emotional development also involve social and emotional initiatives. Choosing a particular toy and taking it down from a shelf, for instance, is quite different from approaching a peer and asking her if she wants to play. "Initiative involves pretending, inventing, creating, taking risks, and playing with others" (p. 166). These activities or accomplishments have physical components, but their content or emphasis is largely social and emotional. They involve children's direct interactions with other people or other people's reactions to their behaviors and accomplishments (pretending, inventing, creating, taking risks, playing with others . . .).

continued

TABLE 4–6   Preschoolers' Social/Emotional Issues/Tasks (Continued)

"Friendship"

Preschoolers' meaning of friendship changes dramatically from when they were toddlers. Among other things, children become less egocentric as they mature, which means they become increasingly capable of taking into account others' feelings and points of view. They also recognize themselves as distinct from others, and others as distinct from themselves, a prerequisite for forming true friendships.

Parten's (1932) six classifications of play illustrate how children's play changes to include interactions that are progressively more social and cooperative. (See Table 4–7 for a description of Parten's play classifications.) There is an important point about friendships in this stage of cooperative play: "Children at this stage are likely to define 'best friends,' individuals particularly selected for companionship, though the friendships may not be lasting and may be characterized by much friction" (p. 166).

For early childhood program staff, the characteristics of preschoolers' play—as it runs the full gamut of the preschool years—potentially define their relative levels of play and social/emotional development, as well as the developmental needs and tasks that confront them. We say potentially, because being capable of cooperative play, for example, does not prevent a child from engaging in associative play or onlooker behavior, or in any of the other play or social interaction categories.

An appropriate assumption is that a child's typical form of play or social interaction is an adequate indication of where she is in this functional area. Accepting where each child is developmentally in her social interactions, and providing opportunities for play and social interactions of all kinds and at all levels, is basic to an effective early childhood program.

"Prosocial Behavior vs. Aggression"

Aggression, or perhaps more appropriately, assertiveness, seems to be more easily tolerated in toddlers than in preschoolers, primarily because toddlers are trying to establish an identity and are testing their newly found skills and abilities. Toddlers' verbal skills are also still in the making, and their need to act out physically is considerably greater than preschoolers', who are increasingly expected to defend or assert themselves with their mouths rather than their hands. Preschoolers presumably are less egocentric than toddlers, making them more capable of foreseeing the negative consequences of aggressive behavior and the advantages of prosocial behavior.

The relationship of aggression and prosocial behavior to "emotional control and appropriate, constructive expression of feelings" should be noted (p. 167). Here, adults need to acknowledge children's feelings, as well as their own, and help children express their feelings constructively.

"Self-Control"

Self-control is a crucial issue in today's society. Hardly a day goes by that the media do not offer up a news story about someone committing an act of violence because he was angry, frustrated, or simply did not like his victim. Of course, self-control among three-, four-, and five-year-olds generally is not so dramatic as that depicted in the previous example. Nevertheless, a preschooler's regulating his or her own behavior is an important social/emotional issue during early childhood, and it is a long, slow process. Positive guidance and modeling of self-control by adults are important tools in helping preschoolers control their behavior. It is also important to take advantage of preschoolers' cognitive and language skills to help them understand the standards of appropriate conduct.

We believe one should distinguish between self-control resulting from external rewards or fear of punishment, and self-control resulting from internal motivation to do what is right. This is not to say that it is easy to help a child learn self-control through his own internal motivation. It is all too convenient for adults to resort to positive reinforcements (rewards) to strengthen children's desirable behavior, or punishment to weaken or eliminate undesirable behavior.

We can only say that expectation of reward or fear of punishment is not the best foundation for teaching children self-control. At the very least, adults can model self-control, and they can use an authoritative rather than an authoritarian approach to disciplining (teaching) children. An authoritative approach does not use force or threat to get children to behave appropriately (the authoritarian approach), but rather uses firm, gentle reasoning to encourage proper behavior.

Adapted from Gestwicki (1999, pp 165–167). Bold-faced text in quotation marks is quoted verbatim).

TABLE 4–7   Parten's Six Classifications of Play or Social Interaction

1. Unoccupied Behavior
Here the child is not engaging in any obvious play activity or social interaction. Rather, she watches anything that is of interest at the moment. When there is nothing of interest to watch, the child will play with her own body, move around from place to place, follow the teacher, or stay in one spot looking around the room.
2. Onlooker Behavior
Here the child spends most of her time watching other children play. The child may talk to the playing children, may ask questions or give suggestions, but does not enter into play. The child remains within speaking distance so that what goes on can be seen and heard; this indicates a definite interest in a group(s) of children, unlike the unoccupied child, who shows no interest in any particular group of children but only a shifting interest in what happens to be exciting at the moment.
3. Solitary Play
This is play activity that is conducted independently of what anyone else is doing. The child plays with toys that differ from those used by other children in the immediate area—within speaking distance—and she makes no effort to get close to them or to speak to them. The child is focused entirely on her own activity and is not influenced by what others are doing.
4. Parallel Play
Here the child is playing close to other children but is still independent of them. The child uses toys that are like the toys being used by the others, but he uses them as he sees fit and is neither influenced by nor tries to influence the others. The child thus plays *beside* rather than with the other children.
5. Associative Play
Here the child plays with the other children. There is a sharing of material and equipment; the children may follow each other around; there may be attempts to control who may or who may not play in a group, although such control efforts are not strongly asserted. The children engage in similar but not necessarily identical activity, and there is no division of labor or organization of activity, or of individuals. Each child does what he or she essentially wants to do, without putting the interests of the group first.
6. Cooperative or Organized Supplementary Play
The key word in this category is "organized." The child plays in a group that is established for a particular purpose—making some material product, gaining some competitive goal, playing some formal games. There is a sense of "we-ness," whereby one definitely belongs or does not belong to the group. There is also some leadership present—one or two members who direct the activity of the others. This behavior requires some division of labor, a taking of different roles by the group members and support of one child's efforts by those of the others.

Reprinted with permission of Delmar Learning. Bentzen, W. R. (2000, p. 107).

Child Appropriate Social and Emotional Interaction

If anything characterizes the human species, it's relationships. With individual exceptions, we are gregarious creatures who need to associate with others. There is no doubt that nearly every aspect of children's learning and development depends upon interactions with other people. Children's physical and emotional health depend on adults who feed them, protect them from harm, care for them when they are ill, and provide them with an appropriate quantity and quality of psychological care. Cognitive and language development will not occur in the absence of interactions with other people. The development of distinctly human sentiments, such as sympathy, empathy, pride, and joy, depends on human relationships.

In this context, interaction takes on both its more common meaning of two or more people taking each other into account through a social exchange, and its meaning as part of the concept of interaction effects. Bear in mind that interaction effects can occur without direct social interaction whereas, ordinarily, social interactions involve some kind of direct social exchange (see Chapter 1). Five-year-old Abigail might experience an interaction effect merely by watching two of her classmates playing together across the room. She might feel jealousy or resentment because her best friend is playing with someone else. To experience a social interaction, however, she would have to join her two classmates and participate in their play. Not all interaction effects are predictable or desirable.

Social interactions are necessary for relationships to form, and relationships necessarily consist of social interactions. Children first need strong, healthy relationships with adults, and later with other children. The developmental environment is all the relationships that occur in the general environment, and in a child appropriate developmental environment, those relationships should be ones that are important to children. Preschoolers' relationships with other children, adults, and even objects help them to learn how they fit into their interpersonal, physical, and social/cultural world. This is what makes play so important for preschoolers; it's through play that children potentially can experience so many different kinds of relationships. Play helps children get out of themselves, so to speak, and learn to adapt to the demands and needs of others. Gestwicki cites adults' personal relationships with young children as the ". . . necessary first step in the process of identification; children only want to be like adults they care for and who they sense care for them" (p. 167).

Caregivers in an effective early childhood program could look at relationships from the perspective of the social/emotional issues summarized in Table 4–6. As we mentioned earlier, relationships—with people and objects—are absolutely essential to proper growth and development. Children deprived of appropriate human contact may suffer **failure to thrive syndrome.** Failure to thrive syndrome describes ". . . infants and children who do not appear to be ill or abnormal but who do not grow at the expected rates" (Fabes and Martin, 2000, p. 150). Even physical growth can depend upon adequate social and emotional nurturance. An effective early childhood program structures and implements a developmental environment in which relationships with children are well thought out and based on sound knowledge of what children need. They also provide the kinds of interactions that will best meet those needs. Let's look at some child appropriate social/emotional interactions.

Nurturing Individual Identity

"One of the most developmentally inappropriate aspects of any preschool environment is a tendency to treat children as if they were *only* members of a group, restricting attention only to group identity . . .". (Gestwicki, 1999, p. 167; italics original). Group cohesiveness and a sense of community are important, but Gestwicki accurately points out that ". . . developmental appropriateness involves considering the unique characteristics and needs of each child and trying to convey acceptance of that uniqueness" (p. 168).

We believe the most significant content of any child's uniqueness is precisely his characteristics and needs. Uniqueness can take other forms or involve other features, but these features will not come about or thrive if age appropriate and individually appropriate needs are not met and developmental tasks are not accomplished. How, then, does early childhood program staff foster children's individual identities? Table 4–8 summarizes some answers to this question.

A developmental environment offers opportunities for children to experience different kinds of relationships.

Caregivers can help each child feel that he or she is personally worthy of their time and attention by taking time during the day to talk to each child on an intimate, one-on-one basis.

TABLE 4–8 A Developmental Environment that Nurtures Positive Individual Identity

To Nurture Positive Individual Identity, Adults Should
❏ Demonstrate sincere affection for and interest in the children by way of appropriate words and nonverbal cues—such as greeting them warmly at the start of each day, saying personal goodbyes at the end of the day, and showing sincere interest in their activities and "work" products.
❏ Adapt the idea of "teachable moments" to the idea of "speakable" or "interactional moments"—occasions during the day when you can talk to each child on an intimate, one-on-one basis, thereby giving the child the feeling that he or she is personally worthy of your time and attention.
❏ Value and encourage individuality through a child appropriate developmental environment where children recognize such things as each other's accomplishments, their differences and strengths in all developmental areas, and that children with disabilities also have strengths and can achieve meaningful goals.
❏ Address children's individuality with sensitive responsiveness. Children essentially define their own uniqueness, which you must discover by determining what is age-appropriate and individually appropriate for each child. Even though not all characteristics are unique, some uniqueness remains simply because it is Billy, for example, and not Rolf who is demonstrating a particular ability, emotion, or interest. Do not treat any two children as though they were equivalent to each other simply because they are roughly at the same developmental level or perform certain skills at the same level of ability. Every child is unique because of who he or she is.
❏ Respect ". . . individual parents' styles and needs, and use parents' knowledge of their children as a primary source for getting to know individuality" (p. 169).
❏ Encourage and provide opportunities for children to show initiative in selecting activities, equipment, and materials that are personally meaningful to them.
❏ Emphasize personal identity by planning a developmental environment (curriculum) that has personal relevance to children's lives and experiences; help children see the relevance of new experiences to their own lives.

Adapted from Gestwicki (1999, pp 167–169).

A Developmental Environment that Foster's Gender Identity

The formation of a healthy gender identity is a developmental task of preschool children. The present authors doubt that any serious movement toward raising children to be gender-neutral (androgynous) will ever take hold in this country. This belief is not a call for sexism, but rather a call for recognizing and appreciating legitimate and meaningful differences between males and females. Most adults take this position. We should certainly allow and encourage children to recognize and appreciate the differences between boys and girls. Table 4–9 briefly summarizes some of the characteristics of adult-child relationships that will foster gender identity.

Fostering Cultural and Racial Identity

Cultural diversity or multiculturalism is a prominent aspect of our society. In Chapter 2, we discussed respect at considerable length, emphasizing that even infants deserved to be treated with respect despite their limited understanding, maturity, and social and emotional skills. Showing respect for children of all ages should be a central theme and goal of every early childhood program. Respect for the individual, however, necessarily extends to respect for his or her family, social, cultural, racial, or ethnic background. It is not only a matter of showing respect for any given child's back-

TABLE 4–9   A Developmental Environment That Fosters Gender Identity

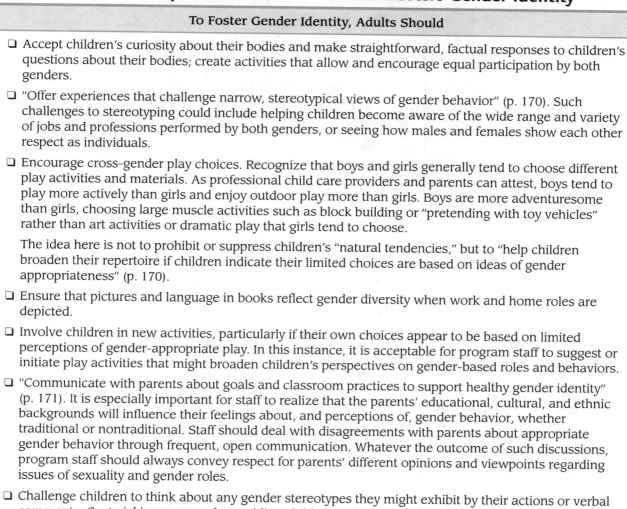

To Foster Gender Identity, Adults Should
❑ Accept children's curiosity about their bodies and make straightforward, factual responses to children's questions about their bodies; create activities that allow and encourage equal participation by both genders.
❑ "Offer experiences that challenge narrow, stereotypical views of gender behavior" (p. 170). Such challenges to stereotyping could include helping children become aware of the wide range and variety of jobs and professions performed by both genders, or seeing how males and females show each other respect as individuals.
❑ Encourage cross-gender play choices. Recognize that boys and girls generally tend to choose different play activities and materials. As professional child care providers and parents can attest, boys tend to play more actively than girls and enjoy outdoor play more than girls. Boys are more adventuresome than girls, choosing large muscle activities such as block building or "pretending with toy vehicles" rather than art activities or dramatic play that girls tend to choose. The idea here is not to prohibit or suppress children's "natural tendencies," but to "help children broaden their repertoire if children indicate their limited choices are based on ideas of gender appropriateness" (p. 170).
❑ Ensure that pictures and language in books reflect gender diversity when work and home roles are depicted.
❑ Involve children in new activities, particularly if their own choices appear to be based on limited perceptions of gender-appropriate play. In this instance, it is acceptable for program staff to suggest or initiate play activities that might broaden children's perspectives on gender-based roles and behaviors.
❑ "Communicate with parents about goals and classroom practices to support healthy gender identity" (p. 171). It is especially important for staff to realize that the parents' educational, cultural, and ethnic backgrounds will influence their feelings about, and perceptions of, gender behavior, whether traditional or nontraditional. Staff should deal with disagreements with parents about appropriate gender behavior through frequent, open communication. Whatever the outcome of such discussions, program staff should always convey respect for parents' different opinions and viewpoints regarding issues of sexuality and gender roles.
❑ Challenge children to think about any gender stereotypes they might exhibit by their actions or verbal comments. Gestwicki recommends providing children with opportunities ". . . to compare their real experiences with their beliefs [which] may eventually cause children to shift their thinking" (p. 171).
❑ Examine their own feelings and attitudes about gender issues. The present authors would characterize this examination as analyzing your possible biases. It is impossible to be completely free of bias if we use the most innocent meaning of bias as a perspective or point of view, which is something everyone has. If you harbor negative biases or prejudices about gender issues, you can't deal with them effectively if you don't acknowledge their existence and aren't aware of how they can affect your relationships with children.

Adapted from Gestwicki (1999, pp 170–171).

ground, but also showing each child that you respect other children's backgrounds. Table 4–10 summarizes some of the things child care staff can do to foster cultural and racial identity.

Prosocial Behavior

Friendships are prime examples of prosocial behavior (though not necessarily in all cases), but prosocial behavior is not limited to friendships. Children and adults alike

Use materials, books, and pictures to foster cultural and racial
identity.

TABLE 4–10   A Developmental Environment that Fosters Cultural and Racial Identity

To Foster Cultural and Racial Identity, Adults Should
❑ Ensure that all books and pictures in the classroom realistically depict the diversity represented by the children in the program, the community, and the whole of the North American population. Diversity should address "racial composition, non-stereotypical gender representation, different abilities, ages, classes, family structures, and lifestyles" (p. 172).
❑ Provide toys, activities, and materials that meet the same requirements as those for books and pictures listed immediately above.
❑ Use parents as a resource for such things as ". . . family stories, songs, drawings, and traditions of their cultural and linguistic background" (p. 172). This once again emphasizes the need for communicating with and involving parents in their children's program. In this instance, using parents as a resource helps them to know that you are paying respect and attention to their children's cultural and racial heritages (p. 172).
❑ Work with bilingual children and their parents to maintain their (children's) home language skills and to foster their learning English within the context of the early childhood program—providing relevant play activities, books, pictures, equipment, materials, and the like.
❑ Use "teachable moments" to reduce children's feelings of "discomfort or prejudice [regarding] what is new or unfamiliar to them" (p. 173). It will require skill and tact on your part to dissuade children from ideas that could lead to bias or prejudice.

Adapted from Gestwicki (1999, pp 172–173).

should learn to extend their socially appropriate, constructive responses to others beyond those they consider their friends. Prosocial behavior essentially consists of giving, helping, empathizing, sympathizing, sharing, giving comfort, and behaving in friendly, generous ways. Prosocial behaviors will not gain a strong foothold during the preschool years. Usually they become well-established during the school years. The preschool years are the time when children can begin forming a foundation for such behaviors. Table 4–11 offers some suggestions for promoting prosocial behavior.

TABLE 4–11:   A Developmental Environment for Promoting Prosocial Behavior

To Promote Prosocial Behavior, Adults Should

❑ Provide equipment and materials that encourage cooperation and joint play activity. There are toys, for example, designed to be used simultaneously by two or more children—wagons, toy cars with two or more seats, age-appropriate board games, and so on. Such materials are good examples of letting physical structures influence or suggest play activities, which can also provide children with opportunities to exercise their initiative.

❑ Provide activities that encourage or require joint, cooperative interactions. Physical equipment and materials generally are the context or props for children's play—they seldom play by twiddling their thumbs—so materials and activities are complementary.

A major difference the present authors see between these first two ways of promoting prosocial behavior is that there are activities that do not involve toys as such. Gestwicki, for instance, mentions such activities as ". . . writing group stories or making cards to send to the sick sister of one child, [which] encourages both turn-taking and opportunities to experience the positive results of cooperation" (p. 175).

❑ Encourage children to ask for assistance from their classmates, and encourage them to give assistance when requested. This recommendation has to do with individual differences in children's abilities and talents.

The present authors also put this recommendation in the context of **instrumental dependency.** All of us are instrumentally dependent on certain other people who are able to do for us what we cannot do for ourselves. Physicians treat us when we are ill, automobile mechanics repair our cars when they are not operating properly, and farmers grow the food we eat. Asking for assistance, when it stems from instrumental dependency, is a natural part of the human condition. It can also foster a sense of healthy interdependence and altruism.

❑ Direct children toward experiences that help them become aware of others' feelings and needs. This recommendation goes hand in hand with Gestwicki's other recommendation to "help children recognize prosocial behavior" (p. 176). Awareness here refers to recognizing the signs that someone needs help, for example, which is really developing a sensitivity to the behavioral cues other people give off. Recognizing prosocial behavior involves understanding what behaviors or responses are actually required in a given situation. Such recognition can be taught in such ways as pointing out ". . . when other children are attempting to show concern or helpfulness" (p. 176).

❑ Reinforce and model prosocial behavior. This is probably one of the easiest recommendations to implement. It does require sensitivity and awareness on the caregiver's part, because he or she has to observe a prosocial behavior in order to reinforce it. It also requires a proper sense of timing; one cannot allow too much time to pass between the occurrence of the prosocial behavior and a reinforcing response. It would be very helpful to specify to the child which of his or her behaviors is being reinforced or rewarded.

One would think that modeling prosocial behavior would be part of a child care provider's normal routine, and it should be. But as Gestwicki implies, modeling prosocial behavior is not just demonstrating it yourself; modeling can also involve ". . . verbally explain[ing] helpfulness and cooperation. . .," thus showing children ". . . the importance of behaving in prosocial ways" (p. 176).

❑ Limit aggressive, antisocial behavior. "You can't say you can't play" (p. 176). This rule is good as far as it goes. It essentially prohibits children from excluding other children in their play, and exclusion is what Gestwicki appears to emphasize. The present authors would merely point out that aggressive, antisocial behavior takes forms other than exclusion—pushing, hitting, verbal insults, disparaging comments, and so on.

continued

TABLE 4–11   A Developmental Environment for Promoting Prosocial Behavior (Continued)

❏ Help children develop empathy. Empathy is the ability to feel or understand what someone else is feeling—it is putting yourself in someone else's shoes. Empathy, however, is primarily cognitive, not emotional; you do not literally have to feel what someone else is feeling, but you do have to have some intellectual appreciation of another's feelings. You can help children acquire this appreciation by verbalizing or defining their own and others' feelings and your concern for them.

To some extent, children learn what to feel in certain situations, but they also have to learn what to call their feelings. It is sometimes risky to try to determine what someone else is feeling. We can't always be sure, for example, whether four-year-old Ralph is angry or frightened by observing only his facial expressions or body postures. Nevertheless, adults do identify what they think children are feeling: "I know you *feel sad* because it's raining and you can't go outside to play. You'll *feel happy* as soon as the rain stops." This kind of verbalization does help children to recognize feelings and occasions that call for empathetic responses.

Adapted from Gestwicki (1999, pp. 175–177).

Self-Control and Emotional Control

Self-control and emotional control are two sides of the same coin, although we can make distinctions between them. A child who is emotionally out of control is not exercising self-control, and it is likely that a child who has poor self-control will also have poor emotional control. We define self-control as controlling or managing one's impulses or behaviors and behaving appropriately in a given situation. Self-control can involve such things as a child obeying the rules even when he is not particularly motivated to do so, or performing an altruistic act for a child he does not particularly like.

Emotional control does not mean having only emotions approved of by adults. "I hate Billy," says three-year-old Katrina. Some adults might respond by saying something like, "Hating someone is wrong, Katrina, and I don't ever want to hear you say that again!" Leaving aside the question of whether Katrina really hates Billy, the strong emotion is very real to Katrina. Yet, she would demonstrate emotional control by not acting on this emotion by being physically or verbally aggressive. Emotional control in this instance is not very different from self-control. Acknowledging Katrina's feelings without judging or scolding her also helps her not to be ashamed of strong emotions and may help her handle them appropriately.

Emotional control also involves the ability to know what one is feeling. Our emotions are an important part of our personalities; they inform us when something is wrong, and they do drive our behavior under certain circumstances. Fear motivates us to avoid or escape a situation; anger can motivate us to protect ourselves and fend off an aggressor. Emotional control requires the ability to identify accurately the feeling and appropriately channel or direct one's responses in appropriate, socially acceptable ways.

Finally, children's emotional control and self-control depend heavily on their perceived and actual ability to deal effectively with a situation. Such ability can be a function of their moods, developmental levels, temperaments, and experiences. Consequently, putting preschoolers into situations that are not individually appropriate or age appropriate can work against emotional and self-control.

A Child Appropriate Cognitive/Language Environment for Preschoolers

Children Qualitatively Different from Adults

There are ongoing differences of opinion regarding the best approach for educating preschoolers. Some argue for formal academic learning. Others such as the National

Child care staff should acknowledge strong feelings and help children handle them appropriately.

Association for the Education of Young Children (NAEYC) argue for developmentally appropriate practices (DAP), the approach we advocate in this book. Play is the hook on which DAP hangs, but play must be properly defined and its principles or characteristics properly applied.

Cognitive and language development seem to follow a definite maturational timetable. Piaget argued that even providing an enriched environment or special experiences could not accelerate cognitive development. His four stages of cognitive development delineate pretty clearly the intellectual/maturational boundaries within which cognitive advancements occur. Therefore, there is no point in trying to teach a preoperational preschooler how to think **operationally** (see glossary for operation) or how to solve conservation tasks; he simply is not ready to function at that level of intellectual reasoning and comprehension. Of course, he needs the experiences that lead up to that level of ability, but any intellectual gains—any movement from one stage to another—is the result of the interaction between experience and maturation, with neither one operating independently of the other.

 SEE FOR YOURSELF

After observing individual preschoolers as well as groups of preschoolers in a child care setting, record specific actions of the children and suggest appropriate caregiver responses to each action. For example, if a preschooler is speaking about a favorite book, the caregiver might engage the child in conversation about the book, listening attentively and sensitively to the child's comments, etc.

Piaget also argued that children essentially construct their own reality, a process that also depends on the interaction between experience and maturation. This is why he so strongly asserted his belief that children's thinking and adults' thinking are **qualitatively different.** Children, he argued, are not merely small adults waiting to "grow up" and become "full-sized" adults. Expecting or demanding that young children function intellectually like adults is inappropriate and developmentally exploitative. Piaget referred to young children as "cognitive aliens" in the world of adult logic and reasoning.

It is very interesting and instructive, though, that Piaget did not view children as "emotional aliens" in an adult world. Children experience many of the same emotions that adults experience—fear, anxiety, shame, humiliation, embarrassment, joy, guilt. Yet, far too often, adults want young children to do such things as internalize rules of conduct. "How many times do I have to tell you," says three-year-old Michelle's mother, "when someone gives you a gift, you say thank you." Michelle's mother wants her to function intellectually like an adult, while at the same time she has no qualms about embarrassing Michelle in front of others. Adults sometimes think that young children do not have the same feelings as they do, that they are too young to experience embarrassment or a sense of unworthiness.

We can't overstress the importance of understanding where preschoolers are in their cognitive, language, and emotional journeys toward adult maturity. An effective early childhood program should neither overestimate preschoolers' cognitive and language abilities, nor underestimate the scope of their emotional repertoire and the intensity of their emotional responses.

What Are the Intellectual Characteristics of Preschool Children?

The years from two to seven are the preoperational years in Piaget's theory of cognitive development. During this period, children undergo dramatic changes in their intellectual functioning, while still experiencing some significant limitations. Children in Piaget's sensorimotor stage primarily relate to their world through physical actions, but children in the preoperational stage, though not fully capable of abstract thought, increasingly relate to their world through mental representations. Compared to sensorimotor children, preoperational children can think more abstractly and express ideas and feelings that are more complicated. Miller (1993) points out that preoperational thought has some distinct advantages over sensorimotor thought: "It is faster and more mobile. It can deal with the past, present, and future in one grand sweep and can recombine its parts to create ideas that refer to nothing in reality (for example, monsters that go bump in the night)" [p. 52]. Let's look at Table 4–12 for some characteristics of preschoolers' intellectual functioning.

Characteristics of the Preoperational Period

Play Briefly Revisited

Play is a consistent theme throughout this chapter. We define play more in terms of certain characteristics or conditions that are essential to play and less in terms of specific activities. Spontaneity, self-selection, and self-direction will fall naturally within the boundaries established by age appropriateness and individual appropriateness.

We are not recommending that adults never guide or monitor children's play activities, or that everything children spontaneously do will have desirable interaction effects. An effective early childhood program is not a hands-off affair for adults. If a developmental environment provides children with opportunities and encouragement to engage in age appropriate and individually appropriate activities, children will play and are likely to experience positive interaction effects. But, it is the program staff that observes the short-term and long-term results of the curriculum and evaluates whether those results are the desired ones.

TABLE 4–12   Characteristics of Preschoolers' Thought

Egocentrism

Egocentrism refers to the young child's inability to take someone else's point of view, to see things from someone else's perceptual or conceptual perspective. Egocentrism is also displayed when preschoolers carry on what Piaget called a collective monologue: each participant in a "conversation" pays no heed to what the others are saying and has no desire to inform or influence the others. Important pieces of information necessary to the listener's understanding are also omitted.

Gestwicki mentions egocentrism's role in the preschooler's inability ". . . to center on more than one aspect of a situation at a time . . ." (p. 247). Egocentrism also leads the preschooler to believe that the world pretty much exists only within his own personal frame of reference, that all objects have the same characteristics he possesses or has experienced.

Implications for Early Childhood Program Staff

Young children's egocentrism should not be confused with the selfishness or arrogance we sometimes attribute to adults who behave egocentrically (egotistically). Children's egocentric behavior is developmentally based and reflects an inability, not an unwillingness, to take someone else's point of view, or to decenter and take into account more than one aspect of a situation at a time. Egocentrism is developmentally appropriate, and children should be afforded ample time and opportunity with people and objects so they will eventually comprehend the world from perspectives other than their own.

Centration, Irreversibility, and Concreteness

Centration, Miller (1993) writes, is ". . . the tendency to attend to or think about one salient feature of an object or event and ignore other features." Centration can be observed when a preoperational child tries to solve Piaget's classic **conservation** of liquid task. The child is shown two identical glasses holding equal amounts of liquid. The contents of one glass are poured into another taller, thinner glass, and the child is asked which of the two glasses contains more liquid. If unable to conserve, a typical answer is that the taller, thinner glass contains more liquid. Unable to *decenter,* the preoperational child *centers* or focuses on the height of the liquid and ignores its width. The child cannot overlook the liquid's visual appearance and understand that what the taller glass has gained in height, it has lost in width.

The ability to decenter allows the child to attend to details while not losing sight of the whole. This ability is required when learning to read and perform mathematical operations—addition, subtraction, multiplication, and division.

Irreversibility is the inability to retrace mentally a series of actions and get back to the original starting point. In the conservation of liquid task, the preoperational child cannot mentally (conceptually) pour the liquid from the tall, thin container back into the short, wide container, thus proving that the amount of liquid has not changed and the container's shape has no effect on the amount of liquid.

Preoperational thinking tends to be concrete. Concreteness means that young children can understand their first-hand experiences with situations, objects, and events, but have trouble with things that are not part of their personal knowledge or experience or that are only described verbally. Such concreteness ". . . ties them to literal interpretation of words and phrases" (Gestwicki, p. 247).

Implications for Early Childhood Program Staff

Taken within Piaget's perspective, here are the most significant practical implications for early childhood program staff. First, accept these characteristics of preschoolers' thought as a normal phase of their development. This is an example of an essential principle of child appropriate practice: view and work with children as they are now and not as you wish them to be.

Second, do not try to speed up their progress through the preoperational stage. Piaget distinguished among three kinds of knowledge; all children should acquire these three kinds of knowledge at a pace dictated by their experiences and the unique pace of their developmental maturation. Here are Piaget's three kinds of knowledge.

continued

TABLE 4–12 Characteristics of Preschoolers' Thought (Continued)

1. **Physical knowledge** is knowledge young children acquire through their interactions with physical objects. Thus, they learn that round things roll quite easily but square things do not; it hurts to bump your head against a hard object but not against a soft one; or you can cut paper with scissors but not glass, wood, or steel. Adults contribute to children's physical knowledge by making appropriate comments about their activities: "See how the round ball rolls across the floor. Now roll it back to me." "Let's see how many of these square blocks we can stack on top of one another."

2. **Social knowledge** is knowledge or ways of doing things that are conventionally agreed upon by the members of a particular group. "You are old enough now to eat your potatoes with a spoon, not your fingers," says three-year-old Lucinda's mother. Four-year-old Mark eventually understands that he does not go to preschool on Saturdays and Sundays. Children acquire social knowledge largely through observation or by adults' direct teaching.

3. The most important knowledge for Piaget was **logico-mathematical** (LM) knowledge. LM knowledge's most important characteristic is that it can't be taught. According to Piaget, children literally construct reality through the interaction of experience and maturation. They eventually understand such things as that the size or shape of a container does not affect the amount of liquid it contains (conservation of liquid or volume), or that how a group of objects is arranged in space does not affect how many of them there are (conservation of number). Children also learn to ignore irrelevant transformations or modifications that have no effect on the original quantity or identity of objects or persons.

Third, provide experiences and teach in ways that are commensurate with how preoperational children learn. Child care staff should accommodate to children's learning styles and cognitive abilities and limitations.

Reasoning

Gestwicki notes the preoperational child's tendency to reason from particular to particular—"The neighbor's dog barks and jumps up on me, so all dogs bark and jump up at me" (p. 247). The preoperational child also tends to assume that events closely related in time have a cause-and-effect relationship—"I sneezed and a book fell off the shelf. My sneezing must have made the book do that."

Symbolic Thought

Symbols are things that represent something else. Waving the American flag represents patriotism; the word *dog* represents a furry, four-legged animal that says "bow wow" and answers to the name Fido; or a stick can represent a rocket ship. Symbolic thought is the ability to form internal, mental representations of events, objects, people, and actions. Importantly, such mental representations can have to do with the real world or a fictitious one (fantasy, for example), and they can be formed without the objects, events, or people being physically present.

Limited Social Cognition

Preoperational thinking also applies to social events and objects. Miller cites as examples of limited social cognition ". . . deficits in role taking and communication resulting from egocentrism, confusions between natural events and human events, and notions about the identity of persons when physical appearances are changed" (p. 56). An example of the latter would be when a child does not recognize his caregiver because she is wearing glasses and a strange hat, things he has never seen her wear.

Piaget paid particular attention to social cognition in relation to moral judgments. As Miller points out, "A preoperational child judges the wrongness of an act according to external variables, such as how much damage was done and whether the act was punished" (p. 56).

Implications for Early Childhood Program Staff

The implications of all the characteristics of preschoolers' thinking for structuring a developmental environment are similar. Accept children as and where they are now, and plan and implement a curriculum that is in keeping with their developmental levels. At the same time, challenge them to stretch intellectually beyond the limits of their present abilities.

Adapted from Gestwicki (1999, pp. 246–248), and Miller (1993, pp. 53–56).

The interaction effects that each child experiences in a program come from the developmental environment in which both the child care staff and each child participate.

Like everything else preschoolers do, their play is much more complex than toddlers' play. Although their cognitive abilities are becoming more mature, preschoolers will still benefit from carefully constructed play and learning areas containing a variety of open-ended materials that match the children's learning abilities and interests. It is through such materials and their appropriate use that children construct their understanding of the world.

Although play primarily arises from children's own volition and proceeds under their own direction, play is not random or haphazard. Program staff establishes the groundwork for appropriate play activity. It's especially important to remember the role of interaction effects. Only child care staff can provide a general environment, but it is staff and children together who create a developmental environment. Each child creates his or her own developmental environment, and each child's developmental environment creates the interaction effects he or she experiences.

In large part, child care staff should act as facilitators of play who set up child appropriate conditions for play, rather than dispensers of information designed to tell children what and how to play. Facilitating play involves being alert to how children's play unfolds, because in principle, each interaction effect paves the way for more interaction effects. It's easy to think of the general environment as the underlying structure for children's learning, and in a sense it is. But, we can't overemphasize that in the final analysis, a relatively poor general/physical environment can become a relatively good developmental environment. In turn, an excellent general/physical environment can fail to become a good developmental environment. Play appropriate experiences are discussed in Table 4–13.

Early Childhood Program Staff and the Play-Supportive Developmental Environment

We have summarized in Table 4-13 the characteristics of a play-supportive environment, with an emphasis on the role of early childhood staff in providing and maintaining such an environment.

TABLE 4–13   Providing a Play-Supportive Developmental Environment for Preschoolers—the Role of Early Childhood Program Staff

"Creator of the Environment"

This is an absolute requirement for program staff, and although it is true that program staff create the environment—in particular the general or physical environment—children are co-creators of the developmental environment. The developmental environment is dynamic and constantly changing. If five-year-old Jose gets bored with a particular toy or activity, that particular aspect of the developmental environment changes for him, as do the effects of his interactions with that toy or activity.

You do not create a developmental environment, then sit back and let it work. On any given day, the children's interactions with the general environment will create a developmental environment, the particular characteristics of which will last for some time and then possibly change. It's highly likely that at the beginning of the following day, the developmental environment will be quite different from what it was at the end of the previous day. You are therefore constant creators and evaluators of the developmental environment. Additionally, this ongoing evaluation requires you always to consider the practical implications of age appropriateness and individual appropriateness. These determine the effectiveness of the environment you have created.

Six aspects that learning centers (our general and developmental environments) should provide are

❑ *"Choices:"* Choices refers to offering children a number of play options by providing a sufficient number of separate play spaces.

❑ *"Free movement:"* This acknowledges children's need to be active, to move about freely. Having a variety of options in various parts of the classroom allows children to meet this need.

❑ *"Range of developmental differences:"* This adheres to the standards of age appropriateness and individual appropriateness by recognizing and providing for individual differences in interests, abilities, and developmental levels. Again, giving children a number of choices will help accomplish this.

❑ *"Facilitating of play:"* Since play does not predominantly involve adults telling children what to do or how to do it, they are free to "move about among children at play, effectively reinforcing the learning they observe or extending and stimulating discoveries on an individual basis" (p. 253).

❑ *"Cooperative learning:"* Although she does not use the term, Gestwicki is referring to scaffolding in the context of cooperative learning. She cites "opportunities for project work and increasing understanding through interactions with others whose experience and learning may be more advanced. . . ." (p. 253).

❑ *"Initiative:"* This aspect essentially restates one of the characteristics of play, namely that of self-chosen and self-directed activity. Materials should be located in predictable places in order to help children plan and initiate their own activities.

"Observer-and-Recorder"

Observing and recording what takes place in the child care facility might just be the single most important responsibility of program staff. You can have the best of everything—equipment, materials, facility location, highly trained and well-paid staff—but if you do not know what is going on in your program, it all becomes moot. You can know what is going on only if you know how to observe and keep accurate, meaningful records of your observations. Chapters 6 through 8 will provide you opportunities to practice and refine your observation and recording skills.

"Facilitator"

Facilitating children's play is not as easy as it may appear. It is a skill that comes with knowledge and practice. Facilitating play requires knowing when and how to intervene to help children achieve new levels of ability and competence. It is not arbitrarily telling children what to do, or in other ways imposing your ideas concerning play. Some reasons for adults to participate or intervene in children's play include

continued

TABLE 4–13 Providing a Play-Supportive Developmental Environment for Preschoolers—the Role of Early Childhood Program Staff (Continued)

❑ To get children involved with their peers and play materials.

❑ To bolster children's play when it appears to be breaking down. This does not mean taking over, but rather subtly introducing new ideas or materials, changing the children's mood, helping them understand what they are doing, and so forth.

❑ To foster social and cognitive development by guiding children's play to more complex levels. Again, guiding should be done in such subtle ways as questions or casual comments.

❑ To accept the children's invitation to play, which enhances your relationship with them. It also gives you an opportunity to be a participant observer, to get a close-up view of the dynamics of their play behaviors.

"Model"

To model is to take the role of a player. The term *player* has the important connotation of an adult participating in play in much the same way a child would participate, which is as an equal partner. Although children do tell their playmates what to do and how to do it, that does not have the same effect as an adult telling children what to do and how to do it. Modeling, therefore, entails giving children ideas, not by telling or imposing, but by behaving in particular ways and talking to them about what they are doing.

Modeling has an effect only if the children are capable of understanding subtle hints, casual suggestions, or the behaviors that an adult is displaying (modeling). This means that modeling should be commensurate with the children's zones of proximal development. Modeling that is appropriate for preschoolers would not be appropriate for toddlers. Once again, age appropriateness and individual appropriateness become relevant.

"Questioner"

Asking children questions, not to test them, but to challenge them to think, to explore new ways of solving problems or accomplishing goals, is an excellent way to foster cognitive development. Asking appropriate questions can motivate them to analyze their experiences, verbalize their understandings of people and events, and deepen those understandings.

Recall our earlier discussion of Piaget's three kinds of knowledge. Each of these three kinds of knowledge lends itself to different kinds of questions. Physical knowledge is conducive to questions that make the child think about how objects behave: "Why do you think that ball rolls? Do you think that big wooden block will roll across the floor like this ball does?" Social knowledge can support such questions as, "Do you remember why you don't come to school tomorrow?" or "Do you remember what we use to eat our potatoes? What do we call it?"

Logico-mathematical knowledge requires different kinds of questions. Recall Piaget's argument that children literally construct their logico-mathematical knowledge, rather than learning it from someone else. Consequently, you should not use questions to correct the children's "wrong" answers, because there are no wrong answers given their present level of cognitive development. Preoperational children have their own logic, and you should not try to speed up their progress through this stage of cognitive development in an effort to push them (prematurely) into adult-like reasoning.

It might be useful to distinguish between two basic kinds of thinking—**convergent thinking** and **divergent thinking.** Questions that seek specific, concrete, right or wrong answers elicit convergent thinking. Open-ended questions that allow the child's thinking to move in many directions, requiring no specific right or wrong answers, elicit divergent thinking. In most instances, divergent thinking is preferable to convergent thinking.

continued

TABLE 4–13 Providing a Play-Supportive Developmental Environment for Preschoolers—the Role of Early Childhood Program Staff (Continued)

"Responder"
Adults' role as responders is almost intuitively obvious. In one context, acting as a responder is an example of sensitive responsiveness, a characteristic that should prevail in every aspect of an early childhood program. In the context of cognitive development, Gestwicki provides a more specific sense of responding. She writes, "As teachers move and observe children at their play, they see opportunities to reinforce and enrich children's learning experiences. In the role of responder, they individualize their perception of what would help children build on their learning." The following identifies four kinds of responding.
❑ As an appreciative comment regarding children's accomplishments or behaviors
❑ As support "in the form of information, hints, and encouragement as a child struggles with a difficult challenge" (p. 260)
❑ As a means of extending children's play through suggestions or provision of more play materials
❑ As an occasion simply to be available to the children and to show a sincere interest in their activities, helping them to maintain their own interest and activity

Adapted from Gestwicki (1999, pp. 252–260). Bold-faced text in quotation marks is quoted verbatim.

Summary

This chapter discussed the characteristics and needs of the preschool child in the context of the early childhood program environment. We noted that preschool children are very different from infants and toddlers. This is because the time children spend in their preschool years is longer than the time spent in infancy and toddlerhood, thus allowing for more experiences and a potentially greater variety of interaction effects than were previously possible.

Information presented in Table 4–1 showed what would constitute appropriate care for three-, four-, and five-year-olds. In Table 4–2, we presented information regarding children's abilities and needs from two to eight years. This included an extended age range to allow you to anticipate some of the preschoolers' potential future characteristics and abilities.

The remainder of this chapter discussed various child appropriate developmental environments for preschoolers, including the physical environment, which in turn includes environments for developing initiative, for play, and for self-control. We then discussed a child appropriate social/emotional environment, including child appropriate social and emotional interactions. Under this latter category, we discussed such aspects as nurturing individual identity, fostering gender identity, fostering cultural and racial identity, prosocial behavior, and self-control and emotional control.

Finally, this chapter dealt with a child appropriate cognitive/language environment for preschoolers. In this context, we described children as qualitatively different from adults, together with the implications of such differences for early childhood program staff. We also discussed the characteristics of preoperational thinking according to Piaget's theory of cognitive development.

Questions to Consider

1. According to the text, what is the most appropriate way to characterize or describe the preschool years?

2. Why are the interaction effects potentially open to preschoolers so different from those open to infants and toddlers?

3. Why do the authors say that you do not have to remember every possible skill and ability of which preschoolers are capable?

4. What is so important about recognizing that preschoolers tend to be egocentric? How might their egocentricity affect your relationships with them?

5. What do you think is the most important characteristic of logico-mathematical knowledge? Explain.

6. Is responding to a preschooler different from responding to an adult? If your answer is yes, in what ways is it different?

7. Is there any connection between a child's egocentrism and his or her limited social cognition? Explain.

8. What, if any, differences are there between being a cognitive alien and an emotional alien? What do these two terms mean, and what is their significance for early childhood program staff?

Conclusion

This ends Part I of *Seeing Child Care.* To this point, we have given you a foundation on which to build an effective early childhood program. The foundation, or the principles of development and child (developmentally) appropriate practice, is the groundwork and boundaries within which program activities can be structured.

Part II offers four chapters of practical observation exercises. The hands-on activities are critical to your complete understanding and application of the essentials of Part I. Part II gives you the opportunity to observe an early childhood program and evaluate its effectiveness. You will be able to determine children's developmental progress and what they need for their continuing development. You will be able to answer such questions as: Does the professional staff understand how children change over time? Does the staff understand what is age appropriate, individually appropriate, and socially/culturally appropriate for each child in the program? Do the general and developmental environments account for and appropriately meet each child's developmental needs and tasks?

To make these assessments, you must have trained observation skills in order to make sense of the information gathered during a program day. Part II provides observation and recording techniques, and tips to help you understand what you are seeing and hearing as you observe children and staff interact. You will also be able to evaluate what kind of developmental environment has been created, the interaction effects that the environment is producing, and how to keep accurate, meaningful records of what transpires during a program day.

The extent to which you use this knowledge and understand its application will help you "see" the essence of child care and determine a program's effectiveness. You're well on your way.

For additional information on assessing the effectiveness of child care programs, visit our Web site at **http://www.earlychilded.delmar.com**

Part II

Chapter 5

Observation and Recording Practices for Child Care Programs

See How To

* differentiate among the selected observation and recording methods

* discuss the similarities and differences among the selected instruments

* determine which method is most appropriate in a given situation

* judge which methods are more appropriate for the preservice and the in-service child care workers to use in specific situations

Methods of Observing and Recording Characteristics of Child Care Programs: An Introduction

Of the several possible methods for observing and recording characteristics of child care programs, we have selected three that we feel are most appropriate for use: (1) narrative description, (2) event sampling, and (3) checklists and rating scales. Each of these methods has its own features, uses, advantages, and disadvantages, and each is appropriate in a specific observation context. For example, a rating scale might be appropriate to judge whether the characteristics of a safe infant environment are present in a given child care setting. Before examining these methods more closely, let us first consider several characteristics of observation and recording methods.

Bentzen (2000, p. 84), citing Goodwin and Driscoll (1980) among others, discusses several attributes of these methods labeled (1) open versus closed, (2) degree of selectivity, and (3) degree of observer inference required. Note the clarification that follows.

Open vs. Closed

The concepts of "raw data" and "data" are central to understanding whether a recording method is open or closed. Simply stated, "raw data are descriptions of behavior and events as they originally occurred" (Bentzen, 2000, p. 85). If you were to observe four-year-old Ahmad take a puzzle down from the shelf, dump the puzzle pieces onto a table, and proceed to put the puzzle together, and then record exactly that sequence of behaviors in as much detail as possible, you would have an example of raw data. The chief advantage of raw data is that they are available for further analysis at some future time. You could re-create more or less precisely what occurred at an earlier time. The adjective *raw* essentially means unchanged or uninterpreted. A recording technique that preserves raw data is referred to as an open technique.

If, on the other hand, you were to observe that same sequence of behaviors but summarize your observations by placing a check mark next to a checklist category, "Child plays with puzzle," you would have converted the original raw data into data. At some future time, that check mark would tell you virtually nothing about the details and subtleties of Ahmad's puzzle-playing behavior. From that check mark, you could not infer anything about such things as the child's demeanor or puzzle-assembly skills, or the extent of his task orientation. A recording technique that loses raw data is a closed technique.

Degree of Selectivity

Selectivity simply refers to the amount of observational data you record. For example, in the narrative description, you are not at all selective because you would record in as much detail as possible everything you have observed during a particular period of time. The event sample, in contrast, is highly selective because you determine ahead of time the specific behaviors you are interested in and which ones you want to record; you essentially ignore everything else. If you were interested in observing the cooperative behaviors among a group of three-year-olds, such behaviors would be the event, and you would not record any behaviors other than cooperative ones. You would not be oblivious to aggressive behaviors or solitary play behaviors, for instance, but at that time they would not be the subject of your recording. At a later time and perhaps for a different purpose, those behaviors could become the events of choice and subject to recording.

Degree of Observer Inference Required

Inference means essentially the same thing as interpretation. Recall from our earlier discussion that interpretation of observational data is essential if such data are to have any meaning or usefulness. Bentzen (2000) defines inference as . . . drawing a conclusion based on data, premises, or evidence (p. 87). It is the continual task of early childhood program staff to draw conclusions from what they observe in the classroom. Such conclusions form the foundation for child appropriate practice.

Different recording techniques require different degrees of inference or interpretation at different times in the observation/recording process. The narrative description technique requires no inference before or during the recording session. Since any and every behavior is of interest in this technique, you need not make any decisions about what to observe and what to ignore. Inference may subsequently be required when you are reading your observation report and want to derive meaning and draw conclusions from your observational data. Therefore, inference is low or nonexistent at the start of the narrative description but may be high at the end when you need to make sense out of your raw data.

The event sample and checklist require relatively high degrees of inference before you begin recording. In the event sample, you should decide ahead of time whether what is occurring in the classroom meets your definition of the event you have chosen to observe and record. For example, does four-year-old Mark's interaction with five-year-old Gabriella match your definition of cooperative behavior? If it does, you would record the details of that interaction. If it does not, you would essentially ignore it. Your decision, however, would have to be immediate and occur prior to recording details of the interaction. The same conditions apply to the checklist, except the checklist does not involve writing down the details of the behavior.

The Narrative Description

The narrative description is an objective record, or description, of a behavior or sequence of behaviors that has occurred over some length of time. (It is also called running record.) You, the observer, determine the length of the recording session, which can be influenced by such things as your mood, level of energy and physical condition, and skill at writing down detailed descriptions of behavioral events.

The basic purpose of the narrative description is to record as much objective detail as possible about what is taking place in the early childhood classroom during a particular period of time. Nothing should be excluded from the observational record. An advantage of a narrative description is that it is a rich source of potentially valuable information. When done skillfully, the narrative description captures the context of children's and staff's behavior and the subtleties and nuances of their interactions. It thus provides a basis for meaningful interpretation of behavior and for intelligent planning of the curriculum (developmental environment). Another advantage of the narrative description is its simplicity, at least in principle. It is not always easy to observe classroom happenings accurately and thoroughly enough to provide meaningful information. Yet this kind of description requires no special preparation, except knowledge and skill, and no tools but pencil and paper.

The two essential characteristics of this recording technique are objectivity and detailed descriptions. The objective behavioral description should contain no inter-

FIGURE 5–1   Narrative Description

Observer's Name	Robin Crowley (Student)
Setting Observed	Infant Room (Physical Environment)
Observation Context	Little Friends Child Care Center
Date of Observation	April 5, 2003 Time Begun 9:30 a.m. Time Ended 9:40 a.m.

**Objective Behavioral Description (OBD) and Interpretation:
Narrative Description**

OBD:

Floor coverings are soft carpeting with vinyl-covered, high-density mats near climbing toys. An infant-safe mirror is mounted, at infant's eye level, to the wall behind a grab bar. Windows are placed high enough that they are inaccessible to the children. All toys are infant-appropriate, with no sharp edges or toxic materials. Staff-child ratio is 1:3, ensuring ample supervision of infants. Infants, secured in their high chairs with safety belts, are supervised and assisted during lunch time.

Interpretation:

This infant environment appropriately ensures the safety of the children. The cushions and vinyl-covered, high-density mats near the soft climbers assure protection should a child take a tumble while attempting to climb up the two soft blocks. The lack of sharp edges on toys and no toxic materials protect the infants while mouthing their toys. The staff provide excellent supervision of the children and provide a safe, comfortable environment for the infants.

pretations or inferences, only accurate descriptions of behavior as you have observed them. Interpretations, which are made after the recording is completed, should be written in a special section, separate and distinct from the descriptions themselves. See Figure 5–1.

 ## Event Sampling

In the context of observing in a child care setting, the event sample refers to those events or characteristics that are selected to be observed in the child care environment. These events can be grouped into particular categories, such as the characteristics of a safe infant environment. Bentzen (2000), citing Goodwin and Driscoll (1982), summarizes the recording technique used in event sampling as "the immediate coding of the occurrence of certain events (p. 116)." However, Bentzen (2000, p. 116) further cites Lay-Dopyera and Dopyera (1982) and Gander and Gardner (1981), stating that you could describe the event in detail. Thus, you could use a coding scheme, a narrative description, or a combination of these two.

For our purposes, event sampling can be either an open or a closed method, depending upon whether a narrative description or a coding scheme is used. When the narrative description, which preserves the raw data, is used, the event sample remains an open method. When only a coding scheme is used, the method remains closed.

Since only specific characteristics, or events, which are chosen in advance of the observation, are observed and recorded, there is a high degree of selectivity in event sampling. There is also a high degree of inference in the event sampling method, since you must decide if a particular event or characteristic belongs in a particular category. Does "constant supervision of infants who are never left unattended" belong in the category "characteristics of a safe infant environment"? You must decide whether constant supervision is an appropriate characteristic of a safe infant environment.

Writing a narrative description (running record) requires objectivity and detailed descriptions.

This staff member uses the children's naptime to categorize events she wants to observe and record.

FIGURE 5–2 Event Sample (using coding scheme)

Observer's Name	Seri Ullerol (Student)
Setting Observed	Infant Room (Healthy Infant Environment)
Observation Context	Little Friends Child Care Center
Date of Observation	May 4, 2003 Time Begun 10:20 a.m. Time Ended 10:35 a.m.

Directions: Check (X) all characteristics observed during this 15-minute period.

Characteristics of Healthy Infant Environment

❑ Staff religiously adhere to standards of "adult hand-washing after coughing, sneezing, wiping a child's nose, changing diapers, and before handling food or bottles; after washing, adults use paper towels to touch faucets or waste containers."

❑ There is strict adherence to licensing standards for cleanliness of the diaper changing area; staff provide a clean and covered surface for each diaper change.

❑ Food and bottles are refrigerated until they are used.

❑ Infants' hands are washed frequently, with individual washcloths.

❑ Toys and surfaces are washed every day, or more frequently when children are sharing and mouthing toys.

❑ Parents and staff remove street shoes before they walk on floors where infants lie.

❑ Individual cribs are kept clean.

❑ Accurate records are kept of up-to-date infant immunizations.

❑ Infants who shows signs of illness are excluded in keeping with the "standards and symptoms defined by the program."

❑ Only prescribed medicines are administered to infants with permission and instructions from the parents.

Adapted from Gestwicki (1999, pp. 50, 76).

A major advantage of event sampling is how it can combine the efficiencies of immediate coding schemes and complete narrative descriptions (Bentzen, 2000, p. 118). See Figure 5–2 for an example of an event sample that uses a coding scheme.

 ## Checklists and Rating Scales

Checklists are used to record the occurrence of particular characteristics in a given context. If your checklist concerns adequate nutrition for toddlers, you would want to observe those criteria in an appropriate setting, such as snack time or at the lunch table.

Checklists require some structure, so the characteristics to be observed in a particular situation should be clearly established beforehand. Since they reduce the raw data to a tally that indicates the presence or absence of a particular characteristic or event, checklists are a closed method. Degree of selectivity is high since the characteristics to be recorded are selected before the observation begins. Checklists are very efficient since they can be quickly applied and used in a child care environment. See Table 5–1 for a Safe Infant Environment Checklist.

A rating scale is an instrument that is used to record the relative degree to which a child care environment possesses certain characteristics or criteria. What is measured falls along a continuum, since it can be assigned a number of different values or qualities. For example, you might want to judge the degree to which a toddler child care setting provides an appropriate environment for sensorimotor exploration. You might judge this appropriateness of the environment according to five different degrees of appropriateness: Always, Usually, Sometimes, Seldom, and Never.

Rating scales are more complicated than checklists, since checklists merely indicate whether the environment is appropriate for sensorimotor exploration. A rating scale, however, tries to judge how well, or to what degree, the environment is appropriate for sensorimotor exploration. As with the checklist, rating scales require structuring. They

TABLE 5–1   Safe Infant Environment Checklist

| Child Care Center's Name _____ | Room No. _____ |
| Observer _____ | Date _____ |

SAFE INFANT ENVIRONMENT CHECKLIST			
Characteristics of Safe Infant Environment	Yes	No	Sometimes
❑ Mirrors and windows that will not break and either windows that open only from the top or protection from windows that open at the bottom.			
❑ No electrical cords to trip or chew on; electrical outlets that are covered.			
❑ Protection from anything that could burn or scald (for example, light bulbs, heaters, radiators, hot water faucets).			
❑ Plants that are not poisonous.			
❑ Unreachable hazardous chemicals such as medicines, cleaning substances.			
❑ No broken or damaged toys, toys with easily removable small parts, or toys painted with lead or other toxic materials.			
❑ Furniture that is stable and cannot be pulled over or fall; furniture should meet consumer protection standards to prevent infants from getting their heads stuck.			
❑ Any sharp edges that could injure if fallen on or bumped into are covered or padded			
❑ Knowledgeable staff concerning emergency procedures, such as CPR and first aid, location of emergency numbers and equipment, and evacuation procedures—such as fire drill.			
❑ Constant supervision of infants who are never left unattended; high-chairs, strollers, and changing tables are fitted with proper restraints.			
❑ Infants are supervised as they eat and drink; they are never left with a propped up bottle; are given properly sized finger foods.			
❑ Infants are not overprotected; infants are provided safe ways to practice a challenging skill (for example, cushioning with a pillow a child's possible fall from a step he is interested in, rather than prohibiting him from climbing at all).			

Adapted from Gestwicki (1999, pp. 75–76).

are also closed, because they reduce raw data to a tally indicating the degree to which the characteristic is present. Both the degree of selectivity and the degree of inference required are high because (1) the characteristics to be recorded are identified before the observation begins, and (2) the observer has to decide whether or not a particular characteristic is present and to what extent, before rating that characteristic. See Table 5–2 for an Infant Mobility Environment Rating Scale.

TABLE 5–2 Infant Mobility Environment Rating Scale

Child Care Center's Name _____ Room No. _____

Observer _____ Date _____

INFANT MOBILITY ENVIRONMENT RATING SCALE					
Characteristics of Appropriate Environment for Fostering Infants' Mobility	Always	Usually	Sometimes	Seldom	Never
❑ Infants are confined to cribs only when necessary for their safety or when they do not need extra space to roll over. Otherwise, they are placed in a safe space on the floor where they can play and move about freely. • Infants need a safe environment and, unless contraindicated, they need to move about freely.					
❑ Nonmobile infants are protected from mobile ones. Creative solutions include the use of movable barriers such as cushions, boxes, or gates. • Again, infants need a safe environment.					
❑ Adults regularly lie down on the floor to get the infant's perspective on her environment. Potential hazards and the "need for verbal restrictions" are eliminated before they become an issue. This makes the environment "an inviting place, rather than one where babies continually have to be removed or restricted." • Infants need sufficient but reasonable freedom to move about safely and to explore. They also need an appropriately stimulating environment.					
❑ Adults keep in mind that the size a space needs to be is relative to the size of the infant. Adults help infants feel secure by sectioning larger spaces into smaller spaces that are appropriate to their needs and abilities. • Infants need a trustworthy, nonthreatening environment.					

Adapted from Gestwicki, 1999, p. 72.

At a child care staff meeting, members discuss emergency procedures.

Summary

We have discussed three methods of observing and recording characteristics of child care programs: (1) narrative description, (2) event sampling, and (3) checklists and rating scales. Each is appropriate to use in various observation contexts, as discussed in this chapter. Whereas the narrative description preserves raw data for future and further interpretation, the other methods, that is, the event sample, the checklist, and the rating scale, are more efficient to use since they reduce one's observations to a tally or mark.

〰〰〰 Through Their Eyes

Cathy Bentley, lead teacher in the infant room at Suny Plattsburgh Early Care and Education Center, is responsible for three infants ranging in age from seven to twelve months. While seven-month-old Chen Lee struggles to pull himself up while grasping Cathy's arm, twelve-month-old Caressa has already begun taking her first unsupported steps. Eight-month-old Tim enjoys the freedom of crawling all around the room. Cathy sometimes uses removable barriers to protect Chen Lee from the more mobile Caressa and Tim. Frequently, she finds herself lying on the floor to better accommodate the infants' need for mobility. This close proximity to the children also reinforces a trustworthy, nonthreatening environment. This scenario offers an excellent opportunity to evaluate the effectiveness of the infants' mobility environment by using the rating scale found in Table 6–5 (Chapter 6). How many of the characteristics mentioned in Table 6–5 are illustrated in this scenario? What other caregiving behaviors could Cathy have reported that would further enhance the infants' mobility environment?

For additional information on assessing the effectiveness of child care programs, visit our Web site at **http://www.earlychilded.delmar.com**

Chapter 6

Observation and Recording Exercises for the Infant Child Care Program

See How To

* ascertain whether the infant environment is safe and healthy

* determine whether the child care environment adequately provides for infants' nutrition needs

* assess whether the child care environment adequately meets infants' needs for an appropriate sensory environment

* judge whether the child care environment is child/developmentally appropriate to meet infants' needs for an adequate and optimal social/emotional environment

* determine whether the child care environment is child/developmentally appropriate to meet infants' needs for an adequate and optimal cognitive/language environment

* assess whether the child care environment is child/developmentally appropriate for fostering infants' mobility

* determine whether the child care environment fosters appropriate attachment patterns along with appropriate caregiver behavior

* decide whether the child care setting fosters a trustworthy environment for infants

* ascertain whether the child care setting fosters an environment for respectful caregiving practices for infants

* assess whether the child care setting fosters an environment for sensitive responsiveness to infants

Introduction

The observation and recording exercises presented in the next three chapters parallel the information and concepts covered in Chapters 2, 3, and 4, which focus on infant, toddler, and preschool child care programs, respectively. Following Gestwicki's (1999) protocol, we divide the developmental environment into three domains: the *physical environment,* the *social/emotional environment,* and the *cognitive/language environment.* Within each of these domains we apply appropriate, selected methods of observing and recording characteristics of child care programs and environments as discussed in Chapter 5.

Because preservice college students may be required to record their observations in greater detail than time permits for in-service child care professionals, use of the narrative description might be more appropriate for the preservice audience. However, should child care professionals wish to record their observations in greater detail to be saved for later analysis, the narrative description would be appropriate for them, too. The basic purpose of the narrative description is to record in as much objective detail as possible what is taking place in the early childhood classroom during a specific time period. By capturing the context of the interactions between the children and the staff, this method provides a basis for meaningful interpretation of what is observed and for appropriate planning of the developmental environment. Conversely, in-service child care professionals may require a more expeditious method of determining whether the child care environment adequately meets children's needs. The objectivity of the event sample's coding scheme or the ease of recording responses using a checklist or a rating scale make these instruments, once developed, more time-effective for use by busy professional child care staff.

EXERCISE 6–1: CHARACTERISTICS OF A SAFE INFANT ENVIRONMENT

Background Information

As discussed earlier, infants need an environment that is safe. The safety of the physical environment requires, among other things, unbreakable mirrors and windows (or at least windows that can be securely opened and closed); inaccessible electric cords; electric outlets that are covered; and protection from anything that could burn or harm, such as light bulbs, hot water faucets, hazardous chemicals, unstable furniture, and sharp objects or edges. Infants also need space that does not restrict their movement or natural curiosity.

Observation Objective

The purpose of this exercise is to ascertain whether the infant environment observed is safe.

Procedure

Using the summary of the characteristics of a safe infant environment, shown in Table 6–1, indicate on the checklist provided whether the infant setting observed is generally considered safe.

An event sample may also be used to describe in greater detail the characteristics of a safe infant environment shown in Table 6–1. For example, the observer might describe the condition of mirrors and windows in the infant room and comment on their condition, placement, etc., as regards safety of the infant. A narrative description of the electrical cords and outlets in the infant room might include whether or not they are accessible to the infants in the room; it might also indicate whether the electrical outlets are covered, a reflection of the safety of the infant room. As each characteristic is noted, described, and assessed, the observer can then judge whether the infant room observed provides a safe environment. Preservation of this raw data allows for further study of the infant setting with recommendations for improvement.

 EXERCISE 6–2: ELEMENTS OF ADEQUATE INFANT NUTRITION

Background Information

Adequate infant nutrition is essential for both the physical and the social/emotional development of the young child. Table 6–2 provides an infant nutrition checklist, adapted from an article titled "Appropriate diet for age" found on the Web site at http://WebMD.com. These elements of adequate infant nutrition are based on increments of two to four months of age and include developmental indicators of readiness for solid food as well as recommendations for feeding solid food.

Observation Objective

The purpose of this exercise is to determine whether the child care environment adequately provides for infants' nutrition needs.

Procedure

Using the infant nutrition checklist shown in Table 6–2, indicate whether the nutritional needs of the infant are adequately met. Because the ages of the children in the infant room vary, and because their needs may be met in different ways (e.g., breast vs. bottle fed), use only the portion of the checklist that reflects the age of a given infant. Because the infant may be in the child care setting for only a relatively small portion of the day, information about how her nutritional needs are provided for by the

TABLE 6-1   Safe Infant Environment Checklist

| Child Care Center's Name _____ | Room No. _____ |
| Observer _____ | Date _____ |

SAFE INFANT ENVIRONMENT CHECKLIST			
Characteristics of Safe Infant Environment	**Yes**	**No**	**Sometimes**
❑ Mirrors and windows that will not break and either windows that open only from the top or protection from windows that open at the bottom.			
❑ No electrical cords to trip or chew on; electrical outlets that are covered.			
❑ Protection from anything that could burn or scald (for example, light bulbs, heaters, radiators, hot water faucets).			
❑ Plants that are not poisonous.			
❑ Unreachable hazardous chemicals such as medicines, cleaning substances.			
❑ No broken or damaged toys, toys with easily removable small parts, or toys painted with lead or other toxic materials.			
❑ Furniture that is stable and cannot be pulled over or fall; furniture should meet consumer protection standards to prevent infants from getting their heads stuck.			
❑ Any sharp edges that could injure if fallen on or bumped into are covered or padded.			
❑ Knowledgeable staff concerning emergency procedures, such as CPR and first aid, location of emergency numbers and equipment, and evacuation procedures—such as fire drill.			
❑ Constant supervision of infants who are never left unattended; high-chairs, strollers, and changing tables are fitted with proper restraints.			
❑ Infants are supervised as they eat and drink; are never left with a propped up bottle; are given properly sized finger foods.			
❑ Infants are not overprotected; infants are provided safe ways to practice a challenging skill (for example, cushioning with a pillow a child's possible fall from a step he is interested in, rather than prohibiting him from climbing at all).			

Adapted from Gestwicki (1999, pp. 75–76).

TABLE 6–2   Infant Nutrient Checklist—Birth to One Year of Age

Child Care Center's Name _____   Room No. _____

Observer _____   Date _____

ADEQUATE NUTRITION CHECKLIST			
Elements of Adequate Infant Nutrition	**Yes**	**No**	**Sometimes**
Birth to Four Months of Age			
❏ During the first four to six months of life, breast milk or formula will meet infant's nutritional needs.			
❏ Breast milk is recommended for the first six months, but a fortified formula is satisfactory.			
❏ A breast-fed newborn may nurse 8 to 12 times per day (every two to four hours) or on demand.			
❏ By four months, frequency of breast feeding is likely to reduce to four to six times per day, but quantity per feeding will increase.			
❏ Formula fed infant may need to eat six to eight times per day, beginning with two to five ounces of formula per feeding (16–35 ounces per day).			
❏ With age, frequency of formula feeding decreases and quantity increases to about six to eight ounces per feeding.			
Four to Six Months of Age			
❏ Infant should consume 28 to 45 ounces of formula; transition to solid foods imminent.			
Developmental Indicators of Readiness for Solid Food			
❏ When birth weight has doubled.			
❏ When infant has good control of head and neck.			
❏ When infant can sit up with some support.			
❏ When infant can show she is full by turning her head away or not opening her mouth.			
❏ When infant shows interest in food when others are eating.			
Recommendations for Feeding Solid Food			
❏ Start with iron-fortified baby rice cereal; mix with breast milk or formula to a thin consistency. With greater mouth control, mix to a thicker consistency.			
❏ Give cereal two times per day, starting with one or two tablespoons of dry cereal prior to mixing with milk. Increase gradually to three or four tablespoons of cereal. *CAUTION:* Do not give cereal in a bottle unless recommended by a pediatrician.			
❏ Introduce other iron-fortified instant cereals when infant is routinely eating rice cereal. Introduce only one new cereal per week and watch for any intolerance.			

continued

TABLE 6–2 Infant Nutrient Checklist—Birth to One Year of Age (Continued)

Child Care Center's Name _____	Room No. _____
Observer _____	Date _____

ADEQUATE NUTRITION CHECKLIST			
Elements of Adequate Infant Nutrition	Yes	No	Sometimes
Six to Eight Months			
❑ Offer breast milk or formula three to five times per day. Milk consumption will decrease as solid food becomes a source of nutrition.			
❑ Following a variety of baby cereals, introduce fruit juices, strained fruits and vegetables. "Use infant-packed juices or unsweetened vitamin C rich-juices such as apple, grape, and orange." *CAUTION:* To avoid tooth decay, do not give juices in a bottle at bedtime. Also, do not give orange juice until infant is at least nine months of age if the family has a history of allergy to orange juice.			
❑ Introduce one strained fruit or vegetable at a time; wait two to three days in between to check for allergic reactions.			
❑ Begin with plain vegetables and plain fruits; for example, green peas, potatoes, carrots, sweet potatoes, squash, beans, beets, bananas, applesauce, apricots, pears, peaches, and melons.			
❑ Offer fruits and vegetables in servings of two to three tablespoons; offer about four servings per day.			
Eight to Twelve Months of Age			
❑ Offer breast milk or formula three to four times per day.			
❑ Introduce strained or finely chopped meats. If the infant is breast-fed, start meats at eight months of age in order to get iron into his or her diet.			
❑ Offer only one new meat per week in three to four tablespoon servings.			
❑ Increase servings of fruits and vegetables to three to four tablespoons, four times per day.			
❑ Offer eggs three to four time per week, but only the yolk to avoid possible sensitivity to egg whites.			
❑ Do not give children under the age of one any dairy products, although cheese, cottage cheese, and yogurt may be given in small amounts.			
One Year of Age			
❑ After one year of age, vitamin D or four percent whole milk may replace formula or breast milk. Do not give children younger than two years of age low-fat milk (two percent or skim).			
❑ The one-year-old child should be getting much of his or her nutrition from "meats, fruits and vegetables, breads and grains, and the dairy group."			
❑ Provide a variety of foods to ensure adequate intake of vitamins and minerals.			

Adapted from a WebMD.com article titled "Appropriate diet for age."

parent should also be considered in judging the adequacy of the child care setting in meeting infants' nutritional needs.

A narrative description of how the infant's nutritional needs are met could be used to gain more specific insights as to how the child care setting addresses the individual needs of the infants therein. For example, keeping a detailed record of the infant's daily food intake at the child care center and supplementing that information with the daily intake provided by the parent will provide a more complete nutritional picture. This information should be useful in assessing how adequately the infant's nutritional needs are met in the child care environment.

 ## EXERCISE 6–3: CHARACTERISTICS OF A HEALTHY INFANT ENVIRONMENT

Background Information

A healthy infant environment is a basic requirement of infant caregiving. Besides meeting licensing requirements, the child care center requires that parents and caregivers attend to many safety and health-related details. Among these is the importance of personal hygiene, including strict standards for cleanliness in feeding, changing, and bathing infants. Also included is the cleanliness of toys, cribs, and any surfaces the infant contacts. Finally, there should be specific procedures to follow when a child becomes ill.

Observation Objective

The purpose of this exercise is to determine whether the infant environment is healthy.

Procedure

Using the summary of the characteristics of a healthy infant environment shown in Table 6–3, indicate on the rating scale provided whether the infant setting observed is generally considered healthy.

Event sampling may be used to describe in greater detail the characteristics of a healthy infant environment as shown in Table 6–3. For example, the observer may discuss the standards of adult hand-washing after coughing, sneezing, wiping a child's nose, and changing diapers, and before handling food or bottles. A narrative description of the cleanliness of individual cribs and toys can provide important details concerning whether the infant environment is healthy. An in-depth description of any or all of the listed characteristics can allow for an analysis of whether the setting meets the criteria for a healthy infant environment.

Using the narrative description, the observer can describe the infant environment in great detail, citing specific ways the setting does or does not meet the criteria for good health. These data can be preserved for further analysis with recommendations for how to address any deficiencies in the environment.

 ## EXERCISE 6–4: CHARACTERISTICS OF AN APPROPRIATE INFANT SENSORY ENVIRONMENT

Background Information

Infants need an environment in which they can explore independently. They need an environment with appropriate materials to examine their surroundings and to use all their senses. They need space that is not unnecessarily restrictive, but still remains safe.

Observation Objective

The purpose of this exercise is to assess whether the child care environment adequately meets infants' needs for an appropriate sensory environment.

TABLE 6–3   Healthy Infant Environment Rating Scale

Child Care Center's Name _____	Room No. _____
Observer _____	Date _____

HEALTHY INFANT ENVIRONMENT RATING SCALE					
Characteristics of Healthy Infant Environment	Always	Usually	Sometimes	Seldom	Never
❑ Staff religiously adhere to standards of "adult hand-washing after coughing, sneezing, wiping a child's nose, changing diapers, and before handling food or bottles; after washing, adults use paper towels to touch faucets or waste containers" (p. 76).					
❑ There is strict adherence to licensing standards for cleanliness of the diaper changing area; staff provide a clean and covered surface for each diaper change.					
❑ Food and bottles are refrigerated until they are used.					
❑ Infants' hands are washed frequently, with individual washcloths.					
❑ Toys and surfaces are washed every day, or more frequently when children are sharing and mouthing toys.					
❑ Parents and staff remove street shoes before they walk on floors where infants lie.					
❑ Individual cribs are kept clean.					
❑ Accurate records are kept of up-to-date immunizations.					
❑ Infants who shows signs of illness are excluded in keeping with the "standards and symptoms defined by the program" (p. 50).					
❑ Only prescribed medicines are administered to infants with permission and instructions from the parents.					

Adapted from Gestwicki (1999, p. 76).

Procedure

Using the summary of the characteristics of an appropriate infant sensory environment shown in Table 6–4, place a check on the rating scale provided to indicate the extent to which these characteristics are observable in the infant setting.

You may also use an event sample to allow for a more detailed description of specific characteristics of the infant's sensory environment. A discussion of materials used in the room for exploration may elicit specific suggestions as to how the environment or the materials themselves could be modified to better meet the needs of the children. For example, if certain homemade toys seem to have greater appeal to the infants, perhaps the infant room can be made more sensorily enticing by adding other homemade toys.

TABLE 6–4   Infants' Sensory Environment Rating Scale

Child Care Center's Name			Room No.		
Observer			Date		

INFANTS' SENSORY ENVIRONMENT RATING SCALE					
Characteristics of an Appropriate Infant Sensory Environment	Always	Usually	Sometimes	Seldom	Never
❑ Provide infants with materials they can explore independently, ". . . using the areas and furniture twenty-four inches above the floor."					
❑ Prepare an environment that uses all the infant's senses.					
❑ Use commercial toys as well as homemade ones that appeal to infants' senses. Continually check all toys for safety.					
❑ Remove things that infants cannot directly understand in order to avoid sensory overload.					
❑ Do not use cribs as an environment for sensory stimulation.					

Adapted from Gestwicki (1999, p. 74).

EXERCISE 6–5: CHARACTERISTICS OF AN APPROPRIATE ENVIRONMENT FOR FOSTERING INFANTS' MOBILITY

Background Information

Except when they are sleeping, infants should not be confined to their cribs. They should be placed in a clean, safe space (usually on the floor) where they can play, explore, and move about freely. Nonmobile infants should be protected from mobile ones using creative barriers such as cushions to separate them. Adults should remove potential hazards from the environment to eliminate the need for verbal restrictions, thereby making the infant room an inviting place where babies can feel safe and secure.

Observation Objective

The purpose of this exercise is to assess whether the child care environment is child/developmentally appropriate for fostering infants' mobility.

Procedure

Using the summary of the characteristics of an environment appropriate for fostering infants' mobility, shown in Table 6–5, indicate on the rating scale provided whether the infant setting observed is generally appropriate in this regard.

By using the narrative description, the observer may note in much greater detail the specific ways the infant setting is or is not an appropriate environment for fostering infants' mobility. For example, you might describe the placement (e.g., in her crib or on the floor) of the infant at various times during the observation and make a comment as to the appropriateness of this placement relative to the infant's activity at the time, such as nap time or play time. Such in-depth descriptions allow the observer to save these raw data for later analysis and interpretation.

TABLE 6–5 Infant Mobility Environment Rating Scale

Child Care Center's Name _____			Room No. _____		
Observer _____			Date _____		

INFANT MOBILITY ENVIRONMENT RATING SCALE					
Characteristics of Appropriate Environment for Fostering Infants' Mobility	Always	Usually	Sometimes	Seldom	Never
❏ Infants are confined to cribs only when necessary for their safety or when they do not need extra space to roll over. Otherwise, they are placed in a safe space on the floor where they can play and move about freely. • Infants need a safe environment and, unless contraindicated, they need to move about freely.					
❏ Nonmobile infants are protected from mobile ones. Creative solutions include the use of movable barriers such as cushions, boxes, or gates. • Again, infants need a safe environment.					
❏ Adults regularly lie down on the floor to get the infant's perspective on her environment. Potential hazards and the "need for verbal restrictions" are eliminated before they become an issue. This makes the environment "an inviting place, rather than one where babies continually have to be removed or restricted" (p. 72). • Infants need sufficient but reasonable freedom to move about safely and to explore. They also need an appropriately stimulating environment.					
❏ Adults keep in mind that the size a space needs to be is relative to the size of the infant. Adults help infants feel secure by sectioning larger spaces into smaller spaces that are appropriate to their needs and abilities. • Infants need a trustworthy, nonthreatening environment.					

Adapted from Gestwicki, 1999, p. 72.

 EXERCISE 6–6: ATTACHMENT PATTERNS OF THE INFANT

Background Information

As noted in Chapter 2, Muzi (2000) describes three basic attachment patterns: *securely attached, avoidantly attached,* and *ambivalently attached.* A fourth pattern of insecure attachment is subsequently described (Muzi, 2000, p. 206) as *disorganized-disoriented attachment.* These patterns can indicate possible characteristics of the parent-child relationship that led to a particular pattern. Likewise, they can also be used to identify the types of adult-child interactions that are most likely, and least likely, to contribute to a positive, child appropriate social/emotional developmental environment.

Observation Objective

The purpose of this exercise is to determine whether the child care environment fosters appropriate attachment patterns along with appropriate caregiver behavior.

Procedure

Using the attachment patterns rating scale provided in Table 6–6, rate the typical child's behavior followed by the contributing caregiver behavior. Securely attached children are more likely to engage in the type of adult-child interactions that would contribute to a positive, child appropriate social/emotional environment than are avoidantly or ambivalently attached children. Likewise, the contributing caregiver behavior toward a securely attached child is characterized by reliable, consistent responsiveness.

Either an event sample or the narrative description could be used to describe the child's behavior in much greater detail, using the examples of attachment patterns given in Table 6–6.

TABLE 6–6   Attachment Patterns Rating Scale

Child Care Center's Name _____ Room No. _____ Observer _____ Date _____					
ATTACHMENT PATTERNS RATING SCALE					
Child's Typical Behavior Followed by Contributing Caregiver Behavior	Always	Usually	Sometimes	Seldom	Never
Securely Attached					
Child's Typical Behavior					
❑ Uses mother/caregiver as a secure base for exploration. He comes back to caregiver if he needs reassurance.					
❑ Becomes upset when caregiver leaves the room, and play decreases. Greets caregiver with pleasure when she returns; is easily comforted and stays close to caregiver for a period of time, then resumes play. Definitely prefers the company of the caregiver to that of a stranger.					
❑ Child is "usually cooperative and free of anger" (Papalia, et al., p. 246).					
Contributing Caregiver Behavior					
❑ Caregiver is very responsive to child's signals and needs. She feeds child when he is hungry and comforts him when he is distressed.					
❑ Care is reliable and consistent. Mothers of securely attached infants "responded promptly, consistently, and appropriately to infant signals and held their babies tenderly and carefully" (Berk, p. 426).					

continued

TABLE 6–6   Attachment Patterns Rating Scale (Continued)

Child Care Center's Name _____	Room No. _____
Observer _____	Date _____

ATTACHMENT PATTERNS RATING SCALE					
Child's Typical Behavior Followed by Contributing Caregiver Behavior	Always	Usually	Sometimes	Seldom	Never
Avoidantly Attached					
Child's Typical Behavior					
❏ Child ignores or is unresponsive to the caregiver while playing with toys.					
❏ Child may or may not appear distressed when caregiver leaves the room (Papalia, et al., report that babies who are avoidantly attached rarely cry when the mother/caregiver leaves); in either case, the child does not seek contact when the caregiver returns.					
❏ Child turns away or averts his eyes when caregiver tries to pick him up. If picked up, child often fails to cling to the caregiver (Berk, p. 424).					
❏ Child tends to be angry, does *not try to* reach out when in need (Papalia, et al., page 246).					
❏ Child does not like to be held, but dislikes being put down even more (Papalia, et al., page 246).					
Contributing Caregiver Behavior					
❏ Caregiver is insensitive to and rejects the child's needs.					
Ambivalently Attached					
Child's Typical Behavior					
❏ Child rarely explores his environment.					
❏ Child shows distress when caregiver leaves the room, but is ambivalent or uncertain when caregiver returns.					
❏ Upon caregiver's return, child reaches out and clings to her, then quickly and angrily pushes caregiver away, "sometimes kicking and swiping at them" (Muzi, p. 207).					
❏ Child shows two essentially contradictory behaviors: Because of her uncertainty, the child wants her mother around continually; at the same time, the child angrily rejects her mother because of her unreliability and inconsistency.					
Contributing Caregiver Behavior					
❏ Caregiver is insensitive to and rejects the child's needs.					

continued

TABLE 6-6 Attachment Patterns Rating Scale (Continued)

| Child Care Center's Name _____ | | | Room No. _____ |
| Observer _____ | | | Date _____ |

ATTACHMENT PATTERNS RATING SCALE

Child's Typical Behavior Followed by Contributing Caregiver Behavior	Always	Usually	Sometimes	Seldom	Never
Disorganized-Disoriented Attachment					
Child's Typical Behavior					
❏ Main found that in a laboratory situation (the Strange Situation experiment), disorganized-disoriented infants "appeared dazed or disoriented and sometimes depressed" (In Muzi, p. 207).					
❏ These children cannot seem to find ways to get close to their mothers. "Sometimes they approach her backward and even stand still and stare into space when she is coming close" (Muzi, p. 207).					
❏ Papalia, Olds, and Feldman (1999) report that disorganized-disoriented infants ". . . often show inconsistent, contradictory behaviors. They greet the mother brightly when she returns but then turn away or approach without looking at her. They seem confused and afraid. This may be the least secure pattern" (p. 246).					
Contributing Caregiver Behavior					
❏ According to Muzi, disorganized-disoriented children often have been abused.					
❏ Papalia, Olds, and Feldman, on the other hand, note that it is often the parents who have ". . . suffered unresolved trauma, such as loss or abuse" (p. 247).					

Adapted from Muzi, 2000, pp. 206–207, and Papalia, Olds, and Feldman, 1999, pp. 246–247.

 EXERCISE 6–7: CHARACTERISTICS OF AN ENVIRONMENT FOR ATTACHMENT

Background Information
An appropriate environment for attachment contains comfortable seating and floor spaces where adult caregivers can relax and enjoy interaction with infants. There should be a designated private area for parents to attend to their babies. Arrangement of work areas in the infant room should be such that adult caregivers can supervise the space and still care for a single baby at the same time. Feeding and diapering areas should not contain any distractions that would keep the infant from focusing on the adult.

Observation Objective
The purpose of this exercise is to ascertain whether the child care setting fosters an environment for attachment.

Procedure

Using the summary of the characteristics of an environment that fosters attachment between the infant and the adult shown in Table 6–7, indicate on the rating scale provided whether the child care setting is generally appropriate.

A narrative description allows the observer to discuss in detail those characteristics of the infant setting that are most conducive to the development of secure attachments in infants. For example, are there comfortable spaces where the adult caregiver can enjoy one-to-one interaction with the infant in a relaxed setting? Is there an appropriate designated area where parents can interact privately with their babies? Is the infant setting arranged conveniently so that, while attending to an infant, the caregiver can simultaneously supervise the room? Preserving this information allows for subsequent examination of the infant setting while making recommendations for improvement.

 ### EXERCISE 6–8: CHARACTERISTICS OF A TRUSTWORTHY ENVIRONMENT FOR INFANTS

Background Information

Attachment and trust are closely connected as they relate to the infant environment. Both are essential components of the adult-child relationship. For infants to learn to trust they need reliable, consistent adults who will attend to their needs in a timely fashion. An environment that nurtures trust is characterized by the adult's consistent responsiveness to the infant's needs.

Observation Objective

The purpose of this exercise is to decide whether the child care setting fosters a trustworthy environment for infants.

TABLE 6–7 Characteristics of an Environment for Attachment Rating Scale

Child Care Center's Name _____	Room No. _____
Observer _____	Date _____

ENVIRONMENT FOR ATTACHMENT RATING SCALE					
Characteristics of an Environment for Attachment	Always	Usually	Sometimes	Seldom	Never
❑ Facility contains comfortable chairs and floor spaces where adults can "relax and enjoy one-to-one interaction with babies" (p. 71).					
❑ There is a designated place for parents to interact privately with their infants.					
❑ Location of work areas is such that staff can supervise the room and still care for an individual infant and have access to all necessary materials.					
❑ Caregiving areas where feeding and diapering take place contain nothing that would distract infants from focusing on the adult.					

Adapted from Gestwicki, 1999, p. 71.

Procedure

Using the summary of the characteristics of a trustworthy environment for infants, shown in Table 6–8, indicate on the rating scale provided whether the infant environment observed is generally appropriate in this regard.

The event sample may be used here to describe in detail how the infant's needs are consistently responded to, and by the same adults; how daily schedules for feeding, sleeping, and playing are individually appropriate to each infant's needs; how the program adheres to a small adult-child ratio, in accordance with developmentally appropriate practice; and so forth. The detailed descriptions gleaned from such an event sample may be preserved for later analysis.

≋ Through Their Eyes

Cathy Bentley has been the lead teacher in the infant room at Suny Plattsburgh Early Care and Education Center for the past seven years. She typically has three infants in her care, which ensures her availability to respond to their needs immediately. Seven-month-old Chen Lee has been one of "Cathy's babies" since he was six weeks old and he has formed a secure attachment with Cathy. The other infants, eight-month-old Tim and twelve-month-old Caressa, have each been in Cathy's care since they were two months old. They, too, have formed close relationships with Cathy, who sees a trustworthy environment as a safe, familiar place for infants. Cathy reports that she establishes trust between herself and her infants by consistently responding to their needs in a timely fashion. She also notes that she keeps the general environment—the equipment and materials and their locations and arrangement—as constant as possible so that the infants find the environment entirely predictable. She also slowly introduces the infants to new equipment and materials and gives them ample time to familiarize themselves with the new items and their locations.

 ## EXERCISE 6–9: RESPECTFUL CAREGIVING PRACTICES

Background Information

Respect is a critical element of trust. As discussed in Chapter 2, respect includes explaining even to very young infants what you are about to do and what the child can expect of the adult (Gonzales-Mena and Eyer, 2001). They contend that caregivers must respect the needs of infants as important.

Observation Objective

The purpose of this exercise is to ascertain whether the child care setting fosters an environment for respectful caregiving practices for infants.

Procedure

Using the summary of the characteristics of caregiving practices that indicate respect for infants, shown in Table 6–9, indicate on the rating scale provided whether the infant setting being observed is generally appropriate in this regard.

TABLE 6–8   Characteristics of a Trustworthy Environment Rating Scale

| Child Care Center's Name _____ | | | Room No. _____ | | |
| Observer _____ | | | Date _____ | | |

TRUSTWORTHY ENVIRONMENT RATING SCALE

Characteristics of a Trustworthy Environment for Infants	Always	Usually	Sometimes	Seldom	Never
❑ Infants' needs are consistently responded to, and by the same adults.					
❑ Daily schedules for feeding, sleeping, and playing are individually appropriate to each infant's "needs, temperament, and natural rhythms" (p. 68).					
❑ One primary caregiver is assigned to the same group of infants in order to facilitate the caregiver's close relationship with the infant and his or her family. ("The purpose of primary caregiving systems is to give each infant and family an opportunity to develop a special relationship of mutual trust and respect" [p. 69]).					
❑ The program adheres to a small adult-child ratio—DAP recommends one adult caring for three infants (see, for example, Bredekamp and Copple, 1997, p. 80).					
❑ In order to ensure that responsiveness is consistent and that infants' needs are met, there is regular communication among all staff members and parents.					
❑ Staff see a trustworthy environment as a safe, familiar place for infants. The patterns of things in the environment are predictable—there is ". . . a place for everything, easily restorable from the clutter of infants' active exploration. Clearly marked storage bins, trays, baskets, and boxes help return things to the same places for babies to find again. Rituals of repeated experiences form the predictable sequence that even babies can comprehend . . ." (p. 69).					
❑ In order to protect infants from constant verbal restrictions that might threaten their emotional security, restrictions and prohibitions, such as gates or the removal of forbidden or dangerous objects, are built into the physical environment.					
❑ Berk (2000) reports that interactional synchrony, which is a "special form of communication," supports babies' feelings of trust. International synchrony is described as "a sensitively tuned 'emotional dance,' in which caregiver-infant interaction appears to be mutually rewarding. The caregiver responds to infants' signals in a well-timed, appropriate fashion. In addition, both partners match emotional states, especially the positive ones" (p. 426).					

Adapted from Gestwicki, (2001, pp. 68–69; also see Berk, 2000, p. 426).

TABLE 6–9   Respectful Caregiving Practices Rating Scale

Child Care Center's Name _____   Room No. _____

Observer _____   Date _____

RESPECTFUL CAREGIVING PRACTICES RATING SCALE

Characteristics of Caregiving Practices that Indicate Respect for Infants	Always	Usually	Sometimes	Seldom	Never
❏ Infants are allowed to establish their own schedules for sleeping, feeding, and playing. Adults do not assume that they know best and that infants should conform to adults' timetables. Caregiver also respects the needs and decisions of individual families.					
❏ Caregiver always assumes that infants' needs are real, and he or she responds promptly to infants' cries. Caregiver makes it clear to the infant that his message has been received.					
❏ Infants are allowed to take the lead when communicating their needs and desires; caregiver tries to interpret their communication. Caregiver also assumes that nonverbal infants will have their own means of communicating. (Gonzales-Mena and Ever [2001, p. 14] include this advice in their third principle of caregiving: "Learn Each Child's Unique Ways of Communicating and Teach Them Yours.")					
❏ Caregiver allows infants time to "solve a problem, soothe themselves, or find something interesting to do" (p. 138) before intervening.					
❏ Caregiver assumes and allows infants' active participation in routine caregiving activities. Caregiver gives infants cues and observes their readiness to participate.					
❏ Infants' preferences for, and aversions to, particular people are respected, especially when they are able to exhibit stranger anxiety.					
❏ Caregiver takes infants' emotions seriously; he or she helps infants find ways of coping with, and acknowledging, their feelings.					
❏ Caregiver respects cultural differences regarding what is appropriate care for infants. Such differences are explored with the families and compromises are reached to accommodate the families' views and the standard practices of the child care facility.					

Adapted from Gestwicki, 1999, pp. 138–139.

A narrative description detailing how the specified caregiving practices indicate respect for infants could address the following: how infants are allowed to establish their own schedules for sleeping, feeding, and playing; how the caregiver responds promptly to infants' cries; how the caregiver allows the infant to amuse himself before intervening; and how the caregiver respects cultural differences regarding what is appropriate care for infants.

 EXERCISE 6–10: SENSITIVE RESPONSIVENESS

Background Information
Sensitivity and responsiveness are essential to the positive development of an appropriate social/emotional environment for infants. Key concerns focus on infants'

TABLE 6–10   Sensitive Responsiveness Rating Scale

| Child Care Center's Name _____ | Room No. _____ |
| Observer _____ | Date _____ |

SENSITIVE RESPONSIVENESS RATING SCALE					
Characteristics of Sensitive Responsiveness to Infants	Always	Usually	Sometimes	Seldom	Never
❑ Caregiver lets infants determine for themselves what kinds and degrees of physical stimulation they can tolerate and enjoy. Caregiver is sensitive to what the infant actually likes and dislikes and does not impose his or her own preconceptions of what the child should like or dislike.					
❑ Caregiver uses what others have learned about infants' styles and experiences. Caregiver communicates with parents and others to enhance his or her own understanding of infants' individual personalities.					
❑ Caregiver recognizes that sensitive responsiveness necessarily involves ". . . reciprocal interaction. Caregivers have to practice turn-taking behavior, taking time in play and caregiving interaction to pause and allow the baby to participate and respond." Such "pauses" permit the caregiver to observe how the infant is reacting and to modify her behavior accordingly.					

Adapted from Gestwicki (1999, p. 140).

temperaments, moods and feelings, communication styles, and other affective qualities that distinguish one child from another. It is important to remember that a caregiver must be sensitive to the infant's needs and respond accordingly.

Observation Objective

The purpose of this exercise is to assess whether the child care setting fosters an environment for sensitive responsiveness to infants.

Procedure

Using the summary of the characteristics of sensitive responsiveness, shown in Table 6–10, indicate on the rating scale whether the infant setting observed is generally characterized as sensitively responsive.

A narrative description of the infant environment might include caregiver behaviors that permit the infant to determine for himself what kinds of physical stimulation he might enjoy. It might also address how the caregiver communicates with parents to enhance his or her understanding of infants' individual personalities.

Chapter 7

Observation and Recording Exercises for the Toddler Child Care Program

See How To

* determine the degree to which the toddlers' needs are met in the child care environment

* ascertain whether the child care environment adequately provides for the development of toddlers' autonomy

* assess whether the child care environment is child appropriate for fostering toddlers' sense of separateness

* judge whether the child care environment is child appropriate for fostering toddlers' physical movement in the child care setting

* determine whether the child care setting is child appropriate for fostering an environment for learning toddler self-help skills

* ascertain whether the child care setting fosters an appropriate environment for toddlers' sensorimotor exploration

* decide whether the child care setting provides an appropriate environment for fostering the development of toddlers' autonomy

* determine whether the child care setting provides an appropriate environment for promoting toddlers' cognitive/language skills

Introduction

The observation and recording exercises presented in this chapter are derived from the information discussed in Chapter 3, focusing on the physical/motor, social/emotional, and cognitive/language development of the toddler. Within these three domains we apply appropriate methods of observing and recording characteristics of toddler programs and environments.

EXERCISE 7–1: TODDLERS' NEEDS

Background Information

With toddlerhood comprising the period of one to three years, the toddler's needs extend well beyond those of the infant. From basic health, safety, and nutrition needs to an increasing need for opportunities to acquire motor, language, and cognitive skills, the toddler years represent a period of ever-increasing growth and development of the young child. As the toddler grows, his need to develop independence, autonomy, and self-control come into sharp focus. Pam's sense of individuality is increasing as is her awareness that she is a member of a group of toddlers in the child care setting. Bob's need for an organized environment to help him develop self-help skills as well as a challenging environment that promotes further growth and development is expanding.

Observation Objective

The purpose of this exercise is to determine the degree to which the toddlers' needs are met in the child care environment.

Procedure

Using the summary of toddlers' needs Table 7–1, indicate on the rating scale the degree to which toddlers' needs are met in the child care setting observed. A narrative description might provide additional details about the opportunities observed for the toddler to acquire motor, language, and other cognitive skills. In-depth coverage of the occasions for exploration and play with other children may offer a rich analysis of the

TABLE 7–1   Toddlers' Needs Rating Scale

Child Care Center's Name _____   Room No. _____

Observer _____   Date _____

TODDLERS' NEEDS RATING SCALE				
	Degree to Which Toddlers' Needs Are Met			
Toddlers' Needs	Very High	Medium	Somewhat Low	Very Low
❑ All the things an infant needs (protection from physical danger, adequate nutrition and health care, etc.)				
❑ Opportunities to acquire motor, language, and cognitive skills				
❑ Opportunities to develop independence				
❑ Opportunities to learn self-control				
❑ Opportunities for exploration and play				
❑ Opportunities to play with other children				
Note: The following needs are adapted from Gestwicki (1999, pp. 83–84).				
❑ Acceptance for who he or she is				
❑ ". . . adults who can enjoy the exuberance and striving of the toddler to move to a sense of self"				
❑ Help with achieving separation or detachment from the persons to whom she is attached				
❑ Help to achieve a sense of individuality, "while maintaining safety and rights" of the toddler as a member of a group				
❑ Protection from his or her "immaturity and impulsiveness," but with assurance that she will be allowed to explore and learn while still in Piaget's sensorimotor stage				
❑ Safety, but without unnecessary restrictions that frustrate him				
❑ Flexibility that accounts for and meets her changing needs				
❑ Flexibility of space and equipment that will allow the accomplishment of several purposes—". . . play as well as routine caregiving, practicing skills of new walkers, and relentless climbers"				
❑ Variety to "provide for different toddlers doing different things and individual exploring, as well as for expanding the world beyond the confines of the four walls of the toddler room"				
❑ An environment that can be easily restored to order to provide him with the "security of familiar objects being in familiar places"				
❑ An organized environment to help her acquire self-help skills and avoid frustrating delays				
❑ A challenging environment that prevents boredom and promotes further growth and development				

quality of the social environment in the toddler room. An event description allows for a detailed narrative description of the toddler room setting. Are there opportunities for exploring an organized environment to help the toddler acquire self-help skills? Is the room environment a challenging one that prevents boredom and promotes further growth and development? Is there sufficient variety of methods and materials to permit different toddlers to do different things?

 ## EXERCISE 7–2: ENVIRONMENT FOR TODDLER AUTONOMY

Background Information

All toddlers' needs or developmental tasks are important. The need for autonomy or independence is related to the accomplishment of other developmental tasks, such as sensorimotor exploration and self-help skill mastery, which would be hard to achieve in the absence of some degree of autonomy.

Observation Objective

The purpose of this exercise is to ascertain whether the child care environment adequately provides for the development of toddlers' autonomy.

Procedure

Using the summary of the characteristics of an appropriate environment for developing toddler autonomy in Table 7–2, indicate on the rating scale provided whether the toddler setting being observed is generally considered appropriate for toddler autonomy.

An event sample may also be used to describe in greater detail the characteristics of an environment appropriate for the development of toddler autonomy. For exam-

TABLE 7–2   Environment for Toddler Autonomy Rating Scale

Child Care Center's Name _____		Room No. _____			
Observer _____		Date _____			

ENVIRONMENT FOR TODDLER AUTONOMY RATING SCALE					
Characteristics of Appropriate Environment for Toddler Autonomy	Always	Usually	Sometimes	Seldom	Never
❑ Appropriately sized furniture and "access to areas that encourage self-help skills"					
❑ Materials arranged in ways familiar and accessible to toddlers so they can get them on their own					
❑ Provisions for toddlers to carry out responsibilities, such as picking up their blocks, putting games back on shelves, and other ways to restore order					
❑ Opportunities to make age and individually appropriate choices					
❑ Places where the toddler can be alone					
❑ Environments that are physically and emotionally safe so as not to unduly restrict exploration					

Adapted from Gestwicki (1999, p. 85).

ple, the observer may note whether the furniture is appropriately sized and provides access to areas that encourage self-help skills. A discussion of whether the materials are arranged in ways that are familiar and accessible to the children so they can get them on their own would also be helpful in assessing the environment for toddler autonomy. Are there opportunities for the children to make age and individually appropriate choices? Places where the toddler can be alone? Is the toddler room physically and emotionally safe so as not to unduly restrict exploration?

 EXERCISE 7–3: ENVIRONMENT TO FOSTER TODDLER SEPARATENESS

Background Information

Separateness refers to the toddler's need and desire to be by himself, not only physically, but also in terms of acquiring an identity or self-concept. In this way the toddler can eventually think of himself as psychologically, emotionally, and intellectually distinct from others. Toddlers should be permitted to select their own toys and activities to suit their moods and activity levels.

Observation Objective

The purpose of this exercise is to assess whether the child care environment is child/developmentally appropriate for fostering toddlers' sense of separateness.

Procedure

Using the summary of the characteristics of an appropriate environment to foster toddler autonomy, shown in Table 7–3, indicate on the rating scale provided whether the toddler setting observed is generally considered appropriate in this regard.

TABLE 7–3 Environment to Foster Toddler Separateness Rating Scale

Child Care Center's Name _____ Room No. _____

Observer _____ Date _____

ENVIRONMENT TO FOSTER TODDLER SEPARATENESS RATING SCALE					
Characteristics of Appropriate Environment to Foster Toddler Separateness	Always	Usually	Sometimes	Seldom	Never
❑ Spaces for play and exploration that are clearly separated and allow each toddler his or her own area away from the other children					
❑ A number of different materials that allow each toddler to make his or her own choice					
❑ Brief opportunities for group interaction, such as "for music, a story, or eating" (p. 86)					
❑ A number of similar toys to permit parallel play while still separate from other children					
❑ "Pictures of family, home, and self to encourage toddlers to feel comfortable with separation and feelings of self" (p. 86)					

Adapted from Gestwicki (1999, p. 85–86).

A narrative description could also be used to explain in more detail how well and to what degree the toddler room is and is not appropriate for fostering toddler separateness. Are spaces for play and exploration clearly separated, allowing each toddler his or her own area away from the other children? Is there a variety of different materials that allow each toddler to make his or her own choice? Are there similar toys to permit parallel play while still separate from the other children? Are there pictures of family, home, and self to encourage toddlers to feel comfortable with separation and feelings of self?

 ### EXERCISE 7–4: ENVIRONMENT TO FOSTER TODDLER MOVEMENT

Background Information

Toddlers' movements—primarily walking and running—proceed practically nonstop, not just for the purpose of getting from one place to another, but also as a means for carrying things from one place to another. Because of their short attention span, toddlers do not linger in any one place for long, and often they explore their space and manipulate objects on the run.

Observation Objective

The purpose of this exercise is to judge whether the child care environment is child appropriate for fostering toddlers' physical movement in the child care setting.

Procedure

Using the summary of the characteristics of an appropriate environment to foster toddler movement, given in Table 7–4, indicate on the rating scale provided whether the toddler setting observed is generally appropriate to foster toddler movement.

TABLE 7–4 Environment to Foster Toddler Movement Rating Scale

Child Care Center's Name _____		Room No. _____		
Observer _____		Date _____		

ENVIRONMENT TO FOSTER TODDLER MOVEMENT RATING SCALE				
Characteristics of Appropriate Environment to Foster Toddler Movement	Always	Usually	Sometimes	Seldom	Never
❏ Classroom furnishings and their spatial arrangements provide clear paths for toddlers' movements and accommodate to their very active exploration style					
❏ Gross motor activities are encouraged by providing proper space and equipment in the classroom					
❏ Toddlers are provided places and accompanying cues that suggest a quiet place where they can be alone					
❏ Toddlers are provided safe outdoor areas and equipment that are commensurate with their skills					
❏ Adults help toddlers acquire physical skills that allow self-management and lessen adults' tendency to overprotect					

Adapted from Gestwicki (1999, pp. 87–88).

A narrative description would be useful also to ascertain whether the room furnishings and their arrangements provide unobstructed paths to accommodate toddlers' very active exploration style; whether toddlers are provided quiet places where they can be alone; whether they are provided safe outdoor areas and equipment appropriate to their skills; and whether the adults help toddlers acquire physical skills that allow self-management, thereby lessening adults' tendency to overprotect.

 ## EXERCISE 7–5: ENVIRONMENT FOR LEARNING TODDLER SELF-HELP SKILLS

Background Information

Self-help skills are an integral aspect of the toddler's development of autonomy. Toddlers cannot be truly autonomous if they cannot accomplish such routine activities as eating, dressing, toileting, and self-hygiene. Because of their messiness in performing these self-help skills, toddlers require time, practice, and the caregiver's patience to do these things efficiently.

Observation Objective

The purpose of this exercise is to determine whether the child care environment is child appropriate for fostering an environment for learning toddler self-help skills.

Procedure

Using the summary of the characteristics of an appropriate environment for learning self-help skills, given in Table 7–5, indicate on the rating scale provided whether the toddler setting observed is appropriate for learning self-help skills.

An event sample may be used to describe in greater detail specific characteristics of the toddler environment that promote the learning of self-help skills. Are child-sized eating utensils provided? Can toddlers easily access toilets and sinks using step-stools

TABLE 7–5   Environment for Learning Toddler Self-Help Skills Rating Scale

| Child Care Center's Name _____ Room No. _____ | | | | | |
| Observer _____ Date _____ | | | | | |

ENVIRONMENT FOR LEARNING TODDLER SELF-HELP SKILLS RATING SCALE					
Characteristics of Appropriate Environment for Learning Self-Help Skills	Always	Usually	Sometimes	Seldom	Never
❑ Toddlers are given durable, child-sized eating utensils and an eating area that is easy to clean					
❑ Toddlers are provided stools or other physical structures that help them reach toilets, sinks, and mirrors					
❑ Toddlers are given as much time as they need or want to participate in self-help activities					
❑ Adults approach toddlers' learning of self-help skills with a positive, accepting attitude					

Adapted from Gestwicki (1999, p. 89).

or other appropriate structures? Are toddlers given as much time as they need or want to participate in self-help activities? Do adult caregivers approach toddlers' learning of self-help skills with a positive, accepting attitude?

≋ Through Their Eyes

Kristina Jackson, lead teacher in the wobbler room at Suny Plattsburgh Early Care and Education Center, has learned that if teachers allow the wobblers to do what they can manage to do for themselves, the children develop a positive sense of self-esteem. After 15-month-old Toni is diapered, she gets her own soap, and washes and dries her own hands. Having a child-sized toilet, sink, and mirror allows her to help herself, and in so doing, she takes pride in her growing sense of independence. Kristina sees the importance of having a positive, accepting attitude in approaching toddlers' learning. Kristina also allows the children to try to solve problems and accomplish tasks for as long as possible on their own before offering help. She says that she tries to distinguish between situations when a child really needs assistance, and when, given just a little more time, the child can accomplish the task on his or her own.

EXERCISE 7–6: ENVIRONMENT FOR TODDLER SENSORIMOTOR EXPLORATION

Background Information

Appropriate sensorimotor exploration requires mobility and autonomy. The toddler requires not only adequate space in which to move about, but also a variety of objects and toys to touch, grab, manipulate, and explore. Ideally, these objects should be open-ended to maximize their use and value to the toddler; that is, the objects should have many other uses beyond the obvious ones. A cardboard box, to the toddler, becomes a home, a car, or a toy container.

Observation Objective

The purpose of this exercise is to ascertain whether the child care setting fosters an appropriate environment for toddlers' sensorimotor exploration.

Procedure

Using the summary of the characteristics of an environment appropriate for sensorimotor exploration, given in Table 7–6, indicate on the rating scale provided whether the toddler setting being observed is appropriate for sensorimotor exploration.

A narrative description can also be used to provide details about the objects and materials in the toddler room that foster sensorimotor exploration. Are these materials and objects changed as needed to prevent boredom? Is symbolic play encouraged

TABLE 7–6   Environment for Toddler Sensorimotor Exploration Rating Scale

Child Care Center's Name _____   Room No. _____

Observer _____   Date _____

ENVIRONMENT FOR TODDLER SENSORIMOTOR EXPLORATION RATING SCALE

Characteristics of Appropriate Environment for Sensorimotor Exploration	Always	Usually	Sometimes	Seldom	Never
❑ Toddlers are provided a variety of open-ended objects and materials that foster sensorimotor exploration; these objects and materials are changed when necessary					
❑ Imitative and symbolic play are encouraged by providing realistic toys and props					
❑ "Simplifies the typical preschool environment, while dividing the space into appropriate areas for active learning"					
❑ Toddlers are offered meaningful experiences with people, together with opportunities to observe their physical surroundings					

Adapted from Gestwicki (1999, pp. 91).

by providing realistic props and toys in the toddler room? Are the children offered meaningful experiences with people together with opportunities to observe their physical surroundings?

 EXERCISE 7–7: ENVIRONMENT FOR FOSTERING TODDLER AUTONOMY

Background Information

Autonomy is an important social/emotional issue of toddlerhood. It is toddlers' striving to become independent, to demonstrate their ability to do things on their own. From a developmental perspective the toddler progresses from autonomy in performing physical tasks to emotional and intellectual autonomy. It is important for caregivers to show their approval and support of these first steps toward independence.

Observation Objective

The purpose of this exercise is to determine whether the child care setting provides an appropriate environment for fostering the development of toddlers' autonomy.

Procedure

Using the summary of the characteristics of an appropriate environment for fostering toddler autonomy, given in Table 7–7, indicate on the rating scale provided whether the child care setting observed is generally appropriate for fostering toddler autonomy.

An event sample may be used to describe how adult caregivers' actions contribute to the development of toddler autonomy. Do the adults allow toddlers to complete

TABLE 7–7 Environment for Fostering Toddler Autonomy Rating Scale

Child Care Center's Name _____ Room No. _____

Observer _____ Date _____

ENVIRONMENT FOR FOSTERING TODDLER AUTONOMY RATING SCALE					
Characteristics of Appropriate Environment for Fostering Toddler Autonomy	Always	Usually	Sometimes	Seldom	Never
❑ Adults allow toddlers to complete their self-chosen age appropriate and individually appropriate tasks. Just the right amount of help is offered if a task is beyond the toddler's present level of ability—a response that is in keeping with Vygotsky's zone of proximal development.					
❑ Adults respond to toddlers' accomplishments with appreciation, admiration, and specific meaningful comments.					
❑ Adults allow toddlers to make choices that are within their capabilities and control—such as choices among food items, toys to play with, or activities to participate in.					
❑ Adults "encourage independent play requiring exploration and mastery" (p. 149). • Recall our promise that autonomy is truly achieved only when the child's behavior is reasonably freely chosen and under his or her control (Gestwicki's term "mastery").					
❑ Adults help toddlers achieve a sense of identity (or self-concept) by calling them by their names, identifying and playing games involving awareness of their body parts, and using mirrors and photographs to enhance toddlers' self-perceptions. • We recommend helping each child recognize the names of the other children, which should help the child recognize him or herself as distinct from the others.					
❑ Adults avoid being overprotective by allowing toddlers as much freedom as they can safely use. "As they can safely use" requires you to consider what is age appropriate and individually appropriate for each child.					
❑ Adults arrange equipment and materials to be accessible to the children with little or no adult help.					
❑ Adults look for signs of a toddler's readiness for toilet training and then gently and patiently accustom him to the toilet and assist him in using it.					
❑ Adults accept and respond sensitively to toddlers' strivings for autonomy. They recognize that toddlers' abilities and needs are changing, and they anticipate these changes and respond accordingly—"anticipatory socialization." Adults also greet these changes with genuine enthusiasm, an indication of sensitive responsiveness.					

Adapted from Gestwicki (1999, pp. 149-150).

their self-selected, age appropriate tasks? Do adults respond to toddlers' accomplishments appropriately? Do the adults permit toddlers to make their own choices within reason, such as choices among toys, food, or activities to participate in?

 ## EXERCISE 7–8: ENVIRONMENT FOR PROMOTING APPROPRIATE COGNITIVE/LANGUAGE SKILLS

Background Information

In an appropriate and effective child care setting, adults provide a developmental environment that supports and encourages language acquisition. A summary of the conditions necessary for fostering language development in toddlers is provided in Table 7–8.

Observation Objective

The purpose of this exercise is to determine whether the child care setting provides an appropriate environment for promoting toddlers' cognitive/language skills.

Procedure

Using the summary of the characteristics of an appropriate environment for promoting toddler cognitive/language skills, given in Table 7–8, indicate on the rating scale provided whether the toddler setting observed is generally considered appropriate for fostering toddlers' language development.

A narrative description could be used to provide insights into how well and to what degree the toddler setting and the adult caregivers contribute to toddlers' language development. Are the teachers responsive to the child's efforts to learn language? Do the caregivers serve as accurate and appropriate models of proper language use? Do they expand the toddler's original utterances of the language and link words with actions and experience? Do they encourage the toddler's use of the language by engaging her in child appropriate conversation?

TABLE 7–8 Environment for Promoting Appropriate Toddler Cognitive/ Language Skills Rating Scale

Child Care Center's Name _____	Room No. _____
Observer _____	Date _____

ENVIRONMENT FOR PROMOTING APPROPRIATE TODDLER COGNITIVE/LANGUAGE SKILLS RATING SCALE					
Characteristics of Appropriate Environment for Promoting Toddler Cognitive/Language Skills	Always	Usually	Sometimes	Seldom	Never
First Principle: "Language Teachers Respond"					
Responsiveness is the critical component of virtually every aspect of effective child care. Gestwicki, however, notes its special importance in toddlers' efforts to learn language. If thirteen-month-old Brandon's initially unsuccessful efforts to pronounce his older brother Anthony's name are met with sensitive responsiveness, several benefits will accrue; his efforts will be positively reinforced, and he will come to learn that language is important and valued; his sense of initiative will be strengthened; and reinforcement of successive approximations to the correct pronunciation will eventually result in Brandon's ability to say Anthony correctly.					
Second Principle: "Language Teachers Model"					
Given our earlier discussion regarding teaching language, we need to make clear our support of Gestwicki's perspective on modeling. As Gestwicki so rightly points out, ". . . toddlers depend on adult speech for their example of vocabulary, as well as for extracting their own understanding of grammar usage. . ." (p. 239).					
We simply want to make clear that providing examples of vocabulary comes closer to the usual meaning of teaching than does providing examples of speech from which children can extract "their own understanding of grammar usage." By repeating words and phrases, adults help toddlers with pronunciation. By emphasizing key words, adults help toddlers learn the names of objects and people. By making clear to whom they are speaking, and by waiting for a response, adults help toddlers learn what Gestwicki calls "the logistics of conversation" (p. 239). Except for such instances of special emphasis, modeling entails fairly ordinary speech under fairly ordinary circumstances. We believe, in other words, that most language modeling occurs when adults simply speak, although their speech must be commensurate with the toddler's ability to understand. It must be age appropriate and individually appropriate.					
We do want to stress that children *must hear the language they are to learn.* Adults, therefore, must meet the child's need to hear language. Young children do not learn a first language the way we adults generally learn a second language—by poring over textbooks, memorizing vocabulary and rules of grammar and syntax. This is the aspect of language teaching that we want to deemphasize.					

continued

TABLE 7–8 Environment for Promoting Appropriate Toddler Cognitive/ Language Skills Rating Scale (Continued)

Child Care Center's Name _____ Room No. _____

Observer _____ Date _____

ENVIRONMENT FOR PROMOTING APPROPRIATE TODDLER COGNITIVE/LANGUAGE SKILLS RATING SCALE

Characteristics of Appropriate Environment for Promoting Toddler Cognitive/Language Skills	Always	Usually	Sometimes	Seldom	Never
Third Principle: "Language Teachers Simplify"					
Simplification does not mean talking baby talk to the toddler. It means avoiding overuse of complex sentences but not avoiding them entirely. As Gestwicki points out, judicious use of complex sentences helps the toddler acquire an understanding of grammatical structures. Appropriate speech simplification occurs within the child's zone of proximal development. Adults' speech should be just far enough above the child's present level of ability to provide him with a model for further learning.					
Fourth Principle: "Language Teachers Expand"					
"Expansion" is related to the zone of proximal development, and it is a very effective way of providing children with a language model. Adults expand when they add vocabulary and ideas to a toddler's original utterances, notes Gestwicki. She further notes that such expansions are important for language and cognitive development. By expanding on the toddler's original utterances, you are providing the child a model or pattern for her own speech, and you are scaffolding by relating the child's ideas and experiences to additional ideas and experiences that are not quite familiar to her, thus requiring her to "stretch" cognitively and linguistically.					
Fifth Principle: "Language Teachers Link Words with Actions and Experience"					
This principle, we believe, has a great deal to do with explicitness and with the power of actions to command a toddler's attention. Verbs—action words—are what give life to writing and speaking. Action words tend to be concrete and specific, especially if adults model or describe the actions the words represent. "Here, Jimmy, let's roll the ball back and forth," says Francine, who then rolls the ball to Jimmy using clear, distinct arm motions. "Now," Francine says, "roll the ball back to me." Gestwicki (1999) cautions that although gestures, pointing, and other nonverbal cues can aid toddlers' language learning, adults should never replace words with gestures. If anything, gestures should accompany words, and she notes further that adults' choice of words should be explicit—for example, by making specific reference to object nouns rather than their pronoun referents ("Take the ball" rather than "Take this").					

continued

TABLE 7–8 Environment for Promoting Appropriate Toddler Cognitive/ Language Skills Rating Scale (Continued)

| Child Care Center's Name _____ Room No. _____ |
| Observer _____ Date _____ |

ENVIRONMENT FOR PROMOTING APPROPRIATE TODDLER COGNITIVE/LANGUAGE SKILLS RATING SCALE					
Characteristics of Appropriate Environment for Promoting Toddler Cognitive/Language Skills	Always	Usually	Sometimes	Seldom	Never
Sixth Principle: "Language Teachers Correct Indirectly"					
Proper grammar and word usage are achieved over time and are fairly consistently preceded by such mistakes as overgeneralization of the rules governing the formation of past tense and plurals that are formed by "ed" and "s," respectively: "He goed" for "He went," or "My foots" for "My feet." Correcting indirectly reflects, we think, the different character of teaching language as opposed to teaching, say, arithmetic or history. When correcting indirectly, the adult simply recasts the toddler's original utterance into the correct form—"Yes, those are your two feet"; he does not say such things as "No, Billy, the plural of foot is an irregular construction, and the singular 'foot' becomes 'feet.' " You can see how ridiculous such a statement would be, given the toddler's relative immaturity of cognitive and language ability. Moreover, the well-known pediatrician, Dr. Terry Brazelton (1974), attributes language delay to undue emphasis on correct speech, when correctness is attempted through repeated direct instruction (p. 240). This principle again illustrates the easy, non-stressful communication style that should be used in "teaching" language.					
Seventh Principle: "Language Teachers Encourage Speech"					
Encouraging speech in this context is a natural, almost spontaneous behavior. Although most of us do not talk constantly, a significant part of many adults' day involves speaking. For the professional child care provider, speech patterns and the occasions for speaking have to be adjusted to be commensurate with what is age appropriate and individually appropriate for each child. Adults also encourage speech by patiently allowing toddlers to verbalize their needs and desires rather than prematurely anticipating them and thus precluding their need to talk.					
Encouraging speech is really not much different from encouraging any other child-appropriate behavior. All encouragement ultimately depends on providing children with an adequate and appropriate general and developmental environment.					

continued

TABLE 7–8   Environment for Promoting Appropriate Toddler Cognitive/ Language Skills Rating Scale (Continued)

Child Care Center's Name _____   Room No. _____

Observer _____   Date _____

ENVIRONMENT FOR PROMOTING APPROPRIATE TODDLER COGNITIVE/LANGUAGE SKILLS RATING SCALE					
Characteristics of Appropriate Environment for Promoting Toddler Cognitive/Language Skills	Always	Usually	Sometimes	Seldom	Never
Eighth Principle: "Language Teachers Talk Face to Face"					
In some respects, talking face to face with toddlers is the equivalent of adults looking each other in the eye when having a conversation. One could argue that talking face-to-face is a sign of respect, interest, and sensitive responsiveness. Toddlers can benefit greatly from this intimate experience with adults. Getting physically down to the toddler's level helps him feel that he is worthy of your personal attention. He can more easily watch your mouth as you pronounce words with which he might have difficulty. Face-to-face conversation gives a toddler the sense that you are talking *to* him in a personal, meaningful way, rather than *at* him in an impersonal, distracted way. As with infants and older children, toddlers need quality time with their primary caregiver. Feeding an infant is a caregiving activity that meets a developmental need. The infant benefits most when the caregiver interacts with the infant in a direct, personal way during the feeding process. Learning language is also a developmental need, and if you meet that need with the same sensitivity as you would an infant's nutritional needs, you will immediately recognize the importance of face-to-face interactions and communications with toddlers.					
Ninth Principle: "Language Teachers Sing, Recite, and Play Games"					
Singing, reciting, and playing games are at the very least interesting ways of using language. Moreover, as Gestwicki points out, "traditional nursery songs, rhymes, and games have lasted" because they are appropriate "for [the] language experiences of toddlers. The rhythm, rhyme repetition, and linking of action and meaning help toddlers acquire understanding and vocabulary" (p. 241). We need say no more.					

continued

TABLE 7–8   Environment for Promoting Appropriate Toddler Cognitive/Language Skills Rating Scale (Continued)

Child Care Center's Name _____   Room No. _____

Observer _____   Date _____

ENVIRONMENT FOR PROMOTING APPROPRIATE TODDLER COGNITIVE/LANGUAGE SKILLS RATING SCALE					
Characteristics of Appropriate Environment for Promoting Toddler Cognitive/Language Skills	Always	Usually	Sometimes	Seldom	Never
Tenth Principle: "Language Teachers Read Books"					
The ability to speak does not automatically entail the ability to read; hearing words and seeing them on the printed page are two quite different things. Among other benefits, reading to toddlers helps them see the connection between the spoken and the printed word. Sustained interest in actual stories will not occur until the toddler is well into the second year (241), but picture books play a vital role in forming associations between words and pictures, thus increasing the toddler's vocabulary. Reading to toddlers, especially on a one-on-one basis, provides another opportunity for adults to spend high-quality time with a child, and such time is another avenue for enhancing a toddler's feelings of self-worth as well as providing him or her with a source of pleasure.					

Adapted from Gestwicki (1999, pp. 230–231). Bold-faced text in quotation marks are quoted verbatim.

For additional information on assessing the effectiveness of child care programs, visit our Web site at **http://www.earlychilded.delmar.com**

Chapter 8

Observation and Recording Exercises for the Preschool Child Care Program

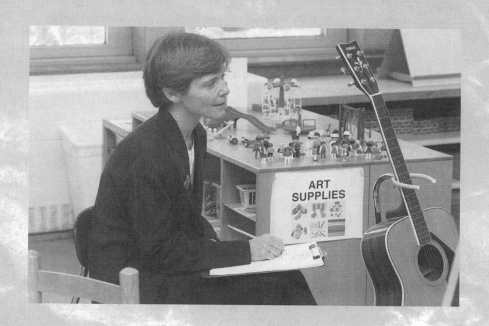

See How To

* determine the degree to which preschool children's needs are met

* ascertain whether the child care setting provides an appropriate environment for promoting initiative in preschool children

* assess whether the child care setting is child appropriate for fostering a play supportive environment for preschool children

* judge whether the child care setting provides an appropriate environment for promoting self-control in preschool children

* determine whether the child care environment provides for the development of child and age appropriate social interaction among preschool children

* ascertain whether the child care setting fosters an appropriate environment that nurtures a positive individual identity in the preschool child

* decide whether the child care setting provides an appropriate environment for fostering the development of gender identity in preschool children

* determine whether the child care setting provides an appropriate environment for fostering cultural and racial identity among preschool children

* judge whether the child care setting provides an appropriate environment that promotes prosocial behavior among preschool children

 ## Introduction

The observation and recording exercises presented in this chapter are taken from the information discussed in Chapter 4, focusing on the physical/motor, social/emotional, and cognitive/language development of the preschool-age child. Within these three domains we apply appropriate methods of observing and recording characteristics of preschool programs and environments.

 EXERCISE 8–1: PRESCHOOL CHILDREN'S NEEDS

Background Information

The preschool-age child is a totally different person from his younger counterpart, the toddler. Because he is continuing to develop at such a rapid rate—physically, emotionally, and cognitively—the preschooler enjoys a much wider range of experiences. She possesses greater knowledge, more complex skills, and a broader array of abilities than she did as a toddler. He is looking forward to building on the foundation he started developing as an infant and a toddler.

The purpose of this exercise is to determine the degree to which the preschool children's needs are met in the child care setting.

Procedure

Using the summary of preschool children's needs given in Table 8–1, indicate on the rating scale provided the degree to which the preschool children's needs are met in the child care setting observed. An event sample might provide additional details of the opportunities observed for the preschooler to acquire more advanced motor, language, and other cognitive skills. In-depth coverage of the opportunities to further expand language skills and to learn cooperation by helping and sharing may offer rich detail of the quality of the social environment in the preschool room.

TABLE 8-1 Preschool Children's Needs Rating Scale

Child Care Center's Name _____   Room No. _____

Observer _____   Date _____

	PRESCHOOL CHILDREN'S RATING SCALE					
		Degree to Which Preschoolers' Needs Are Met				
Age	Preschool Children's Needs	Very High	High	Medium	Somewhat Low	Very Low
2–3½ years	*In addition to the needs of previous stages, they need opportunities to:* ❑ Make developmentally appropriate choices ❑ Engage in dramatic or fantasy play ❑ Read books of increasing complexity ❑ "Sing favorite songs" ❑ Assemble simple puzzles					
3½–5 years	*In addition to the needs of the previous stages or age periods, they need opportunities to:* ❑ Develop and refine fine motor skills ❑ Further expand language skills through "talking, reading, and singing" ❑ "Learn cooperation by helping and sharing" ❑ "Experiment with prewriting and prereading skills"					
5–8 years	*In addition to the needs of the previous stages or age periods, they need opportunities to:* ❑ Develop a concept of numbers, develop reading skills ❑ Solve problems ❑ "Practice teamwork" ❑ Acquire and refine a sense of competency ❑ Question and observe ❑ "Acquire basic life skills" ❑ "Attend basic education"					

Adapted from the "Early Child Development" Web site.

EXERCISE 8–2: ENVIRONMENT FOR PROMOTING INITIATIVE

Background Information

The preschooler should be capable of the activities and behaviors she initiates. Adult caregivers should approve of and encourage the child's initiative. The physical environment should be conducive to the preschooler's making her own choices and decisions; it should encourage him to freely choose his own activities; it should allow children to display their work in the classroom; and it should provide open-ended materials that foster creativity.

Observation Objective

The purpose of this exercise is to ascertain whether the child care setting provides an appropriate environment for promoting initiative in preschool children.

Procedure

Using the summary of the characteristics of a child appropriate environment for promoting initiative, given in Table 8–2, indicate on the rating scale provided whether the preschool setting observed is generally considered appropriate in this regard.

A narrative summary may be used to describe in greater detail those characteristics noted in Table 8–2. The raw data gained would allow for further study of the preschool environment with recommendations for improvement.

 EXERCISE 8–3: PLAY SUPPORTIVE ENVIRONMENT

Background Information

As noted in Chapter 4, play is a developmental need and a means by which children accomplish various important developmental tasks. We view play as the spontaneous, self-selected activities that are developmentally and child appropriate. Adult caregivers in a play supportive environment believe that play is the primary means by which learning occurs. They minimize distractions through appropriate activity centers, and they invite the children's active participation in play through appropriate arrangement of equipment and materials.

Observation Objective

The purpose of this exercise is to assess whether the child care setting is child appropriate for a play supportive environment for preschool children.

Procedure

Using the summary of the characteristics of a play supportive environment shown in Table 8–3, indicate on the rating scale provided whether the child care setting observed is generally considered play supportive. An event sample could allow for more detailed descriptions of the various characteristics discussed in Table 8–3, with the data permitting further examination of the child care setting.

 EXERCISE 8–4: ENVIRONMENT FOR PROMOTING SELF-CONTROL

Background Information

Self-control implies knowing what to do and conforming to societal and cultural expectations of what is appropriate behavior in particular circumstances. It also implies a child's understanding, ability, and motivation to do what she needs to do.

TABLE 8–2   Environment for Promoting Initiative Rating Scale

Child Care Center's Name _____	Room No. _____
Observer _____	Date _____

CHILD APPROPRIATE ENVIRONMENT FOR PROMOTING INITIATIVE RATING SCALE

Characteristics of Child Appropriate Environment for Promoting Initiative	Always	Usually	Sometimes	Seldom	Never
An environment for initiative					
❑ allows and encourages children to freely choose their own play activities by providing activity areas that are clearly defined and labeled • Clearly defined and labeled activity areas help prevent confusion. Confusion should be avoided because it places undue limits on children's initiative. There are times, of course, when even children have to demonstrate initiative in uncertain or ambiguous circumstances. Nevertheless, their play in an early childhood program should not be one of those times.					
❑ puts materials and equipment where children can get them for themselves • Initiative and autonomy go hand-in-hand. Initiative probably is not possible without autonomy. In the case of this second characteristic, suitably placed equipment and materials gives the child overall freedom (autonomy) to choose and the initiative to make particular choices from among a number of options.					
❑ lets children "display their work in the classroom" (p. 102) • Initiative has to be reinforced or rewarded, otherwise it will be discouraged and possibly stifled altogether. When children produce things through their own initiative, adults give value to their productions and their efforts by proudly displaying their work for all to see.					
❑ provides open-ended materials that foster creativity and accommodate all levels of ability • The advantages of open-ended materials are that they simultaneously serve a number of different levels of ability and interest, and they allow varying degrees of initiative. Creativity is really a form of initiative, and to some extent, initiative is a form of creativity. Open-ended materials contribute to both sides of that coin.					

continued

TABLE 8–2   Environment for Promoting Initiative Rating Scale (Continued)

Child Care Center's Name _____   Room No. _____

Observer _____   Date _____

CHILD APPROPRIATE ENVIRONMENT FOR PROMOTING INITIATIVE RATING SCALE

Characteristics of Child Appropriate Environment for Promoting Initiative	Always	Usually	Sometimes	Seldom	Never
❑ "establishes systems that help children make conscious choices for play" (p. 102) • "Systems," for Gestwicki, appears to mean more or less formal or structured ways for children to plan their activities. She includes such things as " 'signing up' for activities . . ." or "planning or choice boards with hooks or pockets for adding a child's name tag to indicate a choice to work in the art area . . ." among other suggestions. Probably no choice is more conscious than one that has been planned ahead of time. There are cognitive and social benefits to be gained by such planning—foreseeing future events and their possible consequences, and delaying gratification or waiting one's turn, for example.					

❑ provides "opportunities for independence and responsible participation in the classroom" (p. 102)
  • You can see how closely related all these characteristics of an environment for initiative are; all of them have something to do with independence and responsible participation. The first characteristic emphasizes clear definition and labeling of activity areas, which support independence and participation.
  • The second emphasizes easy accessibility of the equipment and materials, which also supports independence.
  • The third emphasizes displaying children's work or productions, which certainly would seem to foster responsible participation.
  • The fourth emphasizes open-ended materials, again fostering independence by allowing the child to make choices.
  • The fifth characteristic emphasizes systems for allowing the child to make conscious choices for play, and again, independence is the foundation of conscious choice.					

Adapted from Gestwicki (1999, p. 102)

Observation Objective

The purpose of this exercise is to judge whether the child care setting provides an appropriate environment for promoting self-control in preschool children.

Procedure

Using the summary of the characteristics of an environment for promoting self-control, given in Table 8–4, indicate on the rating scale provided whether the preschool setting

TABLE 8–3 Play Supportive Environment Rating Scale

Child Care Center's Name _____ Room No. _____

Observer _____ Date _____

PLAY SUPPORTIVE ENVIRONMENT RATING SCALE					
Characteristics of Play Supportive Environment	Always	Usually	Sometimes	Seldom	Never
Adults in a play supportive environment					
❑ send a clear message that play is the primary means by which learning occurs • Gestwicki couches this message in "the careful preparation of the physical environment . . .", which includes "well-designed places to play and materials to play with. The placement of centers and the design of the classroom contribute to meaningful play experiences for children" (p. 103). Since the physical (general) environment sets the stage for the developmental environment, the children have to use these places to play and materials to play with in ways that are meaningful to them. Moreover, autonomy and initiative are at least two second-category needs that should be met by children's play behavior.					
❑ protect play and minimize distractions through carefully designed interest or activity centers • This particular criterion helps children focus their attention, but we think it also helps children learn that sometimes environments are designated for specific purposes—the idea that situations are defined in particular ways and therefore suggest or encourage particular behaviors.					
❑ invite active participation and play through proper arrangement of equipment and materials • "Proper arrangement" does not only mean where equipment and materials are located in the classroom, although that is important with respect to accessibility, visibility, and establishing meaningful relationships between different activity centers. Particular arrangements can also suggest related activities within a given activity center. Gestwicki, for instance, notes that "The scales and a box of rocks on a science table suggest an activity; a notepad and pencil arranged beside the telephone in the house corner suggest a beginning plot line" (p. 104). The present authors see this as a form of scaffolding that encourages children to use their initiative and imagination in their choice of play activities without direct suggestions from adults.					

continued

TABLE 8–3　Play Supportive Environment Rating Scale (Continued)

Child Care Center's Name _____	Room No. _____
Observer _____	Date _____

PLAY SUPPORTIVE ENVIRONMENT RATING SCALE					
Characteristics of Play Supportive Environment	Always	Usually	Sometimes	Seldom	Never
Adults in a play supportive environment					
❑ set up activity areas whose size promotes small-group interactive play, but also allows for secluded or solitary play 　• This criterion recognizes that play spaces can be larger than is appropriate for the activity and the developmental level of the children in those spaces. Space that is too large invites children to physically distance themselves from one another so that relatively intimate, interactive play becomes difficult. We believe large spaces also tend to scatter children's focus or attention away from the activities at hand. Large, unoccupied spaces, Gestwicki notes, also encourage running and intrusion by children who are not directly involved in the ongoing activity. 　　Allowing for secluded or solitary play enables children to exercise their initiative and autonomy by freely choosing not to participate in a group activity.					
❑ provide "long time blocks for play" (p. 106) 　• This criterion recognizes the importance of play in children's development. If, as has been said, play is children's work, then they must be given enough time to finish the "jobs" they have undertaken. Ample time also allows the children to terminate play when it suits them, rather than being forced to stop because of externally imposed (and possible artificial) time constraints.					
❑ "function as facilitators of play" (p. 106) 　• This criterion illustrates, we think, the symbiotic relationship between the general and the developmental environment. Although this criterion apparently is meant to stand on its own, everything discussed thus far in Table 8–3 is intended to facilitate play. For the present authors, however, "facilitators of play" incorporates all of the other characteristics of a play-supportive environment while also emphasizing the critical function of an appropriate developmental environment. None of these things is likely to happen on its own.					
❑ "plan outdoor play areas and materials as carefully as indoor play areas" (p. 106) 　• This is only to say that play is no less important outdoors than indoors. Play is important wherever it occurs.					

Adapted from the Gestwicki (1999, pp. 103–106).

TABLE 8–4   Environment for Promoting Self-Control Rating Scale

Child Care Center's Name _____   Room No. _____

Observer _____   Date _____

ENVIRONMENT FOR PROMOTING SELF-CONTROL RATING SCALE					
Characteristics of Environment for Promoting Initiative	Always	Usually	Sometimes	Seldom	Never
An environment for self-control					
❏ is a general and developmental environment that anticipates and prevents "problems caused by boredom, frustration, overcrowding, and fatigue"					
❏ is a general and developmental environment that provide clear signals and expectations for appropriate behavior					
❏ "uses posters and other visual clues to remind children of appropriate classroom behavior"					
❏ provides children with places for private retreat or withdrawal					
❏ respects individual rights and differences and uses equipment and materials that convey such respect					
❏ provides children with the means to express strong emotions—toys and other objects made for vigorous use, for example					
❏ "model[s] opportunities for children to meet for problem solving" • This last feature provides a vehicle or forum for the children to discuss problems and disagreements and try to reach agreeable solutions. This would seem to be similar to a "family council" that meets to solve problems that exist within the family group.					

Adapted from the Gestwicki (1999, p. 107).

observed is generally considered appropriate for promoting self-control. A narrative description may be used to allow for more in-depth details about the characteristics noted in the given table. As these characteristics are described, the observer can then assess whether the room being observed contributes to an environment for self-control.

 EXERCISE 8–5: SOCIAL INTERACTIONS/PLAY

Background Information

Play is the work of the young child. From infancy through the early childhood period, children progress through different stages or classifications of play or social interaction. As indicated in Table 8–5, Bentzen (2000) has summarized Parten's six classifications of play or social interactions. Beginning with the first stage of unoccupied behavior, we can see that the child is not engaging in any obvious play activity or social interaction. Rather, she simply observes what is going on elsewhere in the room.

The next classification, onlooker behavior, involves the child's watching other children play. He may talk to those children who are playing, asking questions or giving suggestions, but he does not enter into play.

During the third play stage, solitary play, the child plays with toys that differ from those used by others in the immediate area, but she makes no effort to get close to them or to speak to them, choosing instead to focus entirely on her own activity. During the fourth stage, parallel play, the child is playing close to other children but is still independent of them. He plays *beside* rather than *with* the other children.

The fifth classification, associative play, involves the child playing *with* the other children, while sharing materials and equipment. The children engage in similar but not necessarily identical activity, doing essentially what each one wants to do, without putting the interests of the group first. In the final play stage, cooperative play, the children are engaged in *organized* play in which the group is established for a particular purpose, such as making a product or playing a formal game. As children move through these play stages, their social skills develop and they are able to progress to increasingly more complex social interactions.

Observation Objective

The purpose of this exercise is to determine whether the child care environment provides for the development of child- and age-appropriate social interactions among the preschoolers.

Procedure

Using Bentzen's (2000) summary of Parten's six classifications of play or social interactions given in Table 8–5, indicate on the rating scale provided whether the child care setting observed generally provides for the development of social interactions among preschool children. An event sample could allow for more detailed description of these play stages discussed in Table 8–5, with the data permitting further assessment of the child care setting.

 ## EXERCISE 8–6: ENVIRONMENT THAT NURTURES POSITIVE INDIVIDUAL IDENTITY

Background Information

Most aspects of children's learning and development depend upon interactions with other people. Interaction involves not only the obvious social exchange of two or more people; it also involves the concept of interaction effects (see Chapter 1). As discussed in Chapter 4, adults' personal relationships with young children are the necessary first step in the process of identification. Developmental appropriateness requires the consideration of the unique characteristics and needs of each child and the attempt to convey acceptance of that uniqueness.

Observation Objective

The purpose of this exercise is to ascertain whether the child care setting fosters an appropriate environment that nurtures a positive individual identity in the preschool child.

Procedure

Using the summary of how adults can nurture positive individual identity, given in Table 8–6, indicate on the rating scale provided whether the preschool setting observed is generally considered appropriate in this regard. An event sample can be used to record details of specific adult-child interactions, such as those described in Table 8–6. As these exchanges are detailed, the observer can then assess the appropriateness of adult-child interactions there.

TABLE 8–5   Social Interactions/Play Rating Scale

Child Care Center's Name _____   Room No. _____

Observer _____   Date _____

SOCIAL INTERACTIONS/PLAY RATING SCALE		Always	Usually	Sometimes	Seldom	Never
Parten's Six Classifications of Play or Social Interactions						
1. Unoccupied Behavior	Here the child is not engaging in any obvious play activity or social interaction. Rather, she watches anything that is of interest at the moment. When there is nothing of interest to watch, the child will play with her own body, move around from place to place, follow the teacher, or stay in one spot looking around the room.					
2. Onlooker Behavior	Here the child spends most of her time watching other children play. The child may talk to the playing children, may ask questions, or give suggestions, but does not enter into play. The child remains within speaking distance so that what goes on can be seen and heard; this indicates a definite interest in a group(s) of children, unlike the unoccupied child, who shows no interest in any particular group of children but only a shifting interest in what happens to be exciting at the moment.					
3. Solitary Play	This is play activity that is conducted independently of what anyone else is doing. The child plays with toys that differ from those used by other children in the immediate area—within speaking distance—and she makes no effort to get close to them or to speak to them. The child is focused entirely on her own activity and is not influenced by what others are doing.					

continued

TABLE 8-5 Social Interactions/Play Rating Scale (Continued)

Child Care Center's Name _____ Room No. _____

Observer _____ Date _____

SOCIAL INTERACTIONS/PLAY RATING SCALE

Parten's Six Classifications of Play or Social Interactions		Always	Usually	Sometimes	Seldom	Never
4. Parallel Play	Here the child is playing close to other children but is still independent of them. The child uses toys that are like the toys being used by the others, but he uses them as he sees fit and is neither influenced by nor tries to influence the others. The child thus plays *beside* rather than with the other children.					
5. Associative Play	Here the child plays with the other children. There is a sharing of material and equipment; the children may follow each other around; there may be attempts to control who may or who may not play in a group, although such control efforts are not strongly asserted. The children engage in similar but not necessarily identical activity, and there is no division of labor or organization of activity, or of individuals. Each child does what he or she essentially wants to do, without putting the interests of the group first.					
6. Cooperative or Organized Supplementary Play	The key word in this category is "organized." The child plays in a group that is established for a particular purpose—making some material product, gaining some competitive goal, playing some formal games. There is a sense of "we-ness," whereby one definitely belongs or does not belong to the group. There is also some leadership present—one or two members who direct the activity of the others. This behavior requires some division of labor, a taking of different roles by the group members and support of one child's efforts by those of the others.					

Reprinted with publisher's permission from Bentzen, W. R. (2000). *Seeing Young Children: A Guide to Observing and Recording Behavior* (p. 107).

TABLE 8–6 Environment that "Nurtures Positive Individual Identity" Rating Scale

| Child Care Center's Name | Room No. |
| Observer | Date |

ENVIRONMENT THAT "NURTURES POSITIVE INDIVIDUAL IDENTITY" RATING SCALE

How Adults Can Nurture Positive Individual Identity	Always	Usually	Sometimes	Seldom	Never
To nurture positive individual identity, adults should					
❏ demonstrate sincere affection for and interest in the children by way of appropriate words and nonverbal cues—such as greeting them warmly at the start of each day and saying personal goodbyes at the end of the day, and showing sincere interest in their activities and "work" products.					
❏ adapt the idea of "teachable moments" to the idea of "speakable" or "interactional moments"—occasions during the day when you can talk to each child on an intimate, one-on-one basis, thereby giving the child the feeling that he or she is personally worthy of your time and attention.					
❏ value and encourage individuality through a child appropriate developmental environment where children recognize such things as each other's accomplishments, differences, and strengths in all developmental areas, and that children with disabilities also have strengths and can achieve meaningful goals.					
❏ address children's individuality with sensitive responsiveness. Children essentially define their own uniqueness, which you must discover by determining what is age appropriate and individually appropriate for each child. Even though not all characteristics are unique but are shared with other children, some uniqueness remains simply because it is Billy, for example, and not Rolf who is demonstrating a particular ability, emotion, or interest. Do not treat any two children as though they were "equivalent" to each other simply because they are roughly at the same developmental level or perform certain skills at the same level of ability. Every child is unique merely by being who he or she is.					
❏ respect "individual parents' styles and needs, and use parents' knowledge of their children as a primary source for getting to know individuality."					
❏ encourage and provide opportunities for children to show initiative in selecting activities, equipment, and materials that are personally meaningful to them.					
❏ emphasize personal identity by planning a developmental environment (curriculum) that has personal relevance to children's lives and experiences; help children see the relevance of new experiences to their own lives.					

Adapted from the Gestwicki (1999, pp. 167–169).

EXERCISE 8–7: ENVIRONMENT THAT FOSTERS GENDER IDENTITY

Background Information

The formation of a healthy gender identity is an important developmental task of pre-school children. The preschool child care environment should encourage children to recognize and appreciate the differences between boys and girls. Characteristics of adult-child relationships that foster gender identity are described in Table 8–7.

Observation Objective

The purpose of this exercise is to determine whether the child care setting provides an appropriate environment for fostering the development of gender identity in preschool children.

Procedure

Using the summary of how adults can foster gender identity, given in Table 8–7, indicate on the rating scale provided whether the preschool setting observed is generally considered appropriate in this regard. A narrative description may be used to provide greater detail about specific ways adults can foster gender identity, using Table 8–7 as a guide.

≋ Through Their Eyes

Preschool lead teacher Amy Scheels says it's an everyday occurrence to see the four- and five-year-old boys delight in dressing up in women's clothing, including hats, dresses, feather boas, and high heels. When she tells Nicky he looks pretty, Noriko objects. You can't tell a boy he's pretty. Amy assures her that dressing up is fun and gives the boys a chance to try on other roles. Likewise, Amy displays posters around the room depicting different family types. Some families have two mommies or two daddies; others have one of each; and others have one mommy or one daddy. By reinforcing that all families are good, she helps the children feel good about their own family, regardless of its composition.

 EXERCISE 8–8: ENVIRONMENT THAT FOSTERS CULTURAL AND RACIAL IDENTITY

Background Information

Showing respect for children of all ages should be an important goal of every early childhood program. This respect extends to the child's family, social, cultural, racial, and ethnic background. Suggested methods of fostering cultural and racial identity are discussed in Table 8–8.

TABLE 8–7   Environment that Fosters Gender Identity Rating Scale

Child Care Center's Name _____   Room No. _____

Observer _____   Date _____

ENVIRONMENT THAT FOSTERS GENDER IDENTITY RATING SCALE					
How Adults Can Foster Gender Identity	Always	Usually	Sometimes	Seldom	Never
To foster gender identity, adults should					
❑ accept children's curiosity about their bodies and make straightforward, factual responses to children's questions about their bodies; create activities that allow and encourage equal participation by both genders.					
❑ "offer experiences that challenge narrow, stereotypical views of gender behavior" (p. 170). Such challenges to stereotyping could include helping children become aware of the wide range and variety of jobs and professions performed by both genders, or seeing how males and females show each other respect as individuals.					
❑ encourage cross-gender play choices. You need to recognize that boys and girls generally tend to choose different play activities and materials. As Gestwicki points out, ". . . boys tend to be more active in their play, while girls tend to play more quietly. Boys appear more interested in outdoor play than girls, and select more adventuresome activities such as block building or pretending with toy vehicles. . . . Girls select art activities and dramatic play more frequently" (p. 170). The idea here is not to prohibit or suppress children's "natural tendencies," but to "help children broaden their repertoire if children indicate their limited choices are based on ideas of gender appropriateness" (p. 170).					
❑ ensure that pictures and language in books reflect gender diversity when work and home roles are depicted.					
❑ involve children in new activities, particularly if their own choices appear to be based on limited perceptions of gender-appropriate play. In this instance, it is acceptable for program staff to suggest or initiate play activities that might broaden children's perspectives on gender-based roles and behaviors.					
❑ "communicate with parents about goals and classroom practices to support healthy gender identity" (p. 171). It is especially important for staff to realize that the parents' educational, cultural, and ethnic backgrounds will influence their feelings about, and perceptions of, gender behavior, whether traditional or nontraditional. Disagreements with parents about appropriate gender behavior must be addressed through frequent, open communication. Whatever the outcome of such discussions, program staff must always convey respect for parents' different opinions and viewpoints regarding issues of sexuality and gender roles.					

continued

TABLE 8–7   Environment that Fosters Gender Identity Rating Scale (Continued)

Child Care Center's Name _____   Room No. _____

Observer _____   Date _____

ENVIRONMENT THAT FOSTERS GENDER IDENTITY RATING SCALE	Always	Usually	Sometimes	Seldom	Never
How Adults Can Foster Gender Identity					
❑ challenge children to think about any gender stereotypes they might exhibit by their actions or verbal comments. Gestwicki recommends providing children with opportunities "to compare their real experiences with their beliefs [which] may eventually cause children to shift their thinking" (p. 171).					
❑ "examine personal feelings about gender-free activities, comments, and attitudes" (p. 171). The present authors would characterize this "examination" as analyzing your possible biases. It is impossible to be completely free of bias, especially if we use the most innocent or innocuous meaning of bias as a perspective or point of view, which is something everyone has. If you harbor negative biases or prejudices about gender issues, you cannot deal with them effectively if you do not acknowledge their existence and are not cognizant of how those prejudices can affect your relationships with children.					

Adapted from Gestwicki (1999, pp. 170–171).

Observation Objective

The purpose of this exercise is to determine whether the child care setting provides an appropriate environment for fostering cultural and racial identity in preschool children.

Procedure

Using the summary of how adults can foster cultural and racial identity, given in Table 8–8, indicate on the rating scale provided whether the preschool setting observed is generally considered appropriate in this regard. An event sample may also be used to allow for more in-depth details about specific ways adults can foster cultural and racial identity.

EXERCISE 8–9: ENVIRONMENT THAT PROMOTES PROSOCIAL BEHAVIOR

Background Information

Prosocial behavior consists of giving, helping, empathizing, sympathizing, helping, sharing, giving comfort, and behaving in friendly, generous ways. Although prosocial behaviors will not become well-established until the school years, children can begin forming a foundation for these behaviors during their preschool years. Table 8–9 provides some adult behaviors that can promote prosocial behaviors in the preschool classroom.

TABLE 8-8   Environment that Fosters Cultural and Racial Identity Rating Scale

Child Care Center's Name _____   Room No. _____

Observer _____   Date _____

ENVIRONMENT THAT FOSTERS CULTURAL AND RACIAL IDENTITY RATING SCALE					
How Adults Can Foster Cultural and Racial Identity	Always	Usually	Sometimes	Seldom	Never
To foster cultural and racial identity, adults should					
❏ ensure that all books and pictures in the classroom realistically depict the diversity represented by the children in the program, the community, and the whole of the North American population. Diversity should address "racial composition, nonstereotypical gender representation, different abilities, ages, classes, family structures, and lifestyles" (1999, p. 172).					
❏ provide toys, activities, and materials that meet the same requirements as for books and pictures listed immediately above.					
❏ use parents as a resource for such things as "family stories, songs, drawings, and traditions of their cultural and linguistic background" (p. 172). This once again emphasizes the need for communicating with and involving parents in their children's program. In the present instance, using parents as a resource helps them to know that you are paying respect and attention to their children's cultural and racial heritages (p. 172).					
❏ work with bilingual children and their parents to maintain their (children's) home language skills and to foster their learning English within the context of the early childhood program—providing relevant play activities, books, pictures, equipment, materials, and the like.					
❏ use "teachable moments" to assuage children's feelings of "discomfort or prejudice [regarding] what is new or unfamiliar to them" (p. 173). It will require skill and tact on your part to dissuade children from ideas that could lead to bias or prejudice.					

Adapted from Gestwicki (1999, pp. 172–173).

Observation Objective

The purpose of this exercise is to judge whether the child care setting provides an appropriate environment that promotes prosocial behavior among preschool children.

Procedure

Using the summary of how adults can promote prosocial behavior given in Table 8–9, indicate on the rating scale provided whether the preschool setting observed is generally considered appropriate for promoting prosocial behavior. A narrative description may also be used to provide greater detail about specific ways adult caregivers can promote prosocial behavior, as discussed in Table 8–9.

TABLE 8–9 Environment that Promotes Prosocial Behavior Rating Scale

Child Care Center's Name _____ Room No. _____

Observer _____ Date _____

ENVIRONMENT THAT PROMOTES PROSOCIAL BEHAVIOR RATING SCALE					
How Adults Can Promote Prosocial Behavior	Always	Usually	Sometimes	Seldom	Never
To promote prosocial behavior, adults should					
❑ provide equipment and materials that encourage cooperation and joint play activity. There are toys, for example, designed to be used simultaneously by two or more children—wagons, toy cars with two or more seats, age-appropriate board games, and so on. Such materials are a good example of letting physical structures influence or suggest play activities, which can also provide children with opportunities to exercise their initiative.					
❑ provide activities that encourage or require joint, cooperative interactions. Physical equipment and materials generally are the context or props for children's play—they seldom play by twiddling their thumbs—and so materials and activities are complementary. A major difference the present authors see between these first two ways of promoting prosocial behavior is that there are activities that do not involve toys as such. Gestwicki, for instance, mentions such activities as "writing group stories or making cards to send to the sick sister of one child, [which] encourages both turn-taking and opportunities to experience the positive results of cooperation" (p. 175).					
❑ encourage children to ask for assistance from their classmates, and, of course, encourage them to give assistance when requested. Gestwicki puts this recommendation in the context of children's differing abilities and unique talents. The present authors would also put this recommendation in the context of instrumental dependency. All of us are instrumentally dependent on certain other people who are able to do for us what we cannot do for ourselves. Physicians treat us when we are ill, automobile mechanics repair our cars when they are not operating properly, and farmers grow the food we eat. Asking for assistance, therefore, when it stems from instrumental dependency, is a natural part of the human condition. It can, we believe, also foster a sense of healthy interdependence and altruism.					
❑ ". . . actively guide children toward awareness of others' needs and feelings" (p. 175). This recommendation goes hand in hand with Gestwicki's other recommendation to "help children recognize prosocial behavior" (p. 176). "Awareness" here refers to recognizing the signals or indications that someone needs help, for example, which is really developing a sensitivity to the behavioral cues that other people give off. "Recognizing prosocial behavior" is understanding what behaviors or responses are actually required in a given situation. Such recognition can be taught in such ways as pointing out "when other children are attempting to show concern or helpfulness" (p. 176).					

continued

TABLE 8–9   Environment that Promotes Prosocial Behavior Rating Scale (Continued)

| Child Care Center's Name _____ | Room No. _____ |
| Observer _____ | Date _____ |

ENVIRONMENT THAT PROMOTES PROSOCIAL BEHAVIOR
RATING SCALE

How Adults Can Promote Prosocial Behavior	Always	Usually	Sometimes	Seldom	Never
❑ reinforce and model prosocial behavior. This is probably one of the easiest recommendations to implement. It does require sensitivity and awareness on your part, because you have to observe a prosocial behavior in order to reinforce it. It also requires a proper sense of timing; you cannot allow too much time to pass between the occurrence of the prosocial behavior and your reinforcing response. It would be very helpful if you specified to the child what behavior you are pleased with or are commending.					
One would think that modeling prosocial behavior would be part of a child care provider's normal routine, and it should be. But as Gestwicki implies, modeling prosocial behavior is not just demonstrating it yourself; modeling can also involve "verbally explain[ing] helpfulness and cooperation. . . ," thus showing children "the importance of behaving in prosocial ways" (p. 176).					
❑ limit aggressive, antisocial behavior. Gestwicki (1999) cites Vivian Paley's (1992) "cardinal rule in her classroom," namely "You can't say you can't play" (p. 176). This rule is good as far as it goes. It essentially prohibits children from excluding other children in their play, and exclusion is what Gestwicki appears to emphasize. The present authors would merely point out that aggressive, antisocial behavior takes forms other than exclusion—pushing, hitting, verbal insults, disparaging comments, and so on.					
❑ help children develop empathy. Empathy is the ability to feel or understand what someone else is feeling—it is putting yourself "in someone else's shoes." Empathy, however, is primarily cognitive, not emotional, you do not literally have to feel what someone else is feeling, but you do have to have some intellectual appreciation of another's feelings. You can help children acquire this appreciation by verbalizing or defining their own and other's feelings and your concern for them.					
To some extent, children learn what to feel in certain situations, but they also have to learn what labels to apply to their feelings. It is sometimes risky to try to determine what someone else is feeling. We cannot always be sure, for example, whether four-year-old Ralph is angry or frightened simply by observing such outward appearances as his facial expressions or body postures. Nevertheless, adults do identify what they think children are feeling—"I know you *feel sad* because it's raining and you can't go outside to play. You'll *feel happy* as soon as the rain stops." This kind of verbalization does help children to recognize feelings and occasions that call for empathic responses.					

Adapted from Gestwicki (1999, pp. 175–177).

Conclusion

Throughout this book, we have provided you with the necessary background information to increase your knowledge of observation and interpretation of what goes on in early childhood programs; the roles of the general and developmental environments; the role of interaction effects; children's developmental needs and how they change over time; the principles that guide and explain developmental change; and what constitutes a child appropriate curriculum. Further, we have provided a variety of observation and recording exercises to help you assess various aspects and components of child care programs.

Insights from these criteria will help you determine how well a child care program measures up to the standards you envision for professional child care programs or for your own child's program. This guide will be helpful in selecting an appropriate child care setting or in improving your own child care program. We are confident that a program that exemplifies these criteria is a child appropriate program.

Although the essence of child care is the knowledge comprising the conceptual and theoretical content presented in Chapters 1 through 4 of *Seeing Child Care,* this knowledge is limited to the degree to which it can be applied. The observation and recording exercises in Chapters 5 through 8 provide opportunities to apply these concepts and theories, thus reinforcing the symbiotic relationship between knowledge and application.

We encourage all readers—professionals, students, and parents—to continue your endeavors to apply these principles that provide a guide to evaluating the effectiveness of early childhood programs.

For additional information on assessing the effectiveness of child care programs, visit our Web site at **http://www.earlychilded.delmar.com**

References

Allen, K. E. & Marotz, L. R. (2003). *Developmental profiles: Pre-birth through twelve* (4th ed.). Clifton Park, NY: Delmar Learning.

Bentzen, W. R. (2001). *Seeing young children: A guide to observing and recording behavior* (4th ed.). Clifton Park, NY: Delmar Learning.

Berk, L. E. (2000). *Child development* (5th ed.). Boston: Allyn and Bacon.

Bredekamp, S. (Ed.). (1987). Excerpts from: *Developmentally appropriate practice in early childhood programs serving children from birth through age 8.* Exp. ed. Washington, DC: National Association for the Education of Young Children.

Bredekamp, S. & Copple, C. (Eds.). (1997). *Developmentally appropriate practice in early childhood programs* (Rev. Ed.). Washington, DC: National Association for the Education of Young Children.

Cowley, G. (1997, spring/summer). The language explosion. *Newsweek,* Special Edition.

Donohue-Colletta, N. (1992) *Understanding cross-cultural child development and designing programs for children.* Washington, DC: Pact Publications.

Fabes, R., & Martin, C. L. (2000). *Exploring child development: Transactions and transformations.* Boston: Allyn and Bacon.

Gestwicki, C. (1999) *Developmentally appropriate practice: Curriculum and development in early education.* Clifton Park, NY: Delmar Learning.

Gonzales-Mena, J., & Eyer, D. W. (2001). *Infants, toddlers, and caregivers* (5th ed.). Mountain View, CA: Mayfield Publishing Company.

Guiness, O. (1976). *In two minds: The dilemma of doubt and how to resolve it.* Downers Grove, IL: Inter Varsity Press.

Hunt, J. McV. (1961). *Intelligence and experience.* New York: The Ronald Press.

Kaplan, A. (1964). *The conduct of inquiry: Methodology for behavioral science.* San Francisco: Chandler Publishing Company.

Miller, P. H. (1993). *Theories of developmental psychology.* New York: W. H. Freeman and Company.

Muzi, M. J. (2000). *Child development through time and transition.* Upper Saddle River, NJ: Prentice-Hall, Inc.

Paley, V. (1992). *You can't say you can't play.* Cambridge, MA: Harvard University Press.

Papalia, D. E., Olds, S. W., & Feldman, R. D. (1999). *A child's world: Infancy through adolescence* (8th ed.). Boston: WCB/McGraw-Hill.

Sprain, J. (2002). "Developmentally Appropriate Care: What Does It Mean?" *National Network for Child Care* [On-line]. Available: http://www.nncc.org

WebMD http://www.WebMD.com

Webster's *New Universal Unabridged Dictionary* (1996). New York: Barnes & Noble Books.

White, B. (1988). *Educating the infant and toddler.* Lexington, MA: Lexington Books.

White, B. (1995). *The new first three years of life.* (Rev. Ed.). New York: Simon & Schuster.

Child Care Resources

Due to the voluminous and ever-changing nature of the laws and regulations governing child care in New York State, we include here the Web address for updated information on such laws and regulations:

http://www.ocfs.state.ny.us

Please refer to your state's laws and regulations with regard to issues such as teacher-child ratios and handling reports of child abuse.

The National Association for the Education of Young Children (NAEYC) also provides information and resources on all aspects of developmentally appropriate practice and curriculum for young children from birth to age eight.

NAEYC
1509 16th Street, NW
Washington, DC 20036-1426
1-800-424-2460
http://www.naeyc.org

Additional On-line Resources for *Seeing Child Care*

1. http://www.NACCRRA.org provides a comprehensive listing of child care educational resources and referral information.

2. Other web sites available from NACCRRA are:

    http://www.childcareaware.org

3. The National Resource Center for Health and Safety in Child Care maintains information on individual states' child care licensure regulations at:

    http://nrc.uchsc.edu/states.html

Observation Sample

Language

Observer's Name _____

Child/Children Observed _____

Child's/Children's Age(s) _____ Child's/Children's Sex _____

Observation Context (home, child care center, preschool, school) _____

Date of Observation _____ Time Begun _____ Time Ended _____

Brief Description of Physical and Social Characteristics of Observation Setting:

OBJECTIVE BEHAVIORAL DESCRIPTIONS (OBD) AND INTERPRETATIONS:

Narrative Description

OBD 1: Child's Sex ☐ Male ☐ Female [Time begun _____ Time ended _____]

Interpretation 1:

OBD 2: Child's Sex ☐ Male ☐ Female [Time begun _____ Time ended _____]

Interpretation 2:

OBD 3: Child's Sex ☐ Male ☐ Female [Time begun _____ Time ended _____]

Interpretation 3:

Continue for as many OBDs as are needed or desired.

Summary Comments on Children's General Language Behavior, Skills, and so on.

Comparisons and Contrasts Between Boys' and Girls' Language Behavior, Skills, and so on.

Example of Rating Scale

Motor Function	Excellent	Very Good	Good	Fair	Poor
Reaches with one hand; grasps an object when offered					
Transfers objects from one hand to another; capable of manipulating objects					
Can stack objects or place one object inside another					
Uses pincer grasp to pick up small objects, food					
Deliberately drops or throws objects but cannot intentionally put an object down					
Shows beginning ability to pull self to a standing position					
Begins to stand alone; leans on furniture for support; "cruises" around obstacles with side-stepping movements					
Creeps on hands and knees; crawls up and down stairs					

Adapted from Allen and Marotz, 2003, p. 63.

Sample Checklist

Name _____ School or Agency _____

Age _____ Group _____ Sex _____ Time of Day _____

Birthdate _____ Observer _____

Directions: Check only those statements that you feel are really true of the child. Do not guess (if you are not certain) or make a premature judgment call.

1. ( ) Vigorous and energetic in his attack on a project
2. ( ) Overcautious, not venturesome, afraid to attempt the untried
3. ( ) Nearly always accomplishes tasks in spite of difficulties
4. ( ) Voice animated, alive
5. ( ) Does not become fatigued easily
6. ( ) Poor concentration (begins and ends activities quickly or abruptly)
7. ( ) Merely copies other children's reactions, not original
8. ( ) Concentrates well at his task
9. ( ) Original and inventive reactions
10. ( ) Curious and questioning
11. ( ) Expresses himself well for his age
12. ( ) Resourceful in dealing with difficult situations
13. ( ) Poor use of language for his age
14. ( ) Patient
15. ( ) Absorbed; self-sufficient in his activity
16. ( ) Restless; a certain dissatisfaction with his own activity
17. ( ) Retiring; wishes to be in the background
18. ( ) Even-tempered
19. ( ) Frequently disturbed; easily upset by the disagreeable or the exciting
20. ( ) Seldom disturbed; sudden changes in mood infrequent
21. ( ) Slow to adjust to a novel experience
22. ( ) Original in play
23. ( ) Is easily distracted from task at hand
24. ( ) Gives up easily; lacks persistence
25. ( ) Submits to any child who takes the initiative
26. ( ) Dominates children of his own age (either sex)
27. ( ) Will submit to a specific child only
28. ( ) Submits to a leader only after a struggle to dominate
29. ( ) Is a follower to one specific group only
30. ( ) Occasionally dominates a group
31. ( ) Usually leads a small group
32. ( ) Decides who shall participate in the group activities
33. ( ) Can organize the activities of a group to carry out a definite purpose
34. ( ) Leads or follows as the occasion demands
35. ( ) Neither leads nor follows; plays alone

Note: Checklists are from actual centers and are intended as examples; not necessarily ideals for all ages.

Sample Checklist with Some Developmental Norms

Child's Name _____ Date of Birth _____

Date _____ Teacher's Name _____

Directions: Check only those statements that you feel are really true of the child. Do not guess if you are not certain.

1. Puts together 3-piece puzzle	_____ Yes	_____ No
2. Snips with scissors	_____ Yes	_____ No
3. Picks up pins or buttons with each eye separately covered	_____ Yes	_____ No
4. Paints strokes, dots, or circular shapes on easel	_____ Yes	_____ No
5. Can roll, pound, squeeze, and pull clay	_____ Yes	_____ No
6. Holds crayons with fingers, not with fist	_____ Yes	_____ No
7. Puts together 8-piece (or more) puzzle	_____ Yes	_____ No
8. Makes clay shapes with 2 or 3 parts	_____ Yes	_____ No
9. Using scissors, cuts on curve	_____ Yes	_____ No
10. Screws together a threaded object	_____ Yes	_____ No
11. Cuts out and pastes simple shapes	_____ Yes	_____ No
12. Draws a simple house	_____ Yes	_____ No
13. Imitates folding and creasing paper 3 times	_____ Yes	_____ No
14. Prints a few capital letters	_____ Yes	_____ No
15. Copies a square	_____ Yes	_____ No
16. Draws a simple recognizable picture (e.g., house, dog, tree)	_____ Yes	_____ No
17. Can lace shoes	_____ Yes	_____ No
18. Prints capital letters (large, single, anywhere on paper)	_____ Yes	_____ No
19. Can copy small letters	_____ Yes	_____ No
20. Cuts pictures from magazines without being more than 1/4 inch from edge of pictures	_____ Yes	_____ No
21. Uses a pencil sharpener	_____ Yes	_____ No
22. Folds paper square two times on diagonal, in imitation	_____ Yes	_____ No
23. Prints name on paper	_____ Yes	_____ No
24. Kicks large ball when rolled to him	_____ Yes	_____ No
25. Runs 10 steps with coordinated, alternating arm movement	_____ Yes	_____ No
26. Pedals tricycle five feet	_____ Yes	_____ No
27. Swings on swing when set in motion	_____ Yes	_____ No
28. Climbs up and slides down 4–6 foot slide	_____ Yes	_____ No
29. Somersaults forward	_____ Yes	_____ No
30. Walks upstairs, alternating feet	_____ Yes	_____ No
31. Catches ball with 2 hands when thrown from 5 feet	_____ Yes	_____ No
32. Jumps from bottom step	_____ Yes	_____ No
33. Climbs ladder	_____ Yes	_____ No
34. Skips on alternate feet	_____ Yes	_____ No
35. Walks balance beam forward without falling	_____ Yes	_____ No
36. Runs, changing direction	_____ Yes	_____ No
37. Jumps forward 10 times without falling	_____ Yes	_____ No
38. Jumps backward 6 times without falling	_____ Yes	_____ No
39. Bounces and catches large ball	_____ Yes	_____ No

Summary of Recording Techniques

Method	Open vs. Closed	Degree of Selectivity	Degree of Inference	Advantages	Disadvantages
Narrative Description (Formal)	Open	Low degree of selectivity	Low at the time of observation; rises during interpretation	• Provides a complete account • Captures context (setting & situation) • It is a permanent record • Usable under many circumstances	• It is time and energy consuming • Can be inefficient regarding representativeness of behavior sample • Requires skill and effort to record all details of behavior
Event Sampling (Formal)	Open or closed, depending on use of coding schemes or narrative description	High degree of selectivity	High initially	• Can preserve raw data • Suitable for infrequently occurring behaviors • Records natural units of behavior • Can combine narrative description with coding schemes	• Not very useful for the infrequent observer—need to be in the setting often enough to see behavior when it occurs
Rating Scales	Closed. The same conditions apply to rating scales as apply to checklists	Highly selective	High degree of inference	• Except for the degree of inference required, rating scale is simple to use • Economical of recording time and effort • Useful for planning experiences and for ongoing comparisons of a child's behavior • Also see advantages of checklists	• Requires a great deal of structuring • Loss of raw data • Requires a high level of inference • Also see disadvantages of checklists
Checklists (Informal)	Closed. Raw data reduced to a tally mark. If used with narrative description or event sampling techniques, raw data can be preserved	Highly selective	High degree of inference	• Useable in many different situations and methods • It is efficient • Can provide "baseline" information to reveal developmental gains or behavioral changes • Can identify behaviors and skills that one might want to observe in more detail later on	• Does not preserve raw data, so details are lost and only action fragments remain in the observation record

Glossary

age appropriateness—A child's level or stage of development. Age appropriateness is based on principles of development that apply to all children from all social and cultural backgrounds—for example, the twelve developmental principles discussed in Table 1–1.

authoritative discipline—Discipline (which means teaching) through the use of firm, gentle guidance that also uses reasoning to explain appropriate behavior to a child.

authoritarian discipline—Discipline or teaching through the use of coercion or intimidation. An authoritarian might say such things as "Do as I tell you because I am bigger than you are and because I say so."

behavioral definition—Defining something by what it does, can or cannot do, or the uses to which it is put—a lawnmower cuts grass, a chair is something you sit in, an infant is someone who does not yet talk and does not yet walk but crawls or creeps to get from one place to another (among other defining characteristics). A behavioral definition uses developmental norms and observations of behavior to determine where a child is developmentally.

centration—Focusing on one particular aspect of a situation and essentially ignoring or overlooking other aspects, even though they might be relevant to a problem's solution. In Piaget's classic conservation of liquid task, the preoperational child typically misunderstands that the appearance of more liquid in the tall, narrow container is compensated for by the greater width of the other, shorter container.

child appropriate practice (CAP)—Carries the same meaning as developmentally appropriate practice, but "child" consolidates into one word the three kinds of appropriateness central to the meaning of developmentally appropriate practice: (1) age appropriateness, (2) individual appropriateness, and (3) social/cultural appropriateness. The authors believe that "development" does not inevitably or necessarily incorporate these three kinds of appropriateness.

convergent thinking—Thinking or reasoning that looks for a specific, concrete answer to a question or problem. In a child care situation, an adult encourages or demands convergent thinking if she accepts only one right answer and rejects all others.

conservation—The ability to understand that if nothing is added to or taken away from an original quantity of something, then that original quantity is preserved or conserved, irrespective of visual appearances to the contrary. For example, how objects are arranged in space has no effect on their number; or the amount of liquid in a container is totally unaffected by the size or shape of that container.

defer imitation—This is the ability to observe someone else's behavior, store that behavior in one's memory, and repeat or imitate it at a later time. Piaget viewed the ability to defer imitation as an important cognitive ability marking the beginning of true thought.

developmentally appropriate practice (DAP)—Any behaviors and activities that are in keeping with a child's level of development, unique personal characteristics, and family and cultural background, and that promote his or her optimal growth and physical, social, intellectual, language, and emotional development.

developmental environment—The environment, or those aspects of it, to which children respond and that produces interaction effects. The developmental environment is dynamic, changing, and essentially is a function of, or created by, the children's unique characteristics interacting with the characteristics of the general environment.

developmental needs—Needs that are the result of the developmental process. Walking, speaking, thinking, are among the developmental needs that nature has "programmed" children to meet. Development is itself a need. Human beings need to develop, to change over time.

developmental norms—Typical patterns of behaviors or levels of ability that characterize children of particular ages or stages of development. Developmental norms can be thought of as the age at which, or the age range within which, children on average acquire certain functions or abilities; for example, the average age at which children first walk or say their first word.

divergent thinking—Divergent thinking is essentially open-ended thinking, which does not necessarily seek or require one specific, correct answer to a question or problem. The child's thinking is allowed to diverge and explore a number of possible answers to a question or problem.

egocentrism—In Piaget's theory, the developmentally based inability to take someone else's point of view or to see a situation from someone else's perspective. The egocentric child sees the world from his or her own relatively limited frame of reference.

failure to thrive syndrome—Can be defined as "infants and children who do not appear to be ill or abnormal but who do not grow at the expected rates" (Fabes and Martin, 2000, p. 150).

first-category needs—Needs that are clearly delineated during children's development. They tend to be highly specific, follow a fairly well-prescribed timetable and sequence, and are strongly influenced by maturational forces. These are needs that we sometimes can express as developmental skills or milestones—for example, the need to roll over, sit up, crawl, creep, walk,

general environment—That which is relatively fixed and constant. It consists of the physical equipment and materials—together with their spatial arrangements and locations—and the people who are present at any given time. The general environment contains the cues or stimuli to which children and adults can potentially and actually respond. The general environment is the one that exists before anyone sets foot in the center or classroom. The general environment, then, is the objective environment.

genotype—The sum total of a child's genetic inheritance.

holophrases or holophrastic speech—The use of a single word to express a desire or idea. For the young child, "milk" might mean "My milk is all gone," "I want more milk," or "There is some milk."

individual appropriateness—Those characteristics that are unique to each child. An individually appropriate developmental environment considers each child's needs, experiences, interests, temperament, personality, developmental level, and anything else that distinguishes her from everyone else.

instrumental dependency—Dependency based on an inability to accomplish a task oneself, thus requiring the help of another more competent person. A young child, for example, might be too short to reach a puzzle on a shelf and must therefore ask for an adult's assistance (the child cannot be instrumental in getting the puzzle for himself).

interaction effects—The consequences—developmental changes, learning, emotions—children experience from being in a particular child care setting at a particular time in their development.

interpretation—Making sense out of what you have observed; giving meaning to your observational data so you can use them to implement an effective early childhood program.

learning styles—The particular way in which an individual learns best. Some individuals, for example, learn more effectively by reading subject matter content, others by hearing it.

logico-mathematical knowledge—Knowledge that, according to Piaget, is constructed by the child and cannot be taught to him by others. LM knowledge has mainly to do with intellectual functioning that involves such mental operations as classification, conservation, and seriation.

need—A need is any experience, opportunity, or task that is commensurate with a child's level of development and ability that if met, contributes beneficially to his growth and development, and if not met, might interfere with, or negatively affect, his growth or development.

observation—Gathering information through one or more of the five physical senses for the basic purpose of determining the effectiveness of an early childhood program.

Observation is accomplished by using specific recording techniques, which are discussed in chapters 5, 6, and 7.

operation—A reversible mental action that essentially brings something back to its original state or condition. The operational child can mentally—as well as physically, of course—pour the liquid from the tall, narrow container back into the short, wide container, thereby restoring the original condition of two identical containers holding equal amounts of liquid.

physical knowledge—Knowledge a child acquires through her interactions with physical objects: round things roll, square things stack on top of one another, and water turns to steam with the application of sufficient heat.

program effectiveness—How well a program understands children's changing abilities and developmental needs, and meets those needs by employing the accepted standards of child appropriate or developmentally appropriate practice (CAP/DAP) and the accepted principles that describe and govern growth and developmental change.

qualitative differences—Differences in kind rather than quantity. Speaking in complete, grammatically correct sentences is qualitatively different from cooing and babbling. Adult speech is not simply more of the earlier infant speech but is qualitatively different from it.

second-category needs—Needs that are more broadly expressed than first category needs and whose sequence and timing are not as clear-cut as the needs in the first category. These include the need for adequate nutrition and health care, the need to explore, and the need for sensory stimulation, among others.

social/cultural appropriateness—Considers the child's social, cultural, and family background. Development always takes place within the context of family, culture, and social class.

social knowledge—Knowledge acquired through observation or being taught by others. Social knowledge is generally knowledge that is agreed-upon by the members of a particular group, society, or culture. Such knowledge is therefore frequently arbitrary and not logically necessary. Logico-mathematical knowledge, on the other hand, is logically necessary.

telegraphic speech—Speaking in two or three word combinations, leaving out words that are not essential to meaning.

zone of proximal development (ZPD)—The ZPD is that level of knowledge, skill, or performance that a child has not yet reached, but with help or additional time and opportunity is achievable.

Index